Early Start Career Series™

People at Work®!

Second Edition

A Student's A–Z Guide to **350** Jobs

D122912

by the Editors at JIST

JIST Works
America's Career Publisher

People at Work!, **Second Edition**
A Student's A–Z Guide to 350 Jobs

© 2005 by JIST Publishing, Inc.

Published by JIST Works, an imprint of JIST Publishing, Inc.
8902 Otis Avenue
Indianapolis, IN 46216-1033
Phone: 1-800-648-JIST   Fax: 1-800-JIST-FAX
E-mail: info@jist.com   Web site: www.jist.com

Note to Educators: *People at Work!* is part of JIST's Early Start Career Series, which includes a student workbook titled *My Career Adventure*, software called *Career-O-ROM-A*, and an instructor's guide. Call 1-800-648-JIST or visit www.jist.com for more information.

Quantity discounts are available for JIST products. Please call 1-800-648-JIST or visit www.jist.com for a free catalog and more information.

Visit www.jist.com for information on JIST, free job search information, book excerpts, and ordering information on our many products. For free information on 14,000 job titles, visit www.careeroink.com.

Acquisitions Editor: Susan Pines
Development Editor: Nancy Stevenson
Editor: Jill Mazurczyk
Cover Designer: Trudy Coler
Interior Designer: Nick Anderson

Interior Layout: designLab, Inc.
Database Work: Laurence Shatkin
Illustrator: Kevin Walters
Proofreader: Linda Seifert

Printed in Canada
00 09 08 07 06 05   9 8 7 6 5 4 3 2 1

Library of Congress Cataloging-in-Publication Data

People at work : a student's A-Z guide to 350 jobs.— 2nd ed.
        p. cm. — (Early start career series)
    ISBN 1-59357-078-3 (alk. paper)
    1. Vocational guidance—Juvenile literature. 2. Career development—Juvenile literature. I. Series.
        HF5381.2.P42 2005
        331.702—dc22

                                2004029566

We have been careful to provide accurate information throughout this book, but it is possible that errors and omissions have been introduced. Please consider this in making any career plans or other important decisions. Trust your own judgment above all else and in all things.

Trademarks: All brand names and product names used in this book are trade names, service marks, trademarks, or registered trademarks of their respective owners.

ISBN 1-59357-078-3

Walk with Dez on His Journey Through Jobs

Dez the Dawg is bored. Dez needs a career to make his life fun. Dez can't just sit around the house all day. But choosing a job isn't easy. There are so many different jobs. Do you know what you would like to do when you get older?

Choosing a career is an important decision. You should choose one that you will like. But how can you choose if you don't know about all of the careers? You need to explore careers now so you can make good choices later.

Reading *People at Work!* is one way to learn about your future. You follow Dez along on the job hunt. Dez searches through 350 different jobs from A to Z in the first part of the book. In the second part, he learns about job families. Each job family includes similar kinds of work.

You learn helpful information from people who work in each job. They tell you what they do each day. You learn where they work and the tools they use. They even tell you what they like about their jobs. Some jobs may sound boring to you. Others may sound exciting. Not all people like to do the same work. Reading about these jobs can help you find the ones you like the best. The workers in *People at Work!* love what they do. They know it's important to have a job you enjoy.

Dez needs money to pay for his food and house. People need money too. *People at Work!* shows salaries in dog bones. How much money you make at a job depends on where you live and how many other people can do the job. People who live in big cities usually make more money. People who know how to do tasks that other people don't can also make more money. The average salary for all jobs is $33,000.

Key to Earnings

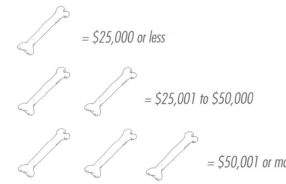

= $25,000 or less

= $25,001 to $50,000

= $50,001 or more

Dez wants a job with a good future. No one knows for sure what careers will have the best outlook because the job market changes all the time. But experts from the government have made predictions based on research. *People at Work!* uses dog paws to show the job growth for each career. The average growth for all jobs is 11 percent through 2012.

Education is very important. Most jobs require at least a high school diploma. Right now you can read and study to prepare for your future. *People at Work!* uses four education levels: high school diploma, training after high school, two-year degree, and four-year degree or more. In training after high school, you get special job-related or technical training.

People at Work! lists the school subjects that are important in each career. You should work extra hard in these subjects. School will help you be a success in any job. Each career also shows the job family to which it belongs, such as business or health.

When you find a job that sounds interesting, learn about its job family later in the book. The "Get a Head Start" and "Look Up These Words" sections give you a feel for the type of work involved in each job family. You may find related jobs that interest you, too. For more information on the jobs in each job family, use the "Find Out More" sections to go online or write letters.

Dez the Dawg wants you to find the perfect career. Finding a job you like is very important to your life.

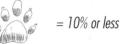

Key to Job Growth

 = 10% or less

  = 11% to 20%

  = 21% or more

able of Contents

JOBS A-Z **1**

Accountants 2
Actors and Actresses 3
Actuaries 4
Administrative Assistants 5
Advertising Account Executives 6
Advertising Directors 7
Aerospace Engineers 8
Agricultural Inspectors 9
Agricultural Scientists..............................10
Aircraft Mechanics 11
Airport Security Workers 12
Air Traffic Controllers 13
Anesthesiologists 14
Animal Health Technicians 15
Animal Trainers 16
Anthropologists 17
Appliance Repairers 18
Appraisers...19
Architects 20
Art Directors 21
Artists...22
Astronauts 23
Astronomers 24
Athletic Trainers 25
Auto Body Repairers 26
Automobile Mechanics............................27
Baggage Handlers.....................................28
Bakery Workers 29

Bank Managers 30
Bank Tellers 31
Barbers...32
Biomedical Engineers 33
Biotechnical Researchers 34
Bookkeepers 35
Bricklayers 36
Broadcast Technicians 37
Building and Home Inspectors................38
Building Contractors 39
Building Maintenance Workers 40
Bus Drivers 41
Business Education Teachers 42
Business Executives 43
Business Service Salespeople...................44
Buyers 45
Cabinetmakers 46
Cable and Satellite TV Installers 47
CAD Technicians.....................................48
Camera Operators 49
Career Counselors 50
Carpenters 51
Caterers 52
Chefs and Dinner Cooks 53
Chemical Engineers 54
Chemical Processing Workers..................55
Chemists 56
Child-Care Workers 57
Chiropractors 58

Civil Engineers...59
Clergy 60
Clothes Designers 61
Commercial Fishers 62
Community Affairs Representatives 63
Compensation Analysts 64
Computer Engineers 65
Computer Graphics Specialists...............66
Computer Security Consultants...............67
Computer Technicians.............................68
Construction Laborers 69
Copywriters 70
Corrections Officers 71
Cosmetologists 72
Court Reporters 73
Craftspeople 74
Credit Analysts..75
Curators...76
Customer Service Representatives...........77
Customs Inspectors 78
Dancers 79
Data Entry Operators 80
Delivery Truck Drivers 81
Dental Hygienists.....................................82
Dental Laboratory Technicians...............83
Dentists 84
Dietitians 85
Directors 86
Dispatchers 87

Dispensing Opticians 88
Domestic Service Workers 89
Drafters 90
Drywall Installers 91
E-Commerce Managers 92
Economists......................93
Editors 94
Education Program Specialists 95
Electrical Engineers 96
Electricians......................97
Electromechanical Technicians 98
Electronic Assemblers......................99
Elementary School Teachers 100
Emergency Medical Technicians............101
Environmental Analysts 102
Ergonomics Engineers 103
Escrow Officers 104
Estimators 105
Executive Assistants 106
Farm Equipment Mechanics 107
Farmers 108
Fashion Merchandisers 109
Fast-Food Service Managers 110
Fiber-optic Engineers 111
Financial Planners 112
Firefighters 113
Fish and Wildlife Specialists.....................114
Flight Attendants 115
Floral Designers 116
Foresters 117
Forklift Operators 118
Front Desk Clerks 119

Fund-Raisers 120
Furniture Designers 121
Furniture Makers 122
Furniture Movers 123
Geologists 124
Gerontologists 125
Glaziers 126
Graphic Designers 127
Grocery Clerks 128
Groundskeepers and Gardeners 129
Hazardous Waste Managers 130
Health and Safety Inspectors 131
Health Therapists......................132
Heating and Cooling
    Systems Mechanics 133
Heavy Equipment Operators 134
Horticultural Workers 135
Hospice Workers 136
Hospital Administrators 137
Hospitality Managers 138
Housekeeping Staff 139
Human Resource Workers 140
Image Consultants 141
Immigration Inspectors 142
Importers and Exporters......................143
Industrial Designers 144
Industrial Engineers 145
Information Abstractors and
    Indexers......................146
Information Technology
    (IT) Managers......................147
Instrument Mechanics 148

Insurance Adjusters 149
Insurance Salespeople......................150
Interior Designers 151
Interpreters and Translators 152
Investigators 153
Jewelers 154
Journalists 155
Kitchen Helpers 156
Landscape Architects 157
Laser Technicians 158
Lawyers 159
Legal Secretaries 160
Liberal Arts Teachers 161
Librarians......................162
Licensed Practical Nurses 163
Loan Officers 164
Locksmiths......................165
Loggers......................166
Machine Tool Operators 167
Machinists 168
Mail Carriers 169
Manufacturing Workers 170
Marketing Directors 171
Market Researchers 172
Massage Therapists......................173
Materials Engineers 174
Math and Science Teachers 175
Mathematicians 176
Meat Cutters 177
Mechanical Engineers......................178
Medical Assistants 179
Medical Equipment Repairers 180

Medical Laboratory Assistants 181
Medical Records Administrators...........182
Medical Records Clerks 183
Medical Secretaries...........................184
Medical Technologists 185
Mental Health Counselors 186
Metallographic Technicians 187
Metal Refining Workers 188
Meteorologists 189
Microbiologists................................190
Midwives 191
Military Enlisted Personnel 192
Military Officers 193
Millwrights.....................................194
Mining Engineers..............................195
Models 196
Molders 197
Musicians 198
Network Administrators......................199
Novelists 200
Nuclear Engineers 201
Nuclear Technicians 202
Nurse Practitioners...........................203
Nurses Aides and Orderlies 204
Occupational Therapists......................205
Oceanographers 206
Office Managers................................207
Operations Research Analysts...............208
Optical Technicians 209
Optometrists 210
Painters 211
Paralegal Assistants 212

Park Rangers 213
Parole and Probation Officers 214
Parts Managers 215
Pathologists 216
Patient Account Representatives............217
Personal Trainers 218
Pest Control Workers 219
Petroleum Field Workers 220
Pharmacist Assistants 221
Pharmacists 222
Photographers 223
Physical Therapists............................224
Physical Therapy Aides........................225
Physician Assistants 226
Physicians.......................................227
Physicists 228
Piano Tuners 229
Pilots 230
Plastic Molders.................................231
Plumbers 232
Podiatrists.......................................233
Police Commissioners 234
Police Officers 235
Political Aides..................................236
Political Scientists.............................237
Politicians.......................................238
Postal Clerks 239
Power Plant Operators 240
Prepress Workers 241
Preschool Teachers 242
Production Assistants 243
Production Planners 244

Production Superintendents..................245
Product Managers 246
Professional Athletes..........................247
Programmers 248
Property Managers 249
Prosthetists.....................................250
Psychiatric Technicians 251
Psychologists 252
Public Health Inspectors 253
Public Health Nurses 254
Public Relations Workers 255
Purchasing Agents 256
Quality Control Inspectors...................257
Radio and Television Announcers 258
Railroad Engineers 259
Range Managers................................260
Real Estate Salespeople........................261
Receptionists 262
Recreation Aides 263
Recruiters.......................................264
Registered Nurses..............................265
Rehabilitation Counselors 266
Respiratory Therapists........................267
Restaurant Managers 268
Retail Salespeople..............................269
Retail Store Managers.........................270
Robotics Technicians 271
Roofers..272
Route Salespeople..............................273
Sales and Service Managers 274
Sales Representatives 275
School Counselors 276

School Principals 277
Securities Clerks.............................278
Security Guards 279
Security System Technicians 280
Seismologists 281
Sewing Machine Operators 282
Sheet Metal Workers 283
Ship Fitters.............................284
Shipping and Receiving Clerks.............285
Ship's Crew Members.........................286
Ship's Officers 287
Shoe Repairers 288
Short-Order Cooks 289
Small Business Owners.........................290
Social Directors 291
Social Scientists 292
Social Service Aides 293
Social Workers 294
Sociologists.............................295
Soil Scientists 296
Solar Energy System Installers 297
Sound Engineers 298
Special Education Teachers...................299
Speech Pathologists and
    Audiologists 300
Stagehands 301
Statisticians 302
Steelworkers 303
Stock Brokers 304
Stock Clerks.............................305
Stunt Performers 306

Surgical Technicians 307
Surveyors 308
Tailors and Dressmakers.....................309
Talent Agents 310
Taxi Drivers 311
Tax Preparers 312
Teacher Aides 313
Technical Illustrators 314
Technical Support Specialists 315
Technical Writers 316
Telecommunications Analysts...............317
Telephone Installers and Repairers 318
Telephone Operators 319
Textile Machine Operators 320
Ticket and Reservation Agents 321
Title Examiners 322
Tool and Die Makers 323
Tour Guides.............................324
Tourist Information Specialists.............325
Trainers and Adult
    Education Teachers 326
Travel Agents 327
Tree Surgeons.............................328
Truck Drivers 329
Ultrasound Technologists 330
Underwriters 331
University and College Teachers.............332
Upholsterers 333
Urban Planners 334
Utility Line Workers 335
Utilization-Review Coordinators 336

Vending Machine Mechanics 337
Veterinarians 338
Vocalists.............................339
Wait Staff 340
Warehouse Workers 341
Water and Sewage Plant Operators 342
Web Designers 343
Webmasters 344
Welders 345
Wireless Technology
    Product Managers 346
Woodworkers 347
Writers 348
X-Ray and Radiologic Technicians 349
Yardmasters 350
Zoologists.............................351

LEARN ABOUT JOB FAMILIES 353

Arts and Entertainment 354
Business 360
Construction 366
Education and Social Services 372
Health 378
Mechanics and Repairers.......................384
Natural Resources 390
Personal Services 396
Production 402
Science and Engineering 408
Technology.............................414
Transportation 420

JOBS A-Z

Accountants

I'm a certified public accountant. But you can call me a CPA for short. CPAs sell accounting and tax services to the public. Let me translate that. We add numbers so you won't have to. We set up bookkeeping systems.

I keep track of small details for businesses. I use a computer to help me. Companies have to keep track of the money they make. They also have to keep track of their costs.

Accountants compare the profits to the money that is spent. I tell a company how it is doing. It is much better to make more than you spend. I keep track of information in a bookkeeping log called a ledger. It's like a diary about money for a business.

Accountants also help people do taxes. I figure out your taxes if you bring me information about your income and expenses. I know many laws about taxes.

BUSINESS

SALARY
 = $25,001 to $50,000

JOB GROWTH
= 11% to 20%

EDUCATION
Four-year degree or more

SCHOOL SUBJECTS

math	science
reading	computers
social studies	business

Actors and Actresses

SALARY

= $25,001 to $50,000

JOB GROWTH

 = 11% to 20%

EDUCATION

Two-year degree

SCHOOL SUBJECTS

drama

reading

math

The theater is my life! I'm an actor. Actors entertain audiences for a living. Most of the work I do is in plays.

Acting isn't easy. You have to be good at watching people. That's how I figure out how to be a character. Actors have to convince you that they are someone else. I remember lots of lines. You wouldn't believe that I was someone else if I read off of a piece of paper. There are a lot of words in a play. I have a good memory.

I am very lucky. I make a living as an actor. Many actors work at other jobs and act in their spare time. I may work on a play for several months. Sometimes I don't work for months at a time.

I try out for each role I play. There is no guarantee that I will get a part. I spend many hours rehearsing. The plays are usually at night. I work many late nights. I perform in front of large groups. That can make you nervous. It doesn't bother me anymore.

I've always enjoyed acting. I put on plays for my neighbors when I was your age. I tried out for every play at school. The best part about being an actor is the applause at the end. It lets me know I have done a good job.

ctuaries

Insurance is a form of protection. People buy insurance policies to protect them when they get in an accident, fire, or flood.

Insurance companies give clients money during an emergency. Insurance companies help pay the hospital bills for sick clients. An insurance company will give you money for damages to your house caused by a fire or a flood.

Where do I fit in? I figure out how much the insurance company will pay. I figure out how much people should pay for policies. I use difficult math every day. I estimate how likely certain accidents are. The cost of insurance is based on the risk of certain things happening.

I decide on a fair price for protection. I want all people to have the insurance they need.

SALARY

= $50,001 or more

JOB GROWTH

= 11% to 20%

EDUCATION

Four-year degree or more

SCHOOL SUBJECTS

math	science
reading	computers
social studies	

Administrative Assistants

BUSINESS

SALARY

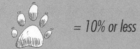

= $25,001 to $50,000

JOB GROWTH

= 10% or less

EDUCATION

Two-year degree

SCHOOL SUBJECTS

math	computers
reading	social studies
writing	

Come into my office! I help the manager of a big company. My name is Eduardo. I'm an administrative assistant.

My boss spends a lot of time out of the office with clients. I meet with her once a day to discuss what needs to be done. Sometimes I make changes in the office to get the work done. Recently, I suggested that we add a new program to our computers.

I talk to my boss's clients when she's not here. I help my boss by working out the details and schedules for her. I help her prepare our budget. I interview people for job openings. I have her meet the people I recommend.

My boss relies on me to keep things in order. She couldn't do her job without me.

Advertising Account Executives

I work with companies to help them advertise their products. I work for a large advertising agency. I am an account executive.

I find new customers and keep our current clients happy. I meet with the managers of companies to discuss advertising plans. They tell me their ideas and how much money they have to spend. I tell the advertising director what the client is looking for. The advertising director works with copywriters and designers to create the ads.

The agency creates a budget for the work. The costs are approved by our client before we do the work. We let the client know exactly what we are doing. I try to keep our clients happy.

I meet with clients so creative teams have more time to write and do designs. I am the business side of an advertising agency.

BUSINESS

● **SALARY**

 = $25,001 to $50,000

● **JOB GROWTH**

 = 11% to 20%

● **EDUCATION**
Two-year degree

SCHOOL SUBJECTS

reading	computers
math	art
social studies	

Advertising Directors

- ## SALARY
  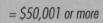
  = $50,001 or more

- ## JOB GROWTH

  = 21% or more

- ## EDUCATION
  Four-year degree or more

SCHOOL SUBJECTS

math	art
reading	writing
computers	social studies

Do you like commercials that are funny? I'm an advertising director at a big company. I plan and supervise advertising to get you interested in buying my products. If something looks good in a commercial, you may want to buy it.

I meet with the marketing and sales managers of my company. We decide what products to advertise. I select the best places for the ads. Sometimes I use magazines. Other ads work better on the radio. I make my decision based on the audience I want to reach.

Right now we are working on a campaign for new cross-training shoes. Most of our ads will appear on TV. I am working with an ad agency that writes and designs the ads. I make sure they do the best job they can. We have a budget. I work with numbers.

My job is important. I make sure that customers know about products. People can't buy products they don't know about.

Aerospace Engineers

You will need me to design a spaceship for you if you grow up to be an astronaut. I work for the government. I design rockets that go into space. Designing a rocket is very difficult. I use a computer to help me.

I am working on a new spaceship right now. This project is top secret. But I can tell you a few things. My spaceship will allow small groups to take vacations to other planets. It will be like a cruise ship in space. Families will be able to travel the galaxies. It will be years before this will happen. I make sure that it is safe and works right.

I do complicated math problems. Science and math are very important when you are designing an airplane or rocket. I sit in my office most of the day doing tests on the computer to make sure it can fly. Sometimes I stay very late working on it. My machines will explore planets that nobody has seen. I can bring you to the moon and stars.

• SALARY

 = $50,001 or more

• JOB GROWTH

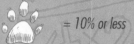 = 10% or less

• EDUCATION

Four-year degree or more

SCHOOL SUBJECTS

science	reading
math	computers
art	

Agricultural Inspectors

SALARY

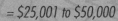

= $25,001 to $50,000

JOB GROWTH

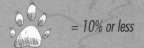

= 10% or less

EDUCATION

Four-year degree or more

SCHOOL SUBJECTS

reading   writing

science   computers

math

I make sure that the food you eat is clean and safe. I work for the U.S. Department of Agriculture. I inspect canneries to make sure they follow health codes.

Fruits and vegetables must be canned under sanitary conditions. Germs could cause people to get sick. I make sure that the canneries wash all of the food. I check to see that they sterilize their equipment. I take my job seriously. People's health depends on my inspections.

I tell the canneries about any problems I find. They listen to what I say and make changes. I can shut down the cannery if they don't. I usually don't have any problems. Companies want to sell clean and healthy food.

I travel to several canneries in a week. I have to be very careful with my inspections. I have many details to look for. I am proud of the important service I do.

Agricultural Scientists

I've developed a new breed of corn. I call it the Incredible Husk. I crossed two breeds of corn to come up with a stronger one. The work I do is called agricultural science. I'm an agronomist.

I wanted to create a corn that doesn't need a lot of water. I wanted something that could grow in dry areas. I wanted the corn to be bug-free. The Incredible Husk is both.

This new corn will feed people in poor countries. They can grow it without complicated irrigation systems or pesticides. It can grow in sandy soil. The Incredible Husk will give food to many hungry people.

I enjoy working in laboratories and outdoors. I work hard to improve the way we grow things.

• SALARY

= $25,001 to $50,000

• JOB GROWTH

= 10% or less

• EDUCATION

Four-year degree or more

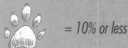

SCHOOL SUBJECTS

science	writing
math	computers
reading	social studies

Aircraft Mechanics

SALARY

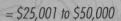 = $25,001 to $50,000

JOB GROWTH

 = 11% to 20%

EDUCATION

Two-year degree

SCHOOL SUBJECTS

reading

math

physical education

industrial arts

I'm sure you've had the family car repaired. Well, where would you go if your airplane wasn't working? You'd come to me. I'm an aircraft mechanic. I do the same things that an automobile mechanic does to your car.

My job is very important. I make sure that airplanes are safe to fly. My work prevents planes from getting in accidents. I look over the plane to see if everything is okay. I use special machines to run tests on the engine. I look over the body of the plane to see if there are any problems. The plane must be very sturdy. I use a rivet gun and a blowtorch to weld the metal on the body together. There can't be any cracks on the surface.

I make sure the inside machinery works the right way. Airplanes are made up of little parts. I check all of them. The landing wheels must be in good shape. The controls in the cockpit must work. A pilot can't fly a plane if there are any problems.

Aircraft mechanics make big machines fly through the air. That's amazing if you think about it.

Airport Security Workers

An airport is busy. Lots of people move through here every day. It's my job to make sure that everybody travels safely.

People walk through a metal detector before getting on planes. When people have something metal in their pockets, like keys or coins, the machine makes a noise. Then the person has to come back and put the metal item in a tray. They walk through again.

I run an X-ray machine that lets me look inside people's bags. I look for anything dangerous. I ask people to take their coats off. I have people open their computers to make sure nothing's hidden.

Most people are happy to help because I protect them. I like my job because I make sure people have a safe trip.

TRANSPORTATION

• SALARY
= $25,000 or less

• JOB GROWTH
= 21% or more

• EDUCATION
Training after high school

SCHOOL SUBJECTS
reading

writing

computers

Air Traffic Controllers

SALARY

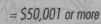 = $50,001 or more

JOB GROWTH

 = 11% to 20%

EDUCATION

Four-year degree or more

SCHOOL SUBJECTS

math   writing

science

reading

Cars have to stop at red lights, or they could get in an accident. Traffic lights protect people and make traffic flow smoothly. I do the same thing for airplanes. I'm an air traffic controller. Of course, we don't have stop signs in the air! I talk to pilots from a control tower. I give them landing and takeoff instructions.

I control many of the planes that come in and out of the airport. I have a radio to talk with each pilot. I know about weather patterns and conditions. I tell the pilot about wind and visibility. I track the flight path of the plane with radar. I prevent collisions by talking with the pilot of every plane. I make sure the runways are clear to land on. I tell pilots when they can take off.

Airplanes could crash if I do not do a good job. I can't make mistakes. Most planes have hundreds of people on board. I help keep them safe.

TRANSPORTATION

Anesthesiologists

I'm an important person in an operating room. I put people to sleep so a doctor can operate. I'm an anesthesiologist. I help people who are having surgery.

I give people anesthesia. It allows them to sleep through the surgery. I wear a scrub suit and a mask to keep out germs. I fit a plastic mask on the patient's face. I turn dials to control oxygen and gases. I make sure the patient breathes normally during surgery. I watch the skin color and eyes for problems. I let the surgeon know if I see bad signs.

I can stop pain when someone needs stitches. I can give the person a shot to make the area less sensitive. Then a doctor can put in the stitches.

I work long hours, but I love my job. I help people when they need it the most.

- **SALARY**
  = $50,001 or more
- **JOB GROWTH**
  = 11% to 20%
- **EDUCATION**
  Four-year degree or more

HEALTH

SCHOOL SUBJECTS

science	writing
math	computers
reading	

Animal Health Technicians

SALARY

= $25,000 or less

JOB GROWTH

= 21% or more

EDUCATION

Two-year degree

SCHOOL SUBJECTS

reading   computers

science

math

I'm an animal health technician. I work for a veterinarian. I am like a nurse at a hospital, except I work with animals.

I had to be certified to take care of animals. I give shots and pills to dogs and cats. I keep the examination rooms clean. I set up equipment so the vet can examine the animals.

Sometimes vets have to operate. I help them with the surgery. I hand them the instruments they need. Sometimes I give animals stitches if the vet has an emergency. I work closely with the vet to take care of the animals.

I help people keep their pets healthy. I work with another technician who isn't certified. Uncertified technicians feed, groom, and clean the animals that stay overnight in our kennels. I love working with animals and helping them feel better.

NATURAL RESOURCES

Animal Trainers

Would you like to take a ride on an elephant? I work with elephants and other animals all day. I'm an animal trainer at Safari Park.

I teach animals how to do tricks and obey commands. It isn't cruel. I only work with the animals that like to be around people. I would never try to teach a porcupine to shake hands! It takes a long time to train animals. You have to earn their trust. Once they trust you, most animals will do tricks. I give them a treat when they do it right.

I'm teaching Dolores the seal how to play the trumpet. She's pretty good with everything but the high notes. I give her sardines when she finishes a song. I give her a pat on the head so she knows I appreciate her work. It's a lot like training your dog. Some animal trainers work only with dogs. They teach them how to work for the police or help blind people.

My job is fun. You have to be patient and love the animals. Trainers know a lot about animal behavior. Animals can be moody just like people. I love working with animals. Training lions and bears is like having wild animals as pets. I can't keep them at home, but I get to spend time with them every day.

SALARY

= $25,000 or less

JOB GROWTH

 = 11% to 20%

EDUCATION

Training after high school

SCHOOL SUBJECTS

reading   computers

science

math

Anthropologists

- ## SALARY

  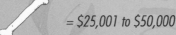

  = $25,001 to $50,000

- ## JOB GROWTH

  = 11% to 20%

- ## EDUCATION

  Four-year degree or more

SCHOOL SUBJECTS

social studies

geography

foreign languages

reading

computers

writing

I've lived in many foreign lands. I've traveled around the world as an anthropologist. I study the physical and cultural patterns of society.

I lived for four years with a tribe of natives in the rain forests of Brazil. Their lives are very different from ours. I had to learn their language. I learned to live like they live. They taught me to hunt. I learned how to make a house out of leaves and branches. I studied their religion. The time I spent in Brazil changed my life.

A university funded my time there. Now I am back teaching and writing a book about my experience. I want the world to know about this tribe. It is important for us to understand how other people live.

The tribe I lived with learned to adapt to the humid rain forest. They treated the land with respect. I think Americans could learn a lot from these people. I hope my book will make many people look at their own lives.

Appliance Repairers

I work for a department store as an appliance repairer. I go to people's houses and fix appliances that they bought from our store.

We sell vacuum cleaners, refrigerators, and washing machines. I know how to fix them all. I usually take appliances apart to find the problem. They have motors inside that make them work. I have special tools for each machine. Most of the time, I just replace a worn part. Sometimes there is a problem with the way the machine was made. Then I arrange for the customer to get a new appliance.

I see many people in one day. Sometimes I work extra hours to get everyone in. I don't mind. I like to tinker with machines. I'm good at what I do.

SALARY

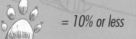 = $25,001 to $50,000

JOB GROWTH

= 10% or less

EDUCATION

Two-year degree

SCHOOL SUBJECTS

math

reading

industrial arts

Appraisers

SALARY

 = $25,001 to $50,000

JOB GROWTH

  = 11% to 20%

EDUCATION

Four-year degree or more

SCHOOL SUBJECTS

math   science

reading   computers

social   writing
studies

BUSINESS

I can tell you how much your jewelry is worth. I work for a jewelry store as an appraiser. I know the value of diamonds, rubies, and emeralds.

I look at each piece closely. Bigger stones are usually worth more money. I check the quality of the stone. I look at the cut and the color. I use a microscope to look for defects. Diamonds sometimes have small cracks inside. I also look at the metal fitting. Gold is worth more than silver.

I write a report for my clients. I tell them what I think the jewelry is worth. I include details to help the customer understand how I came up with the amount. People use my appraisals to insure their jewelry. Insurance companies have to know how much a piece is worth before they insure it.

Appraisers also tell people the value of houses, cars, stamps, coins, and antiques. We have to be experts at what we do.

Architects

I'm an architect for a firm in New York. We've designed some of the tallest skyscrapers in the United States. Right now I'm drawing plans for a new toy store.

I plan many details. I talk to the owners of the company to find out what they want the store to look like. Their new store will be huge. I've already finished drawing the outside of the building. Cities pass building codes for protection. I must know the building laws of this city. Math is an important part of my job. I figure out the exact size of every wall and floor. I have to get my measurements perfect. Otherwise, the building will be unsafe. I wouldn't want people to get hurt.

Buildings are made of many different parts. I plan everything from the air-conditioning systems to where the manager's office will be. I must make the store the way the owners want it. Being good at drawing helps me make the plans on my computer.

Tomorrow, I meet with the people who will build the store to explain the project. I make sure they understand my drawings. My job is very creative. I get to design great buildings. I think kids will like my toy store. It will have a slide that goes down three stories.

- **SALARY**
  = $50,001 or more
- **JOB GROWTH**
  = 11% to 20%
- **EDUCATION**
  Four-year degree or more

SCHOOL SUBJECTS

drawing	computers
math	reading
science	industrial arts
writing	

Art Directors

- ## SALARY

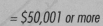

= $50,001 or more

- ## JOB GROWTH

= 11% to 20%

- ## EDUCATION

Four-year degree or more

SCHOOL SUBJECTS

art

computers

reading

social studies

Did you ever wonder how TV commercials get made? I do the art for TV commercials. I work as an art director for a New York advertising agency. Art directors manage people to make art work for magazines, books, newspapers, and TV commercials.

The agency I work for does a lot of commercials. My company has hundreds of clients. I meet with people from the companies to come up with ideas for the ads. They tell me what they need. The copy editor from our agency also sits in on the meeting. He writes what the ad says. I decide what the ad will look like. We come up with a budget to show how much the ad will cost.

I work on lots of ads every day. First, I figure out exactly how everything should look. I work with a team of designers. I get them to develop my ideas. The final sketches have to be approved by a department head and the client. Then the ad goes into production.

The work I do is very creative. It's great to see my ideas on a TV screen. Sometimes it makes me feel like a celebrity.

ARTS AND ENTERTAINMENT

Artists

My first art showing was on my mom's refrigerator. It was a painting of my sister. Now, I hang my paintings in galleries. I'm an artist. Artists paint or make sculptures for a living. We are very creative people.

Artists usually work with one kind of material. I prefer to paint with watercolors. Watercolors are neat because you can see through them. I do most of my paintings in a studio. It has big windows with lots of light. Sometimes I paint outside. Artists don't have to sit at a desk all day. We can work whenever we want. I like to work early in the morning before most people wake up. Sometimes I work after midnight. It depends on how I feel.

Most artists don't become rich. Famous artists can sell art for a lot of money. Artists usually work at other jobs to pay their bills. I sell my paintings at an art gallery. People go to galleries to buy paintings and sculptures.

My art is more than drawing. I turn ideas into pictures. Everyone has his or her own style. My work is unique. I love finishing a painting. Sometimes I spend weeks making one perfect. I am very proud of my work.

 **SALARY** = $25,001 to $50,000

 **JOB GROWTH** = 11% to 20%

EDUCATION Two-year degree

SCHOOL SUBJECTS

art

reading

math

Astronauts

- ## SALARY
   = $50,001 or more

- ## JOB GROWTH
  = 10% or less

- ## EDUCATION
  Four-year degree or more

SCHOOL SUBJECTS

reading	science
math	computers
social studies	writing

TECHNOLOGY

I bet you want to grow up to be just like me. Well, a lot of kids do. I'm an astronaut. In a lot of ways it is fun. But it is also a lot of work.

I went through many years of training. I went to a military service academy and became an officer long before I was an astronaut. They trained me to fly fighter planes on special missions. I was awarded medals. Then I became an astronaut.

I had to go through many physical tests in training. The atmosphere in space is much different than it is on earth. We had to float around in machines that created zero gravity. Some officers didn't pass the tests. They couldn't continue training. I made it through the entire program, but I still haven't gone into space.

The rest of us wait for our turn while we work on other military activities. Astronauts have to know how to use technical space flight equipment. We know all about rockets and the controls in the spacecraft. Some astronauts are scientists. They go up into space to do research.

Being a part of the space program is important to me. One day I hope to have my place in history.

Astronomers

I'm glad you're here. I have something very exciting to tell you. I just discovered a new star. I'm going to call it Zeston. I've been searching for it for a few years. You can see it if you look through my telescope. It's quite lovely. Don't you think? Oh, I almost forgot. My name is Dr. Klyce. I'm an astronomer.

Astronomers use science and math to study the stars, sun, and galaxies. I work in a research lab at a major university. I am in charge of several other scientists working on this project. We are trying to find out everything we can about Zeston. We want to learn about its history and its structure. I wonder what kinds of gases it is made of. My team will spend many hours working with me on this project.

We use a computer to analyze all the data. Scientific research requires a lot of effort. I was the best student in my math and science classes when I was your age. Astronomers know a lot about space and planets. Do you like reading about space? I like the challenge of astronomy. It's really exciting.

SCIENCE AND ENGINEERING

SALARY
= $50,001 or more

JOB GROWTH
= 10% or less

EDUCATION
Four-year degree or more

SCHOOL SUBJECTS

science   reading

math   social studies

computers

Athletic Trainers

- ## SALARY

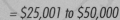

= $25,001 to $50,000

- ## JOB GROWTH

= 21% or more

- ## EDUCATION

Four-year degree or more

SCHOOL SUBJECTS

science	math
reading	first aid
physical education	health

I work with sports teams to keep athletes healthy. I'm an athletic trainer. I help athletes maintain maximum physical fitness.

I develop an exercise program for them. I work with them to strengthen the muscles they need for the sports they play. I help overweight athletes lose weight. I help them with their diets. All athletes watch what they eat. I give massages to relieve soreness, strains, and bruises. Many athletes say that I am their best friend. I work with them to meet their needs. Their health is very important to me.

Sometimes I give them first aid if they get injured in a game or during training. I know how to clean and bandage a wound so it will heal properly. I know how to wrap ankles and knees to prevent injuries. I wrap gauze around them to support the muscles and ligaments.

Playing sports can wear down a body. I work hard to keep athletes going. They have to make it through the entire season. I'm here to work with them along the way.

Auto Body Repairers

I can take that dent out of your fender. I'm an auto body repairer. I fix cars for a living. I work at an auto repair shop. I don't work on engines at all. I only work on the outside parts of cars.

Accidents can smash a car. I can make cars look new again. I can knock a dent out of a car door. I can fix a scratch on the hood. I have a mallet that I use to knock out the dents. I hammer at the metal until it comes out even again. Sometimes cars are really damaged. Then I replace the parts. I may put on a new door or fender or windshield. I make sure the car is safe for traveling. Accidents can make cars unsafe.

I paint the areas I work on to match the rest of the car. I try to make it look as good as it did before the accident. Every job I do is different. It depends on what needs to be done. I never get bored. I have a lot to do.

People appreciate my work. It always makes them happy to see their car back in normal shape. That makes me feel good.

• SALARY

 = $25,001 to $50,000

• JOB GROWTH

= 11% to 20%

• EDUCATION

Training after high school

SCHOOL SUBJECTS

reading	industrial arts
math	
computers	

Automobile Mechanics

SALARY

 = $25,001 to $50,000

JOB GROWTH

 = 11% to 20%

EDUCATION

Training after high school

SCHOOL SUBJECTS

reading   computers

math   industrial arts

physical education

They call me Fixit. That's because I can fix just about anything. I work in an auto repair shop. You should see me if you're having problems with your car. I can tell you why your engine is making that "ping" noise. A computer helps me.

I'll put your car up on a lift and get underneath to check it. Engines have so many parts and wires they confuse most people. Not me. I know car engines inside and out. I could take apart an engine and put it back together with my eyes closed. I can fix problems for you.

I may replace a piston or a rod. I might put in a new transmission or brakes. Different things can go wrong with a car. Cars are complicated machines. I get very dirty working on engines. I usually wear coveralls so I don't mess up my nice clothes. But I don't care about looking good. I'm not a fashion model. I just want to get the job done.

I'm an excellent mechanic. They don't call me Fixit for nothing.

Baggage Handlers

I work at the airport as a baggage handler. I make sure people's bags go to the right airline.

I tag every bag. I check to see if the person's home address and phone number are labeled on the tag. I put a special label on each bag to show where the bag is going. You don't want your luggage to end up in Hawaii if you are going to Kansas. Sometimes I put heavy tape around the bags so they stay secure in transit. I wouldn't want your clothes and personal items to fall out.

I keep track of every bag I handle. I record each one in a computer. Sometimes I load the baggage into the airplane cargo area. I have to be strong to lift heavy bags. I want people to have a nice trip. My job takes care of an important part of traveling.

SALARY

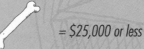 = $25,000 or less

JOB GROWTH

 = 11% to 20%

EDUCATION

High school diploma

SCHOOL SUBJECTS

reading

math

physical education

Bakery Workers

- ## SALARY

= $25,000 or less

- ## JOB GROWTH

= 11% to 20%

- ## EDUCATION
Training after high school

SCHOOL SUBJECTS

reading

math

Mmmmmmm! Doesn't that bread smell good? I make bread, pastries, and cakes for a living. I work in a large bakery. I get here early in the morning so I can make sweet rolls for people's breakfasts.

Maybe I made your last birthday cake. I make lots of cakes every day. I never use a mix. Everything I bake is made from scratch. I start by measuring the ingredients. I'm careful to follow the recipe so it's perfect every time. My cakes would be ruined if I didn't use enough sugar or if I forgot to sift the flour. Then I mix the batter in a huge mixer. It would probably take up half of your kitchen at home! I get the ovens ready. I pour the batter into pans. I have to make sure they are cooked at the right temperature for the right time. I wouldn't want to burn them. I take them out of the oven and let them cool.

My favorite part is frosting them. I write fun messages on top. One man had me write "Have a purrfect birthday ChaCha" for his pet cat. I thought that was a little weird. The hardest part of my job is trying not to sample everything I make. It all looks so good!

Bank Managers

I make sure my bank branch runs smoothly. I'm a bank manager.

I hire bank tellers, loan officers, accountants, janitors, and others to work in my bank. I see that they learn how to do their jobs. They follow the bank's rules. I make sure my bank obeys all banking laws. I make sure that the building is repaired and clean. I keep the money safe. We use a computer to keep track of everything. It must keep everyone's bank balance right.

If something goes wrong, I must stop what I am doing and make it right. I must get along with the people who work for me and the customers. I make a lot of important decisions on my own. I stand by them even if others disagree and get mad.

My job is very hard. I often work late in my office. There are so many different things that I do. I study reports, go to meetings, and talk on the phone. I use a computer to write letters and reports. I know everything that is going on in my bank so I can make the right decisions.

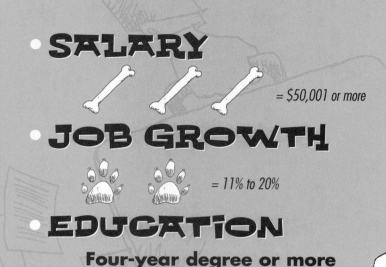

SALARY
= $50,001 or more

JOB GROWTH
= 11% to 20%

EDUCATION
Four-year degree or more

SCHOOL SUBJECTS

science	computers
reading	business
social studies	writing
	math

Bank Tellers

- ## SALARY

= $25,000 or less

- ## JOB GROWTH

= 10% or less

- ## EDUCATION

Training after high school

SCHOOL SUBJECTS

math

reading

computers

BUSINESS

Hi! I'm a bank teller in your town. I stand behind the counter and help people with their checking and savings accounts. I can deposit checks into their accounts. I cash checks for people. I make sure all of the checks are signed. I need to make sure a person is who he says he is. I can look up account balances with my computer using the account number.

Sometimes I help people to put things in safe deposit boxes for safekeeping. When I help people open a new account, I show them how to order checks.

I account for every penny in my drawer. I make sure I count the money accurately. I could get fired if my drawer does not balance. The supervisor looks for any errors. Money is very important in a bank. It has to be exactly right.

Barbers

I work as a barber at Snip-It's Barber Shop. I cut hair all day long. I'll cut it just the way you want it. I use scissors, combs, and clippers. I can take a little off the top. Maybe you'd like a crew cut.

I shampoo the hair before I cut it. I like to cut freshly washed hair. Hair is easier to cut when it's wet. I want it to be nice and even. I don't want you walking out of here looking messy. I can blow dry your hair before you leave. You might not like that wet look. I trim mustaches and shave beards. I went to a special school to learn how to style hair. It's an art.

I keep the barber shop clean. I sweep up the hair on the floor during the day. I clean the scissors and combs after every customer.

I also sell shampoo and conditioner. You can pick up whatever you need right here at Snip-It's. I talk with nice people every day. I can talk and listen to the radio while I work. I'm sure you can't do that at school.

SALARY

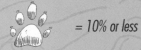 = $25,000 or less

JOB GROWTH

= 10% or less

EDUCATION

Training after high school

SCHOOL SUBJECTS

reading

math

art

Biomedical Engineers

- ## SALARY
   = $50,001 or more

- ## JOB GROWTH
  = 21% or more

- ## EDUCATION
  Four-year degree or more

SCHOOL SUBJECTS

science	reading
math	art
computers	

My work saves lives. I design machines for doctors and labs. My machines help sick people breathe and keep their hearts beating.

Hospitals have lots of machines. Biomedical engineers designed all of them. These machines are very important. Doctors depend on them. I work hard to make the best medical equipment. A lot of planning goes into the designs.

Right now, I am designing a new artificial heart. Designing a heart is very difficult. I know all about the human body and the body's chemistry. I know how a real heart works so I can imitate it. I also have to know engineering.

I run a lot of tests. I have a special computer that copies how it will work. I must make sure that it will work well with the other human organs. It has to be perfect. My job is very important. I create new ways to save people's lives.

Biotechnical Researchers

Hello! I work for a company that makes medicine. I'm doing research on Native American medicine. Native Americans made cures from the plants that grew around them. For years the medical world thought that these cures did not work. We now know that many plants have healing powers.

I work in a lab. I study these plants and mixtures. I do chemical analyses of the plants. I do experiments to see how they react under different conditions.

My findings have been amazing. This company is making three new medicines based on ancient remedies. Doctors around the world are excited about my discoveries. My research is very important. It will help sick people get well. I can't take the credit, though. I'm figuring out what others already knew.

SALARY

= $50,001 or more

JOB GROWTH

= 21% or more

EDUCATION

Four-year degree or more

SCHOOL SUBJECTS

science	writing
math	computers
reading	

Bookkeepers

SALARY

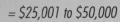

= $25,001 to $50,000

JOB GROWTH

= 10% or less

EDUCATION

Training after high school

SCHOOL SUBJECTS

math

reading

computers

BUSINESS

I keep track of the money this store makes every day. I'm a bookkeeper. I record day-to-day business activities.

I type the numbers into our computer accounting system. I have to type the numbers exactly right. I can't be off by even a penny. I record how many sales we had in cash. I type in how many personal checks we received. I also have to account for credit card sales. I help with the company payroll. I figure out how much we need to pay employees on each pay day. I multiply the money they make in an hour by how many hours they worked. I have to be accurate. If I make a mistake, the person will not get paid the right amount.

I deal with money and finances all day long. I have to be very good with numbers. I've always been good at math. I can add long rows of numbers in my head. Bookkeepers help businesses keep track of money.

Bricklayers

I build walls for a living. Actually, I build a lot more than that. I'm a bricklayer. Bricklayers build things out of bricks.

I lay a row of bricks as a foundation. I use mortar to stick the bricks together. Mortar is another word for cement. I put another row of bricks on top of the first row. I never stack one brick on top of another. I center the new row on two of the bottom bricks. That makes the wall stronger. I use a tool that looks like a spatula to put on the mortar. It's called a trowel. It takes a long time to build something out of bricks. Each one has to be put in place.

I'm working on a chimney for a new house now. I have to look at the architect's blueprints. I have to get the chimney just the right size so the roofers can build around it. Then I go to a new building site.

I work all over the city. I work on a lot of different buildings. Every job is different. Sometimes I make an entire house out of bricks. I stay very active. I've always liked working with my hands.

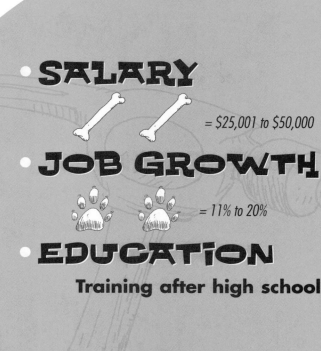

SALARY
= $25,001 to $50,000

JOB GROWTH
= 11% to 20%

EDUCATION
Training after high school

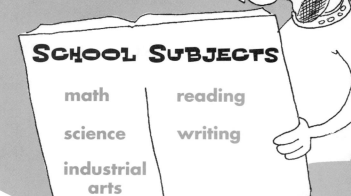

SCHOOL SUBJECTS

math	reading
science	writing
industrial arts	

Broadcast Technicians

SALARY

 = $25,001 to $50,000

JOB GROWTH

= 11% to 20%

EDUCATION

Two-year degree

SCHOOL SUBJECTS

science

reading

math

computers

Come in! I work for a television station as a broadcast technician. I work with the electronic equipment used to send out a television signal. If I don't do my job right, you won't be able to watch your favorite show. I know you don't want that to happen.

I make sure our equipment is running. I have to be very organized. I check the tower to make sure it is sending out the signal. I check our control panels to see if they are working. While shows are on the air, I check monitors to see if everything is okay. I check the signal on the control panel. I can change the color and brightness just like you can on your TV at home. Except, I do it for everyone watching.

Sometimes I work late to get everything right. I do extra work when a big storm has passed by the area. I work hard to get the station running again.

Building and Home Inspectors

Safety first! That's my motto. I'm a building home inspector. I check out your house and school to make sure they are safe.

I look over every inch of the building to find any problems. I look at the walls and the floors. I check the plumbing and the electrical outlets. I make sure that the construction workers have done a good job. Cities pass laws so that houses and offices will be built to be safe. These laws are called building codes. I must see that the codes are obeyed. I know all of them. If someone doesn't follow the codes, the building could collapse or people could be trapped if it caught on fire.

When something isn't right, I file a report. The problems must be corrected. I must be very detailed so the builder knows exactly what to fix. I have to know how to build houses and offices so I can make sure other people are doing their jobs correctly. If a building doesn't pass inspection, I can close it and stop people from going inside. I like my job because I know that I am making the city safer. Without me, people could get hurt by dangerous buildings.

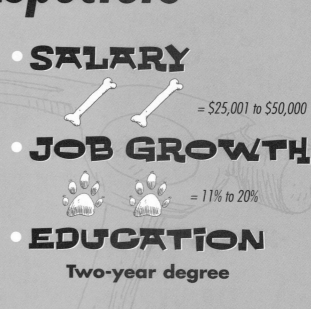

SALARY

= $25,001 to $50,000

JOB GROWTH

= 11% to 20%

EDUCATION

Two-year degree

SCHOOL SUBJECTS

math	writing
science	computers
reading	social studies
industrial arts	

Building Contractors

SALARY

= $50,001 or more

JOB GROWTH

= 21% or more

EDUCATION

Four-year degree or more

SCHOOL SUBJECTS

reading   drawing

computers   math

physical
education

CONSTRUCTION

I'm building a beautiful new house for the Hanks family. They hired me to oversee the work on the building. I'm a building contractor.

Building contractors build houses, theaters, offices, shops, and factories. We take care of all the details for the owner. I look at the blueprints to see what has to be done. I write an estimate of exactly how much it will cost. I include the price of the supplies like lumber, nails, glass, and tools. I figure out how much labor will cost. I hire carpenters, plumbers, and electricians to work on the project.

I sign a contract with the owners. The contract tells the owners how much the project will cost and when it will be done. Once the contract is signed, I get to work. I hire the workers. I purchase materials. I make sure the workers do their jobs correctly. Contractors know the best way to do things. We also know good people to hire and the best materials to buy.

The Hanks are very happy with their new home. If you want to build an office or a house, give me a call.

Building Maintenance Workers

I work at Michael Murphy Elementary School as a building maintenance worker. I keep the school looking beautiful. I also keep it safe. I fix just about anything. I'm a very handy person.

The principal lets me know about any problems with the building. I work on the plumbing and the electrical wires. I make the school look its best. I had to fix the bleachers in the gym the other day. Someone had cracked one of the seats. I replaced it with a new board. I just repainted the school sign in front of the building. It was starting to peel and fade. Sometimes I wash floors or remove graffiti from the building. That makes me mad. People should have respect for this school.

I work hard at my job. Everyone at the school relies on me. I'm the general problem solver. I want this school to be a nice place for the teachers and the students.

SALARY

= $25,001 to $50,000

JOB GROWTH
= 11% to 20%

EDUCATION
High school diploma

SCHOOL SUBJECTS

reading

math

industrial arts

Bus Drivers

- ## SALARY

   = $25,001 to $50,000

- ## JOB GROWTH

  = 11% to 20%

- ## EDUCATION

  Training after high school

SCHOOL SUBJECTS

math

reading

I drive the city bus. Driving might sound like an easy job. It's not. I follow a set schedule every day. People expect to see me at their stop at the same time. They get mad if I'm late. I try to stay on schedule. It's hard if traffic is bad or if it's raining hard.

I don't want to make people late. I'm responsible for getting hundreds of people to work. I have planned stops that I make. People can signal me when they want to get off the bus. They push buttons to let me know. I do a lot of stopping and going. I have to be patient.

I also have to be safe. Bus drivers know how to operate a large vehicle. Driving can be very dangerous. I follow all the traffic laws. If I run a stop sign, I might have an accident and hurt all the people on the bus. I wouldn't want that.

The city keeps buses running almost all the time. I get up very early in the morning to start my shift. Some drivers work way past midnight. We even work on the weekends and holidays. People need us to get where they want to go. I talk to people as they get on and off. I like it when someone tells me to have a nice day. It always makes me smile.

Business Education Teachers

I prepare high school students for the business world. I teach high school students skills like using computers, business writing, and bookkeeping. My classes are important for students who want to work in offices.

I have a computer lab where I teach word processing and spreadsheet software. I teach the proper format for business documents. Students learn how to write contracts and letters. My bookkeeping students learn how to keep track of money. They record figures in a spreadsheet.

I plan what I teach every day. I grade homework. I return it the next day. I let students know how they are doing. We send out report cards every six weeks. I record grades in the school's computer system.

I have some good students. They try very hard to learn the skills. Good students make my job special.

- **SALARY**

= $25,001 to $50,000

- **JOB GROWTH**

= 10% or less

- **EDUCATION**
Four-year degree or more

SCHOOL SUBJECTS

math	writing
computers	social studies
reading	

Business Executives

SALARY

 = $50,001 or more

JOB GROWTH

 = 11% to 20%

EDUCATION

Four-year degree or more

SCHOOL SUBJECTS

math	writing
reading	business
computers	social studies

It's not easy running a large company. I am at the top of the business ladder. Many decisions and problems are brought to me.

I approve the budget for each department. I approve finances for our factories. I make sure every office has supplies. I make sure all the bills are paid. I check over everything that deals with money. I make sure everyone is doing a good job. That's a lot of work. I hire employees. Sometimes I fire people.

I have a staff of department supervisors under me. But I make the final decisions. This company is important to me. I want it to be a success. I make sure we make money. Business is about making money.

I work long hours. Sometimes I feel like I should sleep in my office. I get here early and stay late. But I like my job. My company wouldn't be where it is today without my hard work.

Business Service Salespeople

I travel to companies to ask them to install vending machines for their employees. I'm a business service salesperson for Vend-N-Spend. We provide snacks to people all over the state. We're a snack machine service.

We install vending machines for employees to use. We put in fresh food once a week. We get the money the people put in the machines. The more offices we serve, the more money we make. I work hard to find new locations for our machines. I meet with company managers to get them interested in our service. I tell them how convenient it is for their employees. I have them sign a contract.

I call to make sure my customers are happy with our service. I drive around most of the day. This job takes a lot of travel. It can get pretty hectic.

I use a cell phone and handheld computer to stay in touch on the road. My car is my office.

- **SALARY**
   = $25,001 to $50,000

- **JOB GROWTH**
   = 11% to 20%

- **EDUCATION**
  Two-year degree

SCHOOL SUBJECTS

math   computers

reading

social studies

44   Jobs A–Z

Buyers

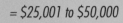

= $25,001 to $50,000

JOB GROWTH

= 10% or less

EDUCATION

Two-year degree

SCHOOL SUBJECTS

math

reading

computers

I buy things from factories so you can buy them later in your favorite store. I'm a professional buyer for a furniture store. I shop for furniture for a living.

My boss tells me the kind of furniture he would like to sell in his store. Then I go to factories and buy tables, chairs, and sofas for our store to sell to you. I have to know what styles people like. I have to know how much you would pay for a sofa. I know furniture. I meet with people at the factories. I arrange payment for the furniture I buy. I make sure all the furniture gets shipped to my store.

I put it out so you can look at it when it arrives. I set up displays that look like living rooms and bedrooms. I did a room where everything looked like it was from Mexico. I even had them hang a fake cow skull on the wall. I like to talk to interior designers to find out the trends. I know all about fabric and different kinds of wood.

I buy furniture that you will want to buy. I love it when someone finds the perfect table or sofa in our store. That means that I have done a great job.

BUSINESS

Cabinetmakers

I work as a cabinetmaker in a factory. I make cabinets for kitchens and bathrooms. I make the cabinets by following a blueprint. The blueprint gives me instructions on what size to make the cabinets.

We make cabinets in many different sizes. I measure the wood. I mark it so I know where to cut. I cut the pieces with a table saw. I wear safety glasses so I don't get anything in my eyes. I put the pieces together with screws and dowels. I make sure that the grains in the boards are a good match. I don't want my work to look sloppy.

I add doors and drawers. I screw the hinges in with a power screwdriver. I sand the surface to make it smooth. I stain the wood to make it a certain color. I put a protective coating on it to keep water from warping the boards.

I build many cabinets in a day. I build them to match my supervisor's orders. I make them in the sizes and colors the company needs. I've always liked working with my hands. I'm glad I have a job where I get to use my carpentry skills.

SALARY
= $25,000 or less

JOB GROWTH
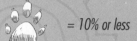
= 10% or less

EDUCATION
Training after high school

SCHOOL SUBJECTS

reading   industrial arts

math

computers

Cable and Satellite TV Installers

SALARY

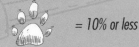

= $25,001 to $50,000

JOB GROWTH

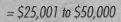

= 10% or less

EDUCATION

Two-year degree

SCHOOL SUBJECTS

reading

computers

math

physical
education

How many TV stations do you get at your house? Cable and satellite companies provide lots of stations to their customers. Instead of an antenna, we hook your house to a cable or satellite. We have cables that run across the city. Our cables are hooked to a satellite dish. We pick up TV channels from space with the satellite dish. Or, we can place a satellite dish on your house.

I run cables into your house or hook up a satellite dish. Your house may already have cables inside. I also repair cable systems. I can improve your TV picture. I may go outside and check the connection from your house. I work with equipment every day. I can find the problem easily most of the time.

I like installing cable and satellite TV. I get to drive from house to house. It's better than sitting in an office.

CAD Technicians

I use a computer to do technical drawings for engineers. I'm a CAD technician. CAD stands for computer-aided design. I work with an engineer. The engineer tells me exactly how the design should look. I use my computer to do the artwork.

Computers are great for technical drawings. I make my lines perfectly straight. The computer measures the lines for me. I make them exactly the right length. I give a printout of the design to the engineer. The engineer looks over my work and tells me how to improve the design. Since I did the artwork on the computer, I can make changes without having to redraw the entire thing.

The engineer uses my drawing to create plans and a budget for the project. CAD technology makes designing machines and buildings much easier. I never have to erase. I make changes just by moving my mouse. I like being a CAD technician. It's like doodling all day.

SALARY

= $25,001 to $50,000

JOB GROWTH

 = 10% or less

EDUCATION

Two-year degree

SCHOOL SUBJECTS

art	computers
math	
science	

48 Jobs A–Z

Camera Operators

- ## SALARY

  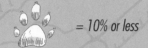 = $25,001 to $50,000

- ## JOB GROWTH

  = 10% or less

- ## EDUCATION

  Four-year degree or more

SCHOOL SUBJECTS

art

computers

reading

math

I'm a photographer for the movies. Instead of shooting still pictures, I shoot movie footage. I'm a camera operator for a big film studio. I use movie and video cameras to record live-action images and sound.

I work closely with directors. They tell me how they want me to shoot each scene. I know a lot about camera equipment. We use different kinds of cameras to create different looks. I know how to work with directors to get the perfect shot. Sometimes we film scenes a few times in a row to get them right.

I work a lot of weird hours. I work at night if we need to shoot after dark. Sometimes I work early in the morning. It depends on what the script calls for. My job is different every day. I don't sit at a desk staring at a computer. I look through a camera lens. I create art.

Think of me the next time you see a movie. Imagine that you're a camera operator shooting every scene. Making movies is pretty exciting.

Career Counselors

Some people think getting a job is easy. Actually, getting a job that you like is one of the hardest things you'll ever do. I try to make getting a good job easier. I'm a career counselor.

I work for a company that helps people find new careers. I talk with them about their interests. I give them tests to match their interests and skills to a career area. Think about your favorite things to do. Now think of a job where you could do those things. If you like to draw, maybe you should become an artist. If you like school, you might make a good teacher. Knowing the things you are best at will help you find a career that you like.

I help people learn interviewing skills and how to write resumes. Job interviews are very important. They determine whether you get the job you want. Resumes are also very important. Resumes summarize all of the things you've done in your life. They mention where you went to school. They mention the jobs you've had.

Have you thought about what you'd like to do when you get older? It's never too early to start thinking about a career. It's a good idea to explore different careers at your age. A career counselor can help you make wise choices.

SALARY

= $25,001 to $50,000

JOB GROWTH

= 11% to 20%

EDUCATION

Four-year degree or more

SCHOOL SUBJECTS

reading   computers

writing

social
studies

Carpenters

- **SALARY**

  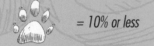 = $25,001 to $50,000

- **JOB GROWTH**

  = 10% or less

- **EDUCATION**

  Training after high school

SCHOOL SUBJECTS

reading

math

industrial arts

CONSTRUCTION

Hi! My name's Sean. I'm a carpenter working on a new house. Carpenters build things out of wood.

That covers a lot of area. We are responsible for the structure of buildings. In a new house, we put up the framework for the walls. We install windows and doors. We put cabinets in kitchens and bathrooms. We add molding around the floor and ceiling. On the outside of the house, we put up siding or build a porch.

I like working with my hands. I can build just about anything if you give me a hammer and nails. Take this house for example. The Simons wanted a ladder that went through a hole in the ceiling up to Sharon's room. She really likes tree houses. I followed the architect's plans to make sure I got it right. I measured the wood with a tape measure. I cut it with my power saw. I nailed the boards in place. I checked to make sure it was sturdy. I wouldn't want Sharon to hurt herself.

I'm sure there are lots of neat things about your home that a carpenter has built. We make houses possible. Carpenters are important people.

Caterers

I make food for special events. I'm a caterer. People hire me to make their weddings, birthdays, and parties a day to remember.

I talk with them to find out what they are looking for. Sometimes people want a special theme. I just threw a "Going Hawaiian" wedding. The food was tropical. We had coconut shrimp and pineapple cake. I work out the details with the clients. We discuss food, drinks, and decorations. They tell me how many people will be there. I come up with a budget. I get the budget approved by the clients.

I have my chefs cook the food. We bring it to the party in vans. I hire servers and bartenders. I try to make the party like being in a restaurant. People hire me because I do a good job. I've thrown wonderful parties. Maybe I could cater a party for you some time.

SALARY

 = $25,000 or less

JOB GROWTH

 = 21% or more

EDUCATION

High school diploma

SCHOOL SUBJECTS

reading

math

art

Chefs and Dinner Cooks

SALARY

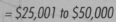 = $25,001 to $50,000

JOB GROWTH

 = 11% to 20%

EDUCATION

Two-year degree

SCHOOL SUBJECTS

reading

math

writing

Ah, you are just in time to taste my newest creation. I call it Tangy Tortellini. Notice its fine color. Notice how the cheese on top is bubbling. And, oh, that smell! I am very proud of the food I create. Like an artist, I combine ingredients to make something beautiful. I am more than a cook. I am a chef.

Chefs develop recipes. We cook food served at the best restaurants. I never make hamburgers and french fries. People like to eat my food. It is unlike anyone else's. I always come up with new ideas. I don't want people to get tired of my restaurant. I work all day in the kitchen. My kitchen is like the one you have at home, except it's much larger. I cook for lots of people.

I follow directions and measure accurately. I don't want to ruin a dish. I have several cooks who work under me. They use my recipes to make the food. I supervise their work.

Notice the food you are eating the next time you go out to dinner. Look at it. Smell it. Taste it. Someone like me created it so you could have a pleasant dinner.

Chemical Engineers

Watch this! I'm designing a rubber ball that will bounce higher than any before. The secret of the bounce is in the chemical in the rubber. I can make the ball bounce higher by changing the chemicals. I'm a chemical engineer.

Chemical engineers find new ways to make drugs, plastics, and detergents. I'm an engineer for a big company. I work in a lab. I mix chemicals to create new compounds. I use my research to create better products.

I figure out how to make thousands of balls once I get the formula right. I come up with a chemical recipe for the ball. The balls have to be made the same way every time. I make sure the workers in the factory understand my instructions. I take samples from the rubber batches to see if the mixture is right. A small error could mess up the balls. No one wants a ball that doesn't bounce.

I create many new products every year. I use my knowledge of chemicals to make life easier.

SALARY
= $50,001 or more

JOB GROWTH
= 10% or less

EDUCATION
Four-year degree or more

SCHOOL SUBJECTS

science	writing
math	computers
reading	

Chemical Processing Workers

- ## SALARY

    = $25,001 to $50,000

- ## JOB GROWTH

    = 10% or less

- ## EDUCATION

    Training after high school

SCHOOL SUBJECTS

reading

math

computers

science

I work with paint all day long. But I've never picked up a brush. I'm a chemical processing worker at the Milwaukee Paint Company. I mix chemicals to make paint for the inside and outside of buildings.

I follow a formula. I use a different formula for outside paint than I use for inside paint. I measure the chemicals accurately. I pour the ingredients into big vats. I use electric mixers to get the paint the right texture. I watch the machines to make sure they work correctly. Sometimes I make adjustments.

I mix paint all day long. I wear a uniform so I don't splash paint on my clothes. Most of the paint I make is white. Workers in another part of the factory make pigments that can be added to white paint. Mixing pigments gives you a rainbow of color choices.

Chemical processing workers work in a lot of different factories. We run machines that make plastics, fertilizers, and rubber materials. I'm sure a factory near you employs workers like me.

Chemists

Shhh! Be very quiet. I'm working on a new secret formula. I work in a lab at a big candy factory. I'm creating a new artificial flavor. It's going to taste like blueberries. I haven't found the right formula yet. At the moment it tastes a little like cherries.

Chemists do research on different ingredients. Chemistry is like working with a recipe. Everything in the world has its own special recipe made from ingredients called elements. I can find out the ingredients of anything by running some tests. I use test tubes, microscopes, and computers to help me.

I know how different chemicals react to different tests. Some ingredients do weird things under bright lights or when heated. That helps tell me what they are.

I get into my work. I know a lot about math and science. Chemistry is very complex. I pay attention to many details. Doing chemistry is like solving a puzzle. I find how things are made. Chemistry is very interesting. It's like being a detective.

SCIENCE AND ENGINEERING

SALARY
= $50,001 or more

JOB GROWTH
= 11% to 20%

EDUCATION
Four-year degree or more

SCHOOL SUBJECTS

science	computers
math	social studies
reading	

Child-Care Workers

SALARY

 = $25,000 or less

JOB GROWTH

  = 11% to 20%

EDUCATION

High school diploma

SCHOOL SUBJECTS

reading   writing

math

computers

Would you like me to read you a story? Oh, I'm sorry. You're a little too old for that. Please forgive me. I'm a child-care worker in a nursery school. I'm used to working with kids who are much younger than you are. I lead them through different activities.

We always have so much fun! We finger-paint and play games and sing songs. I'm sure you're too old to enjoy some of those things. But younger kids like doing them. I teach them how to get along with other kids. My job is to help the kids do everything. Most of them see me as their friend instead of a babysitter. I have to correct them sometimes. I can't let anyone be mean or bad. It wouldn't be fair to the other kids.

We don't just play games all day. I give the children snacks and make sure they take a nap. Smaller kids need to take a nap every day. Child-care workers have to be patient and understanding. Sometimes the kids fuss because they don't want to take a nap. I make sure they have all of their things when it is time to go. Young kids aren't as responsible as you are.

I love the kids I work with. I miss them when they go on to elementary school.

Chiropractors

Do you sit up straight? You should. Posture is very important. I should know. I'm a chiropractor. I diagnose and treat disorders of the spinal column or spine. The spine runs from your skull to your tailbone. The spine is very important.

People come to me when they have a backache. Many of them have been in car accidents. When a car hits another car from behind, it can cause damage to a person's back. I help people feel better again. I examine them in my office. They lie on a table like the one you sit on when you go to the doctor. I look at their spine to see what is wrong.

Many nerves are located near the spine. That's why back injuries are so painful. I suggest treatments for the pain. Sometimes I make backs feel better by giving massages. Sometimes I tell people to exercise or rest. Putting heat on the pain may help. I give patients heating pads to use at home. Sometimes people have back problems because they are overweight. I give them a diet.

I like to help people feel better again. No one should live life in pain.

- **SALARY** = $50,001 or more
- **JOB GROWTH** = 21% or more
- **EDUCATION** Four-year degree or more

SCHOOL SUBJECTS

science	writing
math	computers
reading	

Civil Engineers

- ## SALARY

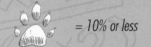

= $50,001 or more

- ## JOB GROWTH

= 10% or less

- ## EDUCATION

Four-year degree or more

SCHOOL SUBJECTS

science	computers
math	reading
social studies	writing

Hi! My name is Pat. I'm a civil engineer. Civil engineers design and build projects like roads and airports. I do a lot of research.

First, I go out to the place where we are planning to build. I look at the land. Later in my office I look at reports and blueprints and photographs taken from the air to make sure it is a good building site. I consider how the building will affect the area. I wouldn't be allowed to build a noisy factory next to a nature preserve. I figure out how to build the project so it will be safe. I wouldn't want anyone to get hurt because I made a mistake.

Then I see if the city can afford the project. I estimate a lot of numbers. Math and science are very important in my job. I am designing a train system between our city and another city 20 miles away. A lot of people drive between the two cities to get to work. A train would help with traffic jams in the morning.

I've spent many late hours in my office over the last few weeks. I draw out the plans on my computer. I've even had to eat at my desk instead of going home for dinner. I am using my knowledge to make the city a better place to live. My train will help people get to work with less stress.

Clergy

There are many different kinds of religions in our country. I'm a minister in my own church. The most important part of my job is helping other people. I teach people about faith and preach sermons. I perform wedding and funeral services. My church members look to me for moral and spiritual guidance. I give them advice.

I visit people who are sick or too old to go to services. I talk with them about religion. Mostly, I just visit them to let them know that someone cares. I represent all of the people in my church to the community. I make sure that our building is taken care of. Places of worship need to be safe and clean. I have to know and be able to understand important religious books. Religious leaders have to like to get up in front of large groups and give speeches.

Ministers like to help and teach people. I work with members of my religion on projects like feeding the homeless and giving clothes to needy families. Clergy work to make the community a nicer place to live. I enjoy teaching people about my religion.

SALARY

= $25,001 to $50,000

JOB GROWTH

= 11% to 20%

EDUCATION

Four-year degree or more

SCHOOL SUBJECTS

reading   writing

math   geography

social studies

EDUCATION AND SOCIAL SERVICES

Clothes Designers

SALARY

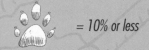

= $50,001 or more

JOB GROWTH

= 10% or less

EDUCATION

Two-year degree

SCHOOL SUBJECTS

art

reading

math

Have you ever thought about the clothes you wear? Someone designed everything that you own. I'm a clothes designer. I work for a clothing company.

I draw pictures of clothes so our factory can make them. I do different designs for each season. I study fabrics and dyes and colors. I draw sketches of my new ideas. I make a pattern for the designs I like the best. A pattern tells me how to cut the fabric for sewing.

I choose a fabric that will be just right. Then I make a sample piece. I have a model try it on. I make changes until it is perfect. Then I draw a pattern for each size. The tailors and dressmakers in our factory use my patterns. They make hundreds of pieces in different colors. Then we ship the clothes to stores.

I have an office upstairs in our factory. I have pieces of fabric and new design sketches everywhere. I like to sketch at a big drawing table. I sit and try to think of new ideas. I have to be original. We have to know how to match fabrics with styles. Fabric is very important. I like to use cotton for summer clothes. I prefer wool for fall jackets and pants. I keep up with the latest fashions. I love creating exciting new clothes.

Commercial Fishers

Do you like to fish? Imagine fishing every day. That's what I do for a living. My job is probably a little different than you would think. I don't sit around with a pole at the end of a pier. I'm a crew member on the Tina Louise. It's a tuna boat that trolls the Pacific Ocean.

Our boat stays out at sea for several days. We use nets instead of poles to catch our fish. We throw our nets into schools of fish. That helps us catch many at once. The nets are really heavy when they're full. We sort through the catch to make sure the fish are all the right size and kind. We must follow fishing laws. The government makes laws to protect wildlife. We can catch only certain fish and in certain amounts. Sometimes we accidentally catch turtles or dolphins in with the fish. I return them to the ocean safely. Then I take the "keepers" and get them ready to be picked up at the dock.

When I was your age I stood on the docks and watched the fishing boats. I always wanted to go out to sea. The ocean is my second home. I like the sound of the waves and the sea gulls. Being on a boat is like heaven. Here's something I bet you didn't know. Tuna are really big. Some weigh several hundred pounds. Now how do those packing plants get them in those little cans?

- **SALARY**
  = $25,001 to $50,000

- **JOB GROWTH**
  = 10% or less

- **EDUCATION**
  High school diploma

SCHOOL SUBJECTS

reading

math

science

ommunity Affairs Representatives

- ## SALARY
  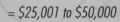
  = $25,001 to $50,000

- ## JOB GROWTH

  = 21% or more

- ## EDUCATION
  Four-year degree or more

SCHOOL SUBJECTS

reading	math
computers	writing
social studies	

I'm a community affairs representative for the local hospital. I work hard to let the people know about the many services we provide.

I like to meet with people to talk about the hospital. I tell them about our cancer facility and our baby delivery room. I encourage them to visit the hospital. I give them tours. It is important for citizens to know about the work we do. We provide health care to thousands of people.

The hospital just opened a new wing. I arranged a party. I invited everyone in the nearby area to attend. I threw the event to get people interested in this hospital. It's my job to make sure that people hear about the things we do. I write articles for the newspaper. I update our Web site. I write a monthly newsletter. It's important that people know about our services.

Compensation Analysts

I deal with money every day. I work for a large accounting company. I'm a compensation analyst.

There are many different positions in this company. We have accountants and managers and janitors. Each one has to be paid. I decide how much money each one should make. I have to look at the position. I look at what the person does. Some jobs require special skills or training. Jobs that require a college education usually pay more. I look at what these positions pay at other companies.

Our firm likes to be fair to its employees. I come up with pay and benefit guidelines. I figure out a salary for each position. I talk with the management about my plan. They approve the salaries. I have to be good with numbers. My job involves many details.

Compensation analysts know about every position at a company. We help people get the money they deserve for the work they do. We also help our companies save money.

BUSINESS

SALARY

= $50,001 or more

JOB GROWTH

= 11% to 20%

EDUCATION

Four-year degree or more

SCHOOL SUBJECTS

math	science
reading	computers
social studies	

Computer Engineers

SALARY

 = $50,001 or more

JOB GROWTH

= 21% or more

EDUCATION

Four-year degree or more

SCHOOL SUBJECTS

math

science

reading

computers

I've just developed a new computer chip. My new chip will be able to store much more information than any others available. Computer engineers like me improve computer technology every day.

Years ago one computer would fill a whole room. Now computers are small enough to be carried in your pocket. That's a big change. I work hard to make better computer equipment.

Think of all the information a computer can store. It's amazing! Computers have changed the way we live. We use computers for almost everything we do. Wireless technology has made computing mobile. The work I do has made computers much easier to use. New systems are very user friendly. They almost tell you what to do.

I enjoy working with gadgets. I need to know about science and mechanics to do what I do. I'm always on the cutting edge!

TECHNOLOGY

Computer Graphics Specialists

Look here! I design video games for a living. I'm a computer graphics specialist. I'm a lot like an artist. But I don't use paint and a brush. I make art by using my computer.

I draw images with my mouse or other special computer parts. I have a camera that can take pictures directly into my computer. I have a scanner to translate photos that have already been taken into computer images.

I change them around once they are in my computer. I change the colors or even the way the pictures look. I could take a picture of you and make it look like you were standing on top of the Empire State Building. I could even make you look blue or draw horns on your head. It's amazing what I can do with a computer.

I have special software to help me animate the pictures. I use this a lot when I'm making a video game. I keep up on the latest software. The technology is changing every day. My job is great. I get to be creative all the time. The only limit is my imagination.

SALARY
= $25,001 to $50,000

JOB GROWTH
= 21% or more

EDUCATION
Two-year degree

SCHOOL SUBJECTS

computers	science
art	reading
math	

Computer Security Consultants

SALARY

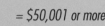

= $50,001 or more

JOB GROWTH

= 21% or more

EDUCATION

Four-year degree or more

SCHOOL SUBJECTS

math	writing
science	computers
reading	

Big companies spend a lot of money on computers. They store important information in them. Banks keep information about customer accounts, for example. Sometimes people try to steal or damage that information. That's where I come in. My job is to help companies protect their computers.

I meet with the company to learn their business. Then I set up software called a firewall to keep people out of the computer network. I add software to detect computer viruses. Computer viruses can damage valuable information.

I make sure all the employees at a company have passwords. Passwords protect each computer from being used by the wrong person. Technology changes all the time. I stay up-to-date. I understand business and technology to do my work. I work with many clients. Every company has different problems I help solve.

Computer Technicians

It's nice to meet you. I'm Alex. I'm the person who fixes office computers when they're on the blink. Computer technicians, like me, are important to offices. We're like computer doctors.

So much information is stored in computers today. Most offices might as well shut down if the computers are broken. I keep offices running smoothly. I can tell you everything there is to know about software drivers and hard drives. I understand many technical terms. I know about electronics. Computers are filled with chips and circuits. I know how they work.

Most problems are easy for me to fix. I can talk a person through many problems over the phone. I also can make a visit to your office or home.

I can open up the computer to see what is wrong. I have to know every piece inside. There are a lot of small parts in a computer. The software that runs a computer can also cause problems. I have to be able to troubleshoot software and hardware problems.

Being a computer doctor is fun. I get to travel around helping people. Computer repairers keep offices up and running. Give me a call if you have a problem.

- **SALARY**
  = $25,001 to $50,000

- **JOB GROWTH**
  = 21% or more

- **EDUCATION**
  Two-year degree

School Subjects

math   computers

reading

science

MECHANICS AND REPAIRERS

Construction Laborers

SALARY

= $25,000 or less

JOB GROWTH
= 11% to 20%

EDUCATION
Training after high school

SCHOOL SUBJECTS
reading

math

physical education

I'll be right with you. I just need to finish stacking this lumber. So you want to know about construction laborers. We do a lot of the physical work to make a building. You have to be very strong to do this job.

I have to lift heavy things. I unload trucks with supplies. I take off 50-pound bags of cement and stacks of bricks. I have to know what all the other workers like carpenters and roofers do so I can bring them the right supplies and tools. I help clean up around here. I can't leave tools and scraps lying around. Workers get hurt at dirty sites.

I really like the work. I'm friends with the other workers. We can talk to each other as we work. I get to spend a lot of time outside. I've built strong muscles doing my job.

My job never gets boring. When we finish a job, we go to another one. Every job is different. I work hard every day, but I don't worry about my job once I go home.

Copywriters

I'm a copywriter. I write the words that go into TV, magazine, and newspaper ads. The words in an ad are called "copy." I get people interested in products. I write ads for all kinds of things.

I've written TV commercials for dolls and action figures. I did a newspaper ad for a line of sports cars. I've even written magazine ads for furniture wax. I work for an advertising agency. I work with the account executive, copy editor, and art director to get my ideas. They give me an outline for my work. Then I sit at my keyboard and come up with the details. I add a little magic to the ads. I try to make every product sound exciting.

I learn all about the subject to write the copy. I talk with the people who sell the product to learn about it. I used the furniture wax on my kitchen table for two weeks to see how it worked.

When I'm done writing, I send the copy to my supervisor to get approval. Sometimes she suggests changes. Everyone at the agency works together to get the job done. Creating ads is a team effort. Listen to the words the next time you see a commercial. They have to be catchy. Copywriters make every day things seem interesting.

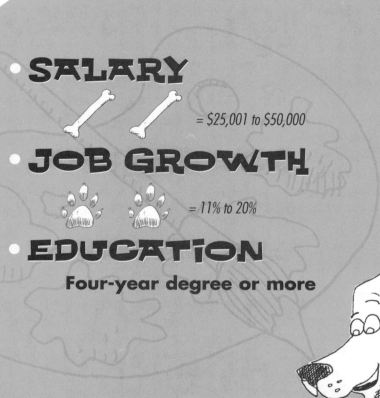

SALARY

= $25,001 to $50,000

JOB GROWTH

= 11% to 20%

EDUCATION

Four-year degree or more

SCHOOL SUBJECTS

reading

computers

writing

math

social studies

Corrections Officers

- ## SALARY
   = $25,001 to $50,000

- ## JOB GROWTH
  = 21% or more

- ## EDUCATION
  Training after high school

SCHOOL SUBJECTS

reading   writing

math

social studies

Nothing gets by me. I'm a corrections officer at the state jail. I watch over the prisoners. The inmates are in prison because they have broken the law. I make sure they behave themselves while they are serving their time.

I walk around the prison keeping guard. I check locks, window bars, doors, and gates. I make sure the prisoners can't escape. I check for weapons. I report anything I see to my supervisor. I write a report about anything that doesn't seem right.

I carry a club in case I run into an emergency. I have to be prepared. This job can be dangerous. I've been caught in some scary situations.

Prisoners don't just sit all day. Some take classes or work at jobs. Sometimes I have to take prisoners around the prison. I may take them to the medical office or to the chapel. I also stand guard at the watch tower. I watch the yard and the fence when prisoners are outside for exercise. I have to keep my eyes open. It's not easy being a corrections officer. The inmates don't appreciate the work I do. I get my job satisfaction from knowing that I am making this community a safer place.

Cosmetologists

You look fabulous! I want to cut your hair. I make people look beautiful all day long. I work as a cosmetologist. Cosmetologists spend their days working on people's hair and skin. People want to look their best. I help them do that.

I can trim your hair when it starts to grow out. I know special haircutting techniques. You can't just chop off hair with scissors! I can help you choose a new style when you get tired of your old one. I know what will look good with the shape of your face. Maybe you would like me to make your hair lighter or darker. I use dyes to change the color. What about making it curly? I can put chemicals in your hair that will do that. I have to be very careful when I use chemicals. I can burn your scalp if I don't use them the right way.

I can help you with your skin. I can give you some lotion to use if it's too dry. I help women apply makeup. I help them choose the right colors and show them how to put it on. Most people like to come to see me. I'll treat you special!

SALARY
= $25,000 or less

JOB GROWTH
= 11% to 20%

EDUCATION
Training after high school

SCHOOL SUBJECTS
reading

math

art

Court Reporters

SALARY

= $25,000 or less

JOB GROWTH

= 11% to 20%

EDUCATION

Training after high school

SCHOOL SUBJECTS

math

reading

computers

I go to court every day. I record every word that is said in the court room. I work for the state as a court reporter.

I use a stenotype machine to type the words that people say. Shorthand is a special language that abbreviates words and phrases. It allows people to take notes much faster. I listen to what people say, and type notes on my keyboard. Some stenotype machines use a computer-aided transcription that puts what I type into an electronic file. Then I can use my computer to work with the notes I take.

I have to be very fast. Sometimes I type 250 words in a minute. Later I rewrite my notes into English. Judges use my reports so they have a record of everything said during a hearing. The report helps them remember every detail. It is important that they have a printed record of exactly what was said.

Court reporters are an important part of the court process. Our notes make it possible for judges and attorneys to review cases when a trial is over. The reports can be used to see if the judge's decision was fair.

I help people get a fair trial. I record the facts and put them in an official record.

Craftspeople

I own my own pottery shop. I make beautiful plates, bowls, and vases out of clay. I fire them in my kiln. I paint them bright colors. I sell everything I make. I get to create art for a living. Some craftspeople run their own businesses. They make and sell things like candles, jewelry, woodcarvings, and pottery.

My shop is called the Mad Potter. I hired two people to help sell my pottery while I'm creating new things in my studio. I have to be both an artist and a business person. I keep track of the money my store makes by using my office computer. I have bills to pay just like any other business. Running a business is a lot of work. Sometimes I place ads in the local newspaper to get customers into the store. I sell my work at art shows and craft fairs. I can make a lot of money by setting up a traveling store to go to festivals.

For me, making money is a lot harder than making art. I work hard to stay in business. I like being the Mad Potter. Seeing someone buy one of my creations always makes me happy.

- **SALARY**

  = $25,000 or less

- **JOB GROWTH**

  = 11% to 20%

- **EDUCATION**

  Training after high school

SCHOOL SUBJECTS

art	computers
reading	
math	

Credit Analysts

- ## SALARY
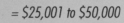
= $25,001 to $50,000

- ## JOB GROWTH

= 11% to 20%

- ## EDUCATION
Four-year degree or more

SCHOOL SUBJECTS

math	science
reading	computers
social studies	

I work for a large national bank. When a company applies for a loan, I check their credit information. I'm a credit analyst.

I look at a company's credit rating and debt information. If it has not paid past bills, we should not loan it money. I check out the growth potential of the company. I compare it to other companies that are the same size. I find out information about their management and how much their stock is worth. Our bank likes to make loans to companies that have a good future.

I write a report that includes all the figures I find. It is important that I write exactly why I do or do not recommend a loan. Then I pass my report on to a loan committee. It reviews the information and application to makes a final decision. Businesses go through this process all the time.

Credit analysts are important in the business world. The information we gather directly affects whether a company receives a loan.

Curators

If you wanted to see a famous painting by Van Gogh, where would you go? You'd probably take a trip to a museum. Museums display lots of famous paintings and sculptures so people can see them up close. I'm a curator at an art museum. Curators organize what you see in museums.

I have a lot of important decisions to make. I decide what exhibits we will have. I also decide where to put each piece of art. I usually group them by when they were created or by the artists. I know a lot about the history of art. I can tell you about famous artists and their work.

I buy new things for the museum. Famous art is really expensive. I decide what people will want to see. Sometimes I work with curators from other museums. We like to trade art so people in another city can see a beautiful piece. I run my museum like a business. I have a big staff to help me with my job. I make sure the museum is perfect when you visit.

Art is important to me. I like knowing that my work presents great art to the average person. Art is meant to be enjoyed.

SALARY
= $25,001 to $50,000

JOB GROWTH
= 11% to 20%

EDUCATION
Four-year degree or more

SCHOOL SUBJECTS

art	writing
reading	geography
social studies	foreign languages

Customer Service Representatives

SALARY

= $25,001 to $50,000

JOB GROWTH

= 21% or more

EDUCATION

High school diploma

SCHOOL SUBJECTS

reading	writing
math	
computers	

I work for a large corporation as a customer service representative. Every one of our products has a phone number on the back. If you have any questions or problems, just call that number. I'll answer the phone and try to help you.

I know all about our products. I can tell you how to use them the right way. I also help you if you are having a problem. Sometimes people have been overcharged. I correct their accounts. I am here to help our customers. My boss says the customer is always right. I do whatever I can to help solve problems.

I let my supervisor know about the calls I receive. The company likes to keep track of any complaints or comments. We want to know what people think about our products. We want people to continue to buy things from us. I work hard to keep up good customer relations.

BUSINESS

Customs Inspectors

If you take a trip to Mexico, you may talk to us to get back into the country. We work as customs inspectors at the U.S. and Mexican border. We check people's cars when they drive across the border into the United States.

We make sure everything they have in their cars is legal. United States law does not allow you to bring certain things across the border. You can bring a few souvenirs without any problem. A piñata would be okay. People are not allowed to bring too much merchandise in for free from Mexico. I would charge you a special tax called a duty if you tried to bring a whole truckload of piñatas. We check cars to make sure people are not bringing harmful things into our country. We look for weapons and drugs.

The United States has customs inspectors at every border and port. Some inspectors check ships that are entering the country. They inspect the entire cargo. The work we do is very important. We were hired by our government to keep this country safe.

Don't worry. We're pretty nice. You won't have any problems with us as long as you're following the law. Just don't try to pull a fast one. We're really good at our jobs. Nothing gets by us.

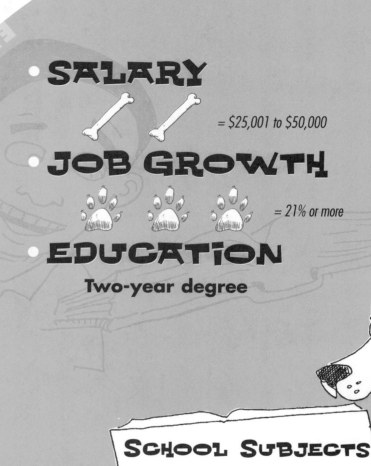

SALARY

= $25,001 to $50,000

JOB GROWTH

= 21% or more

EDUCATION

Two-year degree

SCHOOL SUBJECTS

math

computers

social studies

Dancers

- ## SALARY
   = $25,000 or less

- ## JOB GROWTH
   = 11% to 20%

- ## EDUCATION
  Four-year degree or more

SCHOOL SUBJECTS

dance	music
reading	drama
physical education	

I'm a professional dancer. I've danced in seven music videos. I specialize in modern dance. I move my body and my feet to the beat of music.

I usually work with other dancers. We practice together to get our dance routines perfect. We spend many hours rehearsing. A choreographer plans the routines. We follow the set instructions. We do the moves exactly as we are told. Getting jobs as a dancer isn't all that easy. You have to try out for every part. Auditions can be very rough. Hundreds of dancers compete against each other.

I have to stay in perfect shape. I make sure I eat well, exercise, and get lots of rest. I spend lots of hours dancing by myself. Sometimes I develop routines of my own. I went to school to become a dancer. I had to learn set steps and movements. Professional dancers work very hard. We practice for hours to look relaxed and natural. I have to be careful not to injure myself because dancing can be very hard on your body.

I love being a dancer. I don't make a lot of money. I enjoy what I am doing. One day I hope to teach people your age to dance. There's nothing like the feeling of moving your body along to the rhythm. Dancers bring music to life.

Data Entry Operators

I type information into computers all day long. I'm an expert typist. I work as a data entry operator for a large company. I'm in charge of keeping up our mailing lists.

We mail lots of catalogs to people every year. We keep the addresses up to date. I make changes when people let us know that they have moved. Sometimes we get our catalogs back because the person no longer lives at the address. I take the old addresses out of the system. I also add new names to our records.

We get requests for catalogs every day. I check the details of each entry. I make sure that I have spelled the name right and have the correct street number. I double check the zip code. If I make a mistake it will cost the company money.

I sit at a desk in front of a computer all day long. Sometimes my eyes get a little tired of staring at the screen. It's important that I take breaks to avoid strain. I like my job. I don't have to lift heavy things or work late at night. My feet don't hurt from standing all day. My coworkers are very nice.

BUSINESS

SALARY

= $25,000 or less

JOB GROWTH

= 10% or less

EDUCATION

Training after high school

SCHOOL SUBJECTS

reading

math

computers

Delivery Truck Drivers

SALARY

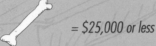

= $25,000 or less

JOB GROWTH

= 21% or more

EDUCATION

High school diploma

SCHOOL SUBJECTS

reading

math

physical education

I've got a truck full of roses, carnations, and daffodils. I deliver flowers for a florist. I'm a delivery truck driver for Bud's Flower Shop. I make many deliveries each day. I make sure each delivery arrives with the flowers fresh and uncrushed.

I pick up floral arrangements from our shop. I make sure each one has an address. I drive around this city so much that I know most of the streets. I keep a map in the glove compartment just in case. I bring the flowers to the door. I make sure I give out the right arrangement. Nothing cheers people up like getting flowers. I see smiling faces all day long.

I used to deliver lumber to building sites, so I had to lift heavy things. Depending on what you deliver, you might have to be in good shape.

Running around the city puts a lot of wear and tear on this truck. I check it before I leave the shop every day. I make sure the air pressure is right in the tires. I look under the hood and check the oil. I wouldn't want to break down when I have a load of flowers. I have the best job. I get to drive around all day.

Dental Hygienists

I like to see healthy smiles. I'm a dental hygienist. I work for Dr. Grinn. Dental hygienists help dentists help you.

I get you ready to see the dentist when you come for a check up. I sit you in the chair. I put a bib around your neck. I don't want you to get your clothes dirty. I clean and inspect your teeth. I give you fluoride to rinse with. Fluoride makes your teeth strong and healthy. You may need to have a cavity filled. I can take an X ray of your mouth. This helps the dentist see what is causing you pain.

I always make sure that I tell Dr. Grinn everything that I see. It is important that your dentist knows all about your teeth. I write down information in a file. Dentist's offices are a little scary to most people. I try to be nice to make it easier.

I'm here to keep you healthy. I want you to have a nice smile.

- ## SALARY
  = $25,001 to $50,000

- ## JOB GROWTH
  = 21% or more

- ## EDUCATION
  Two-year degree

SCHOOL SUBJECTS

science

math

reading

Dental Laboratory Technicians

SALARY

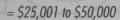 = $25,001 to $50,000

JOB GROWTH

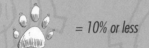 = 10% or less

EDUCATION

Two-year degree

SCHOOL SUBJECTS

reading

math

art

PRODUCTION

Do you have a mouth of healthy teeth? I hope you do. We all want to have a healthy smile. Sometimes people lose their adult teeth. This happens to older people or people who have been in an accident. You don't grow new ones if you lose them. A dentist can have artificial ones made for you. Artificial teeth are called dentures.

Dentists measure people for dentures. They determine the size and kind of teeth the person needs to have made. They make molds and impressions of the mouth. The dentist writes a prescription for the teeth like a doctor writes a prescription for medicine. Dental laboratory technicians read the prescription for directions to make false teeth. We mold plaster and plastic to make new teeth.

We have to be careful to get them the right size and shape. Each tooth in the mouth has a different shape. We use the dentist's impressions and molds to match the rest of the person's teeth. We don't want the false teeth to be noticeable. I work in a lab full of machines. I use molds and polishers and grinders to help me do my work.

My job is fun because I get to make things all day long. Making dentures is a lot like building things out of modeling clay. Every tooth is different. I pay attention to details. I wouldn't want someone to be embarrassed to smile because I didn't do a good job.

Dentists

Don't be afraid of me! Most people are afraid to go to the dentist. They shouldn't be. I don't want any of my patients to be in pain. My job is to help people.

I make sure that your mouth is healthy. I know all about your mouth and teeth. I clean your teeth so they look nice and white. I can fill a cavity. That stops the tooth from hurting. I check your gums and teeth. I use tools that look kind of scary. They really won't hurt you. I have a drill for fillings and some metal picks to check for holes in teeth. Sometimes I give people medicine to make their mouths healthy again. I may put braces on your teeth. That will make your adult teeth grow in straight and pretty.

I write down information about your mouth and put it in a file. I look at the file to tell you when you should come back to see me. I tell people the right way to brush teeth. Brushing and flossing are very important.

I see lots of people every day. I work very hard. I wear a lab coat and rubber gloves to make sure you don't catch any germs.

- **SALARY**
  = $50,001 or more

- **JOB GROWTH**
  = 10% or less

- **EDUCATION**
  Four-year degree or more

SCHOOL SUBJECTS

science	reading
math	computers
social studies	

Dieticians

SALARY

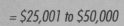

= $25,001 to $50,000

JOB GROWTH

= 11% to 20%

EDUCATION

Four-year degree or more

SCHOOL SUBJECTS

science	reading
math	computers
social studies	

HEALTH

Food is very important. I'm a dietician. I work at your school to plan healthy food for you to eat at lunch. You can blame me when you have to eat broccoli in the cafeteria.

I like french fries just as much as you do. But it isn't good for your body to eat them every day. I went to college to learn all about nutrition. I know all about different foods and how they affect your body. The body needs a good variety of food to work correctly. Otherwise, you would be tired and fall asleep in your classes, even gym.

You have to eat vegetables and fruit. You need protein to give you energy. I let you eat a little sugar. I want you to enjoy your lunch. But if I left it up to you, you would probably eat nothing but candy and cookies. I plan different meals every day so you won't get sick of eating the same thing. Imagine cauliflower five days a week!

My job is very important. I plan balanced meals. Eating right really does make you feel better.

Directors

Lights! Camera! Action! I direct movies for a living. Do you like to watch movies? Directors coordinate everything that happens in movies, plays, and TV programs.

I start out by reading the script. I imagine how the words and the action will appear on the screen. I get ideas for filming. I hire and meet with the cast of the movie. I talk with them about my ideas. Sometimes I make changes to the script to make improvements in a scene. I work with costume designers to have them create exciting costumes for the actors. They're making weird aliens for my new science fiction movie. I meet with special effects experts to explain how I want the spaceships and planets to look. I hire composers to create background music.

I want this movie to look like it is happening on another planet. I get the camera people to film each scene a certain way. I tell them the right camera angles and how much light to use. Directors make movies what they are. We put all the pieces together. The actors and camera people rely on us to tell them what to do.

- **SALARY** = $25,001 to $50,000
- **JOB GROWTH** = 11% to 20%
- **EDUCATION** Four-year degree or more

SCHOOL SUBJECTS

drama computers
science music
math writing
reading

Dispatchers

SALARY

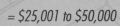

= $25,001 to $50,000

JOB GROWTH

= 11% to 20%

EDUCATION

Training after high school

SCHOOL SUBJECTS

reading

computers

math

writing

I organize deliveries every day. I'm a dispatcher for a nationwide moving company. I tell the drivers where they will go each day. I give them paperwork to organize things. I talk with every driver on the radio to make sure they are on schedule.

Our system is very advanced. I can track a moving truck using my computer. I can estimate the time it will take the truck to arrive at the next city. If a driver needs help, I call local repair people to go to the truck.

If a shipment will be late, I call our customer service person. She calls the customers to tell them about the delay. People want to get their belongings at their new home. I try to make sure we are on time whenever possible.

My job is very stressful. I am responsible for scheduling twenty trucks and moving crews. I must be organized and pay attention to details. I enjoy my work. I run the show and make things work.

Dispensing Opticians

I can find the perfect glasses for you. I'm an expert at choosing just the right frames. I work in an eyeglass shop as a dispensing optician. I don't check your vision. I work with you after you see a doctor and go to buy glasses. This shop has hundreds of frames to choose from. I'm very good at making recommendations.

Maybe you already have something in mind. I can tell you exactly where to find them. I get all kinds of requests. I even had some frames custom-made that had rhinestones and sequins on them. I write down the model number of the frames. Then I measure your face.

I measure the distance between the center of your eyes and the distance between the glasses and your face. I want your glasses to be comfortable. I write an order including the model number of the frame and your doctor's prescription for the lens. Optical technicians grind the lens to make them the right strength.

When you pick up your glasses, I check to make sure they are a good fit. I may make minor adjustments. I work with nice people every day. A lot of people are a little nervous about getting glasses. I like to make them feel at ease.

SALARY
= $25,001 to $50,000

JOB GROWTH
= 11% to 20%

EDUCATION
Four-year degree or more

SCHOOL SUBJECTS
science

computers

math

reading

Domestic Service Workers

SALARY

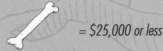

= $25,000 or less

JOB GROWTH

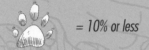

= 10% or less

EDUCATION

High school diploma

SCHOOL SUBJECTS

math

reading

PERSONAL SERVICES

I am an important part of this family. I'm a domestic service worker for the Thompson family. I run the household. I get paid to take care of this family. I do all the laundry and cooking and cleaning.

This house is so big that I stay really busy. I do laundry for seven people. I cook for the family and guests. I have Mrs. Thompson approve the menu. I clean the house every day. I make the beds and dust the furniture. I vacuum and mop.

I also take care of the kids. I make sure they get off to school every morning. I always have to pull Michael out of bed to get him going. That one's a rascal!

I like working for the Thompsons. They're a really nice family. They treat me well. I have my own apartment in the back of the house. Being a domestic service worker is hard work, but there's lots of variety!

Drafters

I get to draw all day long for a living. I work for an architect as a drafter. Drafters take the ideas and rough sketches of architects and engineers and turn them into blueprints and finished drawings. We sketch three-dimensional images like buildings and machines. It's important that people can see what these designs look like from all sides.

Sometimes I draw on a sketch pad. Most of the time I use my computer to sketch out the finished plans. My work has to be very accurate. I make sure my lines are even and meet up exactly right. I have to be careful with measurements. A small error could cause a problem when the construction people start to build. They look at my blueprints and use them as directions for building.

I work closely with my boss to make sure that I am sketching the designs the way they are supposed to be. I have to follow orders. My work involves many details. I also get to be artistic.

I draw every day. I love seeing a finished sketch. I always try to picture what the buildings will look like once they are built.

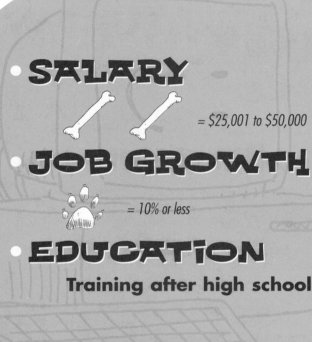

SALARY
= $25,001 to $50,000

JOB GROWTH
= 10% or less

EDUCATION
Training after high school

SCHOOL SUBJECTS

art

math

science

computers

Drywall Installers

SALARY

= $25,001 to $50,000

JOB GROWTH

= 21% or more

EDUCATION

Training after high school

SCHOOL SUBJECTS

math

reading

physical education

industrial arts

Look at the walls around you. Think about how they are made. Walls are built in layers. They have a wooden or metal frame. It is a skeleton for a wall. A layer of insulation keeps out the cold air in the winter and the warm air in the summer. Then a layer of plaster makes up the inside wall. Modern houses use a kind of plaster called drywall. Drywall comes in big, flat sheets.

I put up drywall in buildings for a living. I work for a construction company. I take the big sheets and screw or nail them to the wooden or metal framework in a building. I put up enough pieces to cover all the walls and the ceiling. I sometimes cut holes in the sheets to fit around a window or electric outlet.

Then I fill in the gaps between the sheets with some gooey white "mud" called joint compound. Otherwise, you would have a wall with big seams. I spread compound in the cracks. I put compound over the screw or nail heads. When it dries I sand the joints to make them smooth. Then the wall is ready to be painted.

I work on a lot of different buildings every year. Installing drywall is a good job. I don't have a lot of stress. I have to be strong, because the drywall is heavy to lift.

CONSTRUCTION

E-Commerce Managers

My company sells office supplies online. We have a Web site where people can look at our catalog. They order products and place them in a shopping cart. They pay for the items. We ship them out.

I manage the Web site. Doing business online is called e-commerce. I work with Web designers who design the Web pages. I work with writers who write what you read there. I see to it that the information on our site is accurate. We change the main items every day to keep it interesting. When a customer orders something, the order goes to our warehouse. There are many details to track.

It's important that our site stay up. If we have a crash, nobody can order our products. If we lose orders, we lose money. Customers would be unhappy if we lost their orders. Our site makes it easy for people to shop from their homes.

SALARY

= $50,001 or more

JOB GROWTH

= 21% or more

EDUCATION

Four-year degree or more

SCHOOL SUBJECTS

math	computers
reading	business
writing	social studies

Economists

SALARY

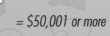 = $50,001 or more

JOB GROWTH

 = 11% to 20%

EDUCATION

Four-year degree or more

I study money for a living. I try to predict what will happen to our economy in the future. The economy is about how many people are unemployed and how much money people make. I look at data from many different sources. I compare the American dollar to the money used in other countries. I spot trends by using computer programs.

I work for the government as an economist. I explain how our country will do financially next year. I write reports explaining how I reached my opinion. I provide facts to support my ideas. The government uses my data to set policies. Sometimes our leaders change the way we deal with other countries based on my advice. They may increase aid to the poor and sick. Our economy changes all the time. Many things affect it.

Economists keep up with what's going on in the world. My estimates are very important. Many companies make decisions based on what economists say. I guess you could say that economists are like money scientists.

SCHOOL SUBJECTS

math	reading
computers	writing
social studies	

EDUCATION AND SOCIAL SERVICES

Editors

I'm a book editor for a large publishing company. Editors work for newspapers, book companies, online publishers, and radio and TV stations. I specialize in fiction. I've worked on some great novels. I find new books to publish. Authors submit manuscripts to book companies. A manuscript is a typed copy of the book. I read the manuscripts to look for the best ones. I have to know what people want to read. I read hundreds of manuscripts every year.

When I find a good novel, I meet with the author about getting publishing rights. The author signs a contract with my company. A contract is a legal document that states how much the author will be paid. Sometimes I ask the author to rewrite parts of the book. I look over the text for misspellings or grammar problems. I work closely with authors to make the books the best that they can be.

I've always liked to read. My job encourages other people to read. I help create great books so people will feel like turning the page. Reading can be exciting. I like to add a little adventure to people's lives.

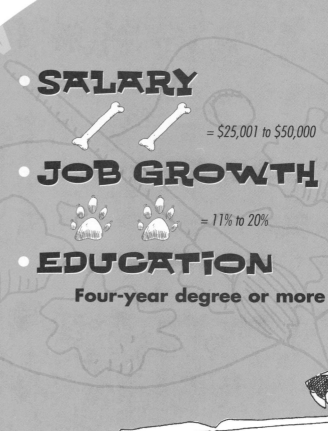

SALARY
= $25,001 to $50,000

JOB GROWTH
= 11% to 20%

EDUCATION
Four-year degree or more

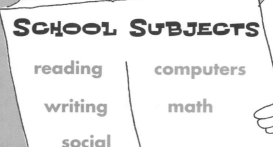

SCHOOL SUBJECTS

reading

computers

writing

math

social studies

Education Program Specialists

SALARY

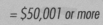 = $50,001 or more

JOB GROWTH

= 11% to 20%

EDUCATION

Four-year degree or more

SCHOOL SUBJECTS

reading   computers

math

social
studies

EDUCATION AND SOCIAL SERVICES

I'm an education program specialist with your school district. That sounds scarier than it is. I help teachers plan their school year. I look at all the schools to make sure they are doing a good job. I want students to learn what they need to know.

The school district expects teachers to teach certain information by the end of the school year. It is important that students do not fall behind. I work closely with the teachers to guide them through the year. I offer training programs to show them how to use new equipment.

My job is very important to me. Hundreds of students go to school in this district. What they learn in one year will greatly affect their futures. I make sure they learn as much as they can. A good education can help a person have a good life.

Electrical Engineers

I work for a large company. I'm an electrical engineer. Electrical engineers design new electrical equipment. We plan and oversee the production of things like TVs, DVD players, and video cameras. I even designed a computer used in many schools.

Computers are complicated. They have many tiny parts. All of the parts have to work together. Electricity makes the parts work. I had to figure out how to get electricity to run the databases. It took me three years to design this computer. I had several engineers helping me. We worked in our office for many hours.

It took a lot of testing. I used math problems to figure out how to get it to work. I drew blueprints so it could be manufactured. It has to be built exactly right. I wouldn't want someone to buy a computer that didn't work. Computers help us do many things. I like developing new technology.

SALARY
 = $50,001 or more

JOB GROWTH
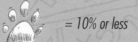 = 10% or less

EDUCATION
Four-year degree or more

SCHOOL SUBJECTS

science	reading
math	computers
art	

Electricians

- ## SALARY

   = $25,001 to $50,000

- ## JOB GROWTH

  = 21% or more

- ## EDUCATION

  Training after high school

SCHOOL SUBJECTS

science	writing
math	industrial arts
reading	

CONSTRUCTION

I'm an electrician. Electricians install and repair anything electrical. I know all about electricity.

You use electricity every day. Your entire house has wires running through it. The wires let you plug in your toaster and TV and lamps. Electricians install the wiring. We fix the wiring if it isn't working right. Every light in your house has a wire that runs from the switch through the wall. I run wires through the walls and hang lighting fixtures.

But electricity can be dangerous. Wires can cause fires or give you a shock. Electricians have to be careful to make your house safe. We check all the wires and outlets in houses. We wouldn't want anyone to get hurt. I have to know building codes to install wiring properly.

Electricity makes your life much easier. You couldn't do your homework at night or watch TV without it. My work makes your house more comfortable.

Electromechanical Technicians

I make and repair altimeters for airplanes. Altimeters tell a pilot how high the plane is flying. An altimeter is an electromechanical device. That means it has both electrical and mechanical parts. I'm an electromechanical technician.

I'm a whiz at fixing machines. Altimeters are very technical. I know how to make them work properly. It is important for a pilot to know the right altitude. A plane might crash into a mountain if the altimeter wasn't working the right way. I check the altimeters in planes to make sure they are accurate. I make adjustments if needed.

Electromechanical devices are also used in some medical equipment. Electromechanical technicians pay attention to the details. Our equipment is quite sensitive. I work hard to make quality machines.

TECHNOLOGY

SALARY
= $25,001 to $50,000

JOB GROWTH
= 11% to 20%

EDUCATION
Four-year degree or more

SCHOOL SUBJECTS

science

reading

math

computers

social studies

Electronic Assemblers

- ## SALARY
   = $25,000 or less

- ## JOB GROWTH
  = 10% or less

- ## EDUCATION
  Training after high school

SCHOOL SUBJECTS

reading	industrial
math	arts
computers	

Have you ever wondered how many parts are inside of a CD player? I could tell you. I build CD players for a living. My name is Lenny. I work in an electronics factory.

I insert the microchips that run the digital display. My microchips tell you what radio station you are listening to or the number of the track on the CD. I use a soldering gun to weld the chips into place. Each one has to be in an exact spot on a player. CD players are very sensitive. The digital display won't work right if I'm not careful. I use a special magnifying glass. Microchips are very small. I need to be able to see what I am doing.

I work with a lot of other people in this factory. We all have our own jobs. We work together to build the CD players. Each of us adds to what the person before did. We pass the product down the line until it is finished. Our supervisor checks each CD player to make sure we did a good job. We can't sell equipment that doesn't work. We build hundreds of CD players every day.

Think about electronics assemblers the next time you listen to your favorite song.

Elementary School Teachers

What grade are you in? I teach fourth grade at an elementary school. I teach kids math and language and science. They'll use the information I teach them for the rest of their lives.

School is very important. I take my job seriously. I want my students to learn everything they need to know. I make lesson plans. I figure out what we are going to talk about before I come to school. I assign chapters out of our textbooks for my students to read at home. I like to discuss what they read. I give my students tests to make sure they understand the information. Tests tell me if they are learning what they need to know.

I'm sure you don't like homework. But it's important that you can do the work on your own. I have homework, too. I always bring papers home to grade. I try to make learning fun. I show movies to my students. Sometimes we play games. School doesn't have to be boring. I learn things from students every day. I want them to grow up to be really smart.

SALARY
= $25,001 to $50,000

JOB GROWTH
= 11% to 20%

EDUCATION
Four-year degree or more

SCHOOL SUBJECTS

math	computers
reading	geography
writing	history
science	foreign languages
social studies	

Emergency Medical Technicians

SALARY

= $25,000 or less

JOB GROWTH

= 21% or more

EDUCATION

Training after high school

SCHOOL SUBJECTS

science

math

reading

physical education

HEALTH

I drive an ambulance for a living. It can be very hard work. We bring injured people to the hospital. We get a call over our radio when someone gets hurt. We put on our flashing lights and turn on the siren. We have to be very fast.

All traffic has to get out of our way. We don't want someone to wait for help. We take care of them wherever they are if they are hurt really badly. Every case is different. Sometimes I see blood at accidents and people crying. I have to stay calm. I have to be able to help with their emergency. We put people on stretchers and carry them into the ambulance to take them to the hospital. We rush down the streets with our sirens on and lights flashing.

We may give a patient first aid while we are driving. We have equipment that helps us keep people alive. We have splints to use on broken bones. We use a monitor to check heartbeats. We rush patients to the emergency room at the hospital. Then a doctor takes over. We go to help someone else.

People need ambulances at every hour of the day and night. Sometimes I work late at night. I don't mind. Saving people's lives is my job.

Environmental Analysts

I care about the animals and plants in this valley. I'm an environmental analyst. Sometimes I'm called an ecologist. I study the way living things exist in their environments.

There are several factories upstream from here. I make sure they don't put this valley in danger. I take soil and water samples. I send them back to a lab to be analyzed for dangerous chemicals.

I check the quality of the air. I look at the plants and trees for diseases and damage. I study the animals and the way they live. I write my findings in reports. I use graphs and charts to make the information clear. I talk with people in government, business, and the citizens of this valley. I want them to know about their environment as well.

This valley is important to me. I want it to be healthy. I also want the people who live here to be healthy. Pollution doesn't just affect forests and animals. It affects everyone.

- **SALARY**
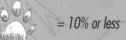 = $25,001 to $50,000

- **JOB GROWTH**
= 10% or less

- **EDUCATION**
Two-year degree

SCHOOL SUBJECTS

science	reading
math	writing
social studies	computers

Ergonomics Engineers

- ## SALARY
  = $50,001 or more

- ## JOB GROWTH
  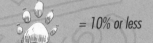 = 10% or less

- ## EDUCATION
  Four-year degree or more

SCHOOL SUBJECTS

science	art
math	reading
physical education	computers

Are you tired of sitting in an uncomfortable chair? I'm designing new desks for your classroom.

In the future, kids will sit at desks designed to fit the shape of their backs. They won't have to slouch to get relaxed. The work I do is called ergonomic engineering.

An ergonomic engineer adapts equipment to people's physical needs. I design desks and chairs so people will be more comfortable. People are more efficient at work when they are relaxed. Some desks cause strain on the back and neck. I study human anatomy to design furniture to match our posture. Back and neck strain can cause a lot of pain.

I use my computer to figure out the best angle to place desktops and the curve of seat backs. Sometimes I add neck supports or knee rests. Ergonomic engineers also create new lighting and air conditioning systems. People spend most of the day at work or in school. I believe we should be comfortable. My work makes daily life better.

Escrow Officers

When people want to buy or sell property, they come to me. I'm an escrow officer at a title company. I work out the details of property sales.

I work for the buyer and the seller. I verify documents. I hold deposit money until the transaction is done. I check to make sure everything is legal. I help the buyer figure out all the expenses. I handle all the payments. I prepare contracts for both people to sign.

I make sure that everything is in order. I check for unpaid mortgages. I file and deliver the deeds after everything is signed.

Escrow officers negotiate property sales. We make buying and selling property much easier. We know all the legal requirements.

BUSINESS

• SALARY

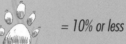 = $25,001 to $50,000

• JOB GROWTH

= 10% or less

• EDUCATION

Two-year degree

SCHOOL SUBJECTS

math	computers
reading	
writing	

Estimators

SALARY

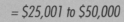

= $25,001 to $50,000

JOB GROWTH

= 11% to 20%

EDUCATION

Four-year degree or more

SCHOOL SUBJECTS

math

reading

social studies

science

computers

BUSINESS

How much do you think it would cost to build a birdhouse? You have to consider the price of wood and nails. What about tools? Maybe you need to buy a hammer or a saw. I ask myself questions like these every day. I'm an estimator.

Estimators figure out the cost of building houses, fixing cars, or manufacturing products. They have to be good at math and managing details. I work in construction. I figure out how much it will cost to build new houses. I have to think about a lot more than you do to build a birdhouse. I look at the architect's blueprints for details. I consider the price of windows, plumbing, wiring, lumber, and tools.

I have to think about labor. I add the cost of hiring carpenters, plumbers, and electricians. I keep track of a lot of different information. I add the figures and put them in a report. I meet with my clients to go over the numbers. I tell them ways to save money. Building a new house is expensive. Estimators are some of the first people who work on building a house.

Executive Assistants

I'm the executive assistant at the Boswell Corporation. I work closely with the president of this company to keep the office running.

I meet with the president to set procedures and policies. I write memos detailing the information. I e-mail the memos to the staff. I help my boss make business arrangements. I schedule meetings. I plan conferences. When our executive board meets, I prepare notes on the meeting to send to our stockholders. Those notes are called minutes.

I manage all the paperwork for the president. I make sure we keep up with important documents and contracts. I even answer a lot of the president's mail. I handle many of his phone calls. My boss trusts my opinions and my work.

Executive assistants are very important to corporations. We keep track of important details and make schedules for everyone to follow. The president wouldn't be able to do a good job without me.

BUSINESS

SALARY

= $25,001 to $50,000

JOB GROWTH

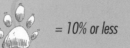

= 10% or less

EDUCATION

Two-year degree

SCHOOL SUBJECTS

reading	writing
math	social studies
computers	

Farm Equipment Mechanics

• SALARY

 = $25,001 to $50,000

• JOB GROWTH

= 10% or less

• EDUCATION

Training after high school

SCHOOL SUBJECTS

reading

math

physical education

computers

industrial arts

I'm a farmer's best friend. I fix tractors and harvesting equipment. I'm a farm equipment mechanic. I make farm calls.

I can come out to a farm to look at equipment. I carry a toolbox with me. Most farm equipment is too large to bring into a shop. I look at the machines and try to run them. A lot of times I can figure out the problem by listening to the machine. I have a good ear for machines. I take the machine apart to get to the problem.

My job is a lot like an auto mechanic's. I repair or replace the defective parts in the engine. Sometimes I just need to clean the parts or add oil. I get the machine operating as quickly as I can.

Farmers rely on their equipment. Farming would be very difficult without machines. I like being out in the country and working with machines.

Farmers

I make my living off the land. I'm a farmer. I run my own farm. I guess you could say that I'm the manager of this farm. I run it as a business.

I hire workers. I keep track of the finances. I buy equipment and supplies. I know all about the crops I plant. I work with scientists to learn the best ways to plant crops. Certain kinds of crops grow best in the soil on my property. I have learned about the best pesticides to use to keep insects away.

I make sure the workers do their jobs. I watch over the way they plant and harvest the crops. I'm proud of my crew. I have to get a good price for my crops. Farmers supply the fruit and vegetables we eat. Farms are an important business.

- ## SALARY

   = $25,000 or less

- ## JOB GROWTH

  = 10% or less

- ## EDUCATION

  Two-year degree

SCHOOL SUBJECTS

science

reading

math

Fashion Merchandisers

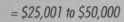

I love clothes! I choose, buy, and sell clothes for a living. That's what fashion merchandisers do.

I travel to big cities and meet with designers to decide what kinds of clothing the store I work for will sell. I buy the clothes from factories. I make sure that the clothes are displayed nicely in my store. I dress the mannequins. I set up displays in our front window. In July I did a window with the theme "Summer Safari." I dressed the mannequins in summer outfits and put zebra and lion masks over their heads.

At the beginning of every season, I plan fashion shows and work with models. I pick the most fabulous clothes for them to wear. I make sure the people I hire do their jobs so the show runs smoothly. Our store's customers like seeing our newest clothes this way.

I have to know how to buy clothing that other people will want to buy. My job is fun. I work with very nice clothes all day long. Many of the people I work with are creative.

BUSINESS

ast-Food Service Managers

Thanks for coming to eat at Healthy and Fast. I'm the manager of this fast-food restaurant. We have the best fast food around. You can get salad wraps and turkey burgers. We make oven-roasted fries that are delicious and healthy.

I make sure that our customers get fast and friendly service. I train my employees to take customers' orders with a smile. We keep the customer happy. I make sure the restaurant stays clean. No one likes to eat at a dirty table.

I train the cooks to make delicious foods without keeping the customers waiting. Fast-food service managers keep their restaurants running smoothly. I make a schedule every week so my employees know when to come to work. We work a lot of hours. I keep records of all the money we make. I count the money in the cash register to make sure the figures balance. I order food and supplies.

I like my job. I talk with nice people every day. I get to wear a cool uniform to work.

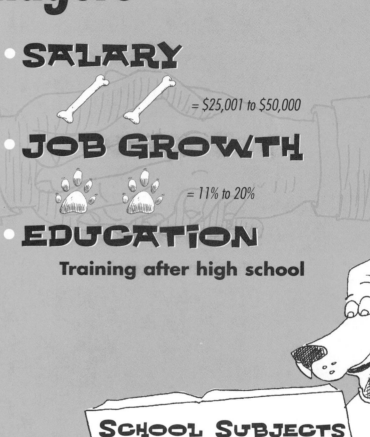

SALARY
= $25,001 to $50,000

JOB GROWTH
= 11% to 20%

EDUCATION
Training after high school

SCHOOL SUBJECTS

math	computers
reading	
social studies	

Fiber-optic Engineers

- ## SALARY
  = $50,001 or more

- ## JOB GROWTH
  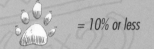
  = 10% or less

- ## EDUCATION
  Four-year degree or more

SCHOOL SUBJECTS

science	reading
math	computers
social studies	

I'm sure you've heard of lasers. I work to develop new products using lasers and other light sources. I'm a fiber-optic engineer. We combine light and electronics. I work for a major research lab.

I'm developing a security system that uses beams of light. The beams cross over the doors and windows. If something crosses the light, it sets off circuits in the alarm system. The circuits notify a computer system that the beam has been broken. No one can pass through the light without setting off the alarm.

Fiber-optic wires use light instead of electricity to transmit information. Light can travel much faster than an electrical current. Fiber optics are a big improvement over old cables. Computer screens use fiber-optic technology. They convert an electrical signal into a beam of light. The light shows you information on the screen.

Fiber optics make it easier for people to communicate through phone lines and computer networks. I am creating the future.

Financial Planners

I spend my day helping other people invest their money. I'm a financial planner.

Most people don't want to work their entire lives. I help them figure out the finances for retirement. I look at how much money they make in a year. I see how much money they have in their savings. Then I look at how much money they will need once they have retired. I help them make investments. Sometimes I suggest that they buy stocks, bonds, or mutual funds. I may tell them to invest in a second home. Everyone has different needs.

I make my decisions based on how much money the people have and what they want to do. Some people may want to buy a new condominium. A lot of my clients want to remain living in the same house. I never tell them what to do. I make suggestions. They choose what they want to do based on what I recommend. I know a lot about money and tax laws.

I help people find ways to save money. I guide their investments so they get the most profit. People rely on me.

- **SALARY**

  = $50,001 or more

- **JOB GROWTH**

  = 21% or more

- **EDUCATION**

  Two-year degree

SCHOOL SUBJECTS

math	computers
science	social studies
reading	

Firefighters

- ## SALARY
   = $25,001 to $50,000

- ## JOB GROWTH
  = 11% to 20%

- ## EDUCATION
  Training after high school

SCHOOL SUBJECTS

reading

math

physical education

Did you hear about that big fire last night? A huge apartment building was in flames. Many people could have been hurt. I'm glad I was there. I'm a firefighter. My job is to put out fires.

I rescue people. I saved many people's lives last night. The fire started at about 2 a.m. I was sleeping in the station. Our alarms went off. All the firefighters had to jump out of bed and get their uniforms on. We wear special suits so we won't get burned or injured. We rushed to the truck.

I jumped in and turned on the siren. We sped down the street to get to the building. Smoke was pouring out of the windows. People were trying to get out. We attached our hoses to the fire hydrants. Some firefighters got up on a ladder to hose down the flames.

I broke a window and climbed inside to check for people. One woman had passed out from breathing the smoke. I helped her outside. I gave her first aid. It took hours to put out the fire. I'm glad we were able to get all the people out. My job is very dangerous. But I know how important it is. I save lives every day.

PERSONAL SERVICES

Fish and Wildlife Specialists

I work in marshes and swamps. I'm a fish and wildlife specialist. I work hard to protect animals and their habitats. I know every mile of this swamp by heart. I travel it every day.

I use an airboat to get around. I take samples of the soil, water, and plants. I send them back to a lab. The lab workers can tell me about pollution levels in the swamp. I make sure chemical plants are not dumping dangerous levels of waste into the water. I keep track of the animals here. Right now, we are studying the deer population. We attached tags to their ears to track them. Each deer has its own number. I record where I see the deer on a map. That tells us where they travel around the marsh.

I work closely with government agencies to protect this land and animals on it. I write reports about my observations. I've helped pass laws to protect the animals here. Fish and wildlife specialists are nature's best friends. We care about the land and animals we protect.

I want this swamp to keep its natural beauty. I want my children to be able to enjoy it as much as I have.

- **SALARY** = $25,001 to $50,000

- **JOB GROWTH** = 21% or more

- **EDUCATION** Four-year degree or more

SCHOOL SUBJECTS

science	math
reading	computers
writing	social studies

NATURAL RESOURCES

Flight Attendants

- ## SALARY
   = $25,001 to $50,000

- ## JOB GROWTH
  = 11% to 20%

- ## EDUCATION
  Training after high school

SCHOOL SUBJECTS

math

reading

social studies

Welcome aboard! My name is Jean. I'll be your flight attendant today. I travel all over the world. I meet new people every day. Doesn't that sound glamorous? It can be. But it's also a lot of work. Flight attendants do much more than serve snacks on airplanes. We make sure that every passenger has a safe flight.

I'm responsible for more than a hundred people on each trip. I make sure they understand all about flying safely. I let them know where the emergency exits are. I tell them what to do in case of an emergency. I have to get all of the passengers out safely. I couldn't leave the plane first even if I were the person closest to the exit.

Flight attendants have to stay very calm. Sometimes the plane rocks in storms. I have to let everyone know that things are okay. I wear a uniform so people will know who I am. I serve food and drinks. I work quickly and give people the drink they asked for. I pick up the trays when they are finished eating. I prepare the passengers for landing. All of them must have their seats upright. The seatbelts must be fastened. I wouldn't want anyone to get hurt.

I'm away from home a lot. I spend the night in hotels when I am on longer trips. I like working with people. I know that some passengers don't like to fly. I try to calm them and ease their minds.

Floral Designers

I work in a flower shop. We have hundreds of beautiful flowers. They come in many different sizes and colors. I arrange them in baskets and vases.

I find the perfect flowers. I may use ones that smell good. Sometimes I pick certain colors. It depends on what people want. I make arrangements in many different sizes. Some have lots of flowers. Other times I may put one rose in a vase. I choose the right flowers for each customer. I add bows and decorations to make them pretty.

Floral designers are artists. We know how to make a bunch of flowers look nice together. People send arrangements to weddings, birthdays, and special events. We keep the flowers in coolers. Coolers are like refrigerators. Most cut flowers do not like heat. I use small scissors to cut the stems. I use clay and foam to make the flowers stand up in vases. I also make arrangements with artificial or dried flowers. I even make corsages for people to wear to dances.

I like working with plants. I am very creative. Going to work is great. I take a deep breath every morning when I go into my shop. I smell a hundred flowers at once.

- **SALARY**
  = $25,000 or less

- **JOB GROWTH**
  = 11% to 20%

- **EDUCATION**
  Training after high school

SCHOOL SUBJECTS

art

reading

math

Foresters

- ## SALARY

  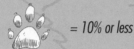 = $25,001 to $50,000

- ## JOB GROWTH

  = 10% or less

- ## EDUCATION

  Four-year degree or more

SCHOOL SUBJECTS

math	reading
science	computers
social studies	

I'm sure you use things made of wood and paper every day. Did you know that boards and paper are made from trees? I work for a lumber company that cuts down trees to make wooden boards and paper. I'm a forester. I protect the forest land.

I care about trees. We need wood to make many important things. We have to cut down trees. But we can't cut down every tree. Trees provide oxygen to the earth. They keep soil from washing away during rainstorms. Animals and birds live in trees.

I make sure that my company plants a new tree for every tree we cut down. I map our land. We can't cut down trees on other people's property. I walk around the woods making maps and checking the trees. The work I do is very important. This lumber company hired me to make sure they don't hurt the environment.

Foresters understand the science of plants and animals. We are responsible for everything that lives in our forest area. If we don't do our jobs, there won't be any forests left. I like knowing that I am helping the earth.

Forklift Operators

I move heavy boxes in a warehouse all day long. It doesn't bother my back at all. I never even touch the boxes. I pick them up with a forklift. I'm a forklift operator.

A forklift is like a tractor. Forklifts make it easy to move heavy things around. They have two metal blades in front that slide under a box or wooden pallet. I raise the "fork" by using levers near my steering wheel. I drive the forklift the same way you drive a car. I have to be careful. I wouldn't want to knock over anything when I'm driving.

I can move boxes that weigh hundreds of pounds from one end of this warehouse to the other in one trip. Forklifts save a lot of time. Forklifts also prevent injuries. People can hurt themselves by trying to lift heavy things.

Being a forklift operator is fun. I like having to guide the "fork" under a stack of boxes. It reminds me of those games at carnivals where you use a lever to make a mechanical claw grab a toy. I have to grab each stack exactly right. I can damage expensive merchandise if I make a mistake. I like working in a warehouse.

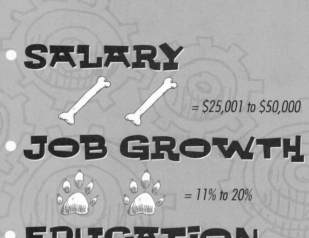

- **SALARY**
  = $25,001 to $50,000

- **JOB GROWTH**
  = 11% to 20%

- **EDUCATION**
  High school diploma

SCHOOL SUBJECTS

reading

math

industrial arts

physical education

Front Desk Clerks

- **SALARY**

   = $25,000 or less

- **JOB GROWTH**

   = 21% or more

- **EDUCATION**

  Training after high school

SCHOOL SUBJECTS

math

reading

computers

BUSINESS

I work at the front desk of the Alpine Village Hotel. I'm a front desk clerk. You'll talk to me if you come for a visit. I register guests and assign them to a room. I look guest information up on our computer system.

I check to see if the guest has a reservation. This is a popular hotel so most of the rooms are reserved. I make sure our guests get the rooms they request. Some of them want to have a view of the mountains. Other guests want to be close to the pool. I am here to help our guests. I can answer any questions. I suggest good restaurants. I tell them about tourist attractions. There are a lot of fun things to do near the Alpine Village.

I help guests check out when they are ready to leave. I look up their room on the computer, and I collect the right amount of money. Most guests pay with a credit card. I have process their cards through our computer. I also have to work a cash register. Some guests pay with cash.

The Alpine Village Hotel is a nice place to work. I like talking with people who are here on vacation. I meet people from all over the world.

Fund-Raisers

Money makes the world go around. Unfortunately, a lot of organizations don't have enough money to operate. I'm a fund-raiser for a homeless shelter. Many people have no place to live and no food to eat. We provide balanced meals to the homeless. We work hard to give them a place to sleep.

Food is very expensive. Our budget is small. I try to get people to give us money to help our cause. Many churches in the area send us checks every week. I also meet with businesses to see if they will help. Several grocery stores have donated food. Other businesses have donated money and supplies.

Volunteers help me raise money. We write letters and make phone calls to people in the community. Many people like to make donations. We just have to make them aware of our good cause. I want everyone in this city to know about our shelter. We provide a needed service.

I work very hard. The organization doesn't have a lot of money for my salary. I do my job because I believe in this cause. Everyone deserves to eat. I'm making this community a better place.

BUSINESS

- **SALARY**
  = $50,001 or more

- **JOB GROWTH**
  = 21% or more

- **EDUCATION**
  Four-year degree or more

SCHOOL SUBJECTS

reading	computers
math	writing
social studies	

Furniture Designers

- ## SALARY

  = $50,001 or more

- ## JOB GROWTH

   = 11% to 20%

- ## EDUCATION

  Four-year degree or more

School Subjects

art	reading
science	writing
math	computers

I've just designed an exciting new bookcase. You can move it around your home and rearrange the shelves to fit any room in your house. I work for a large furniture manufacturer as a designer.

I come up with exciting new ideas for chairs, tables, and beds. Our company likes to make things that are a little different. Our customers like to have a little fun. I draw sketches of my ideas. Sometimes I fill an entire notepad with new designs. I pass my ideas on to a design committee. They pick out the ones the company wants to produce.

I draw designs for all the furniture we will make this year. I tell the factory how to make each piece. The bookcase I designed has lots of curves and angles. I draw these for the people who produce them. I have faith in their work. They did a wonderful job with my "sardine can" bed last year. The finished product looked just like the ones mice sleep on in cartoons.

I work for a great company. I get paid to be creative. I help create the furniture that people are proud to have in their homes.

Furniture Makers

Howdy! My name is Spruce. I make furniture for a living. I can tell you anything about wood. There are many different kinds. You've got pine, oak, and cherry, to name a few. The name of the wood depends on the tree it comes from.

I take wood and make it into furniture. I build dressers, tables, and chairs. I take boards and make them into something useful. I select the best wood so the finished piece will look nice. I wouldn't want big knot holes on the table top. I cut the wood to the right size. I use a lathe to shape the table legs. I fit the pieces together using glue, nails, and screws. I try to get the nails and screws so they don't show. Then I use a sander and steel wool to get the wood smooth. After that I put a stain on the wood using a paint brush.

I have lots of different choices for color. Some people like dark wood. Others like it very light. I put a coat of sealer on it to protect the wood from water. That's how you build a piece of furniture. A lot of work goes into making a table or chair. Every piece of furniture is a work of art.

SALARY
= $25,001 to $50,000

JOB GROWTH
= 10% or less

EDUCATION
Training after high school

SCHOOL SUBJECTS

reading

math

industrial arts

Furniture Movers

- ## SALARY

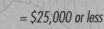 = $25,000 or less

- ## JOB GROWTH

 = 10% or less

- ## EDUCATION

High school diploma

SCHOOL SUBJECTS

reading

math

physical education

I'm a furniture mover with the Box-N-Go Moving Company. I box up people's belongings so they can move to a new home or office. Getting people ready to move is a lot of work.

Think of all the different things you have in your house. Imagine moving them. I pack everything so it is organized and won't break. I want my customers to find everything easily. I wrap dishes in paper and pack them in boxes. I roll up rugs. I remove pictures from the walls. I load furniture into the moving van.

It's a good thing I'm strong. I pick up heavy things every day. I'm careful not to scratch anything. I put padding in the truck for protection. I tie down the big pieces with rope so they won't slide around the truck. I've moved everything from pianos to aquariums. Another mover drives the truck to the new location.

Sometimes we move furniture across the country. Furniture movers unload everything when they get to the right place. We make moving easier. Moving into a new home or office can be very stressful. We handle all the details. I'm an expert mover. I can box up anything. I've turned moving people into a science.

PERSONAL SERVICES

Geologists

Have you ever seen a volcano erupt? I have. I'm a geologist. Geologists study the history of the earth and how it is put together. We look at rocks, minerals, and fossils. They teach us how the earth got to look the way it does.

The earth has a life just like you do. It looks different at different stages. We look at rocks to see how they were made. Some were made by volcanoes. Others were formed by layers of earth built up over many years. I have computer equipment to help me figure out exactly how old a rock is. Imagine that. Even rocks have birthdays.

Geology tells us important things. Geology helps us predict earthquakes. Geologists use chemistry, physics, biology, and math on the job. I use complicated equipment to date the age of rocks and fossils. I've always liked science. My friends called me a science nerd when I was your age. I built volcanoes in a sandbox. I collected cool rocks on the beach.

The history of the earth is amazing. Look at a rock cliff. It looked different a thousand years ago. You would think that mountains and cliffs would stay the same because they are made of rock. They don't. The earth is constantly changing.

SALARY

= $50,001 or more

JOB GROWTH

= 11% to 20%

EDUCATION

Four-year degree or more

SCHOOL SUBJECTS

science	geography
math	computers
reading	

Gerontologists

- ## SALARY

= $50,001 or more

- ## JOB GROWTH

= 21% or more

- ## EDUCATION

Four-year degree or more

SCHOOL SUBJECTS

science

math

social studies

reading

computers

I'm sure you've heard of Alzheimer's disease. It affects some people when they get older. People can lose their memory from it. They can't even live by themselves anymore. They need other people to take care of them.

I'm a gerontologist. I study aging and the problems connected with aging. I also work with elderly people to help them adjust to problems in life. Many of my patients have Alzheimer's. I make sure they get proper health care. People need to watch their health carefully when they get older. I make sure they eat well. Nutrition is very important.

We don't know very much about Alzheimer's disease. I'm writing articles on the information I find from working with people to help other doctors. Scientists use my reports to work toward a cure. We have to understand the disease before we can stop it.

There are other conditions that older people develop. I help study and treat them all.

HEALTH

Glaziers

If you break a window playing softball, you may need me to come fix it for you. I work for a glass company as a glazier. Glaziers cut and fit glass for windows and doors. I put in new windows at homes and offices.

Every job is different. I measure each piece of glass. Windows come in many different sizes. I cut the glass with a special glass cutting tool. It has to be very strong and sharp. I cut a score with the cutter. I have another tool I use to break the glass into even pieces.

I fasten the glass into the window frame with putty and rubber joint seal. I make sure the glass is sealed all the way around. I don't want air or water to get around it. I have to be careful when I work. It is easy to cut yourself on glass. I wear gloves for added protection.

I travel to many different places in a single day. I keep glass in my truck so I don't have to go back to the shop for supplies. I like the work I do. Once you become skilled, being a glazier is pretty easy.

SALARY
= $25,001 to $50,000

JOB GROWTH
= 11% to 20%

EDUCATION
Training after high school

SCHOOL SUBJECTS

reading

math

industrial arts

Graphic Designers

SALARY

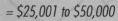

= $25,001 to $50,000

JOB GROWTH

= 21% or more

EDUCATION

Two-year degree

SCHOOL SUBJECTS

art

computers

reading

My name is Art. I'm a graphic designer. Graphic designers plan the way that magazines and books look. I design a magazine. I decide what the cover will look like. I plan each page.

I put words and pictures together. I decide where to put photographs and what kind to use. I work with the magazine editor to make a story look interesting so you will want to read it. I decide which style of type to use. The letters can be large or small. They can be fat or thin. I make the headlines big and colorful. I want them to get your attention. I have a computer that has special design software. I send the magazine to a printer when I finish the design. The printer follows my instructions to make the finished magazine look like it should.

Graphic designers know a lot about color. I loved to draw when I was your age. I even drew pictures for my science class reports. I hoped that would get me a better grade. I went to a special design school after high school. My classes taught me how to make designs out of words and art and photos. Graphic designers make other people's writing look good. I put photographs with stories and articles. I make them pleasing to the eye.

Grocery Clerks

Thank you for shopping at the Food Chain grocery store. My name is Quinn. I work here as a grocery clerk.

I work hard to get you through the checkout line quickly. I don't want people to wait a long time. I stand behind the register and ring up your purchases. The conveyor belt brings the food to me. Everything in this store is computerized. I run the barcode on each item over a scanner. The price comes up in the register. If the price doesn't come up, I call for a price check.

I weigh fruits and vegetables on a scale. I have to know the code for each kind. Mangoes are 7415 and summer squash is 6713. I can't get them confused. I don't want to charge the wrong amount. I pass the groceries down the line to a bagger. I collect payment from customers. I make change if they pay me cash. Many people pay with personal checks. I make sure they write the check for the correct amount and look at their identification card.

I wait on many people every day. It can get pretty hectic sometimes. I am nice to everyone who comes through my line.

BUSINESS

● SALARY

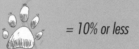
= $25,000 or less

● JOB GROWTH

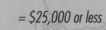
= 10% or less

● EDUCATION

High school diploma

SCHOOL SUBJECTS

math

reading

computers

Groundskeepers and Gardeners

SALARY

= $25,000 or less

JOB GROWTH

= 21% or more

EDUCATION

High school diploma

SCHOOL SUBJECTS

reading

math

physical education

Do you like to go outside and play? I love being outside. I never have to sit at a desk. I'm a gardener for a huge park. I take care of all kinds of plants.

I work with both flowers and shrubbery. Shrubbery is another name for bushes. Gardeners have to know all about plants. The park has different sections. We have a beautiful rose garden. We have ponds with pretty flowering plants called lilies. One section of the garden is filled with cacti, the western plants with needles on them. I have to be careful not to get pricked. I keep the flower beds weeded and watered. I know how much water each plant needs. I have to be careful not to give the cacti too much water. They would die.

I know how to control insects. I don't want them to eat the plants. I trim the shrubbery so it doesn't get too big. I pick up trash to keep the gardens looking nice. I make sure the lawn gets cut.

I spend the entire day in the sun. I like to work in our greenhouse when it is raining. We grow a lot of plants there before they are big enough to plant outside. My gardens are fabulous. It's nice to work in a beautiful garden.

Hazardous Waste Managers

I really care about the environment. I want our planet to be clean for generations to come. That's why I became a hazardous waste manager with the state government. Hazardous waste managers develop rules to protect people and the environment. We do studies around factories to make sure they are not causing pollution.

I take samples of water from nearby rivers and soil from the local fields. I send the samples to a lab for tests. We don't want dangerous chemicals or radiation to get in the air or water. I check factories all over this state. My job is very important. I make suggestions for improving waste disposal methods. I work with them to create new processes.

I collect data on my findings. I use the information to write reports for the government and the people who live around the factories. My work has to be scientific and accurate. Most people who manage factories want to help the environment. Factories can make products without causing damage to the earth. They need to work with the people in their communities and hazardous waste managers.

My job will help preserve our forests and lakes. I'm working hard for the future.

SALARY

= $25,001 to $50,000

JOB GROWTH

= 21% or more

EDUCATION

Training after high school

SCHOOL SUBJECTS

science	math
reading	computers
social studies	

Health and Safety Inspectors

SALARY

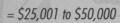

= $25,001 to $50,000

JOB GROWTH

= 11% to 20%

EDUCATION

Four-year degree or more

SCHOOL SUBJECTS

math	writing
reading	computers
industrial arts	

I'm the health and safety inspector for a city in California. I check all of the public buildings here. My job was created to keep people safe. I don't want anyone to be in danger.

I check the areas where employees work. I check the insulation to make sure it isn't asbestos. Asbestos is a dangerous material that we no longer use. I check the machinery at factories. I make sure they have proper safety guards and shields. Sometimes I recommend that employees wear earplugs around noisy machinery. Earplugs can help save their hearing. I check the safety equipment in areas where people work with dangerous chemicals. They must have good fire extinguishers. They also need a special shower to rinse off chemicals that might touch their skin in an emergency.

I note the problems I find. I write detailed reports to give to the supervisors. I include anything I see that is wrong. They have to correct the problems. I wouldn't want anyone to get hurt.

Health and safety inspectors know a lot of rules. They stop many accidents from happening.

Health Therapists

Some people would say that my job is depressing. But not me. I work as a health therapist at a cancer treatment center. I work with the doctors to plan treatments for people with cancer.

I work closely with the patients. I get to know them. I want to provide them with more than medicine. I want them to know that I care. Many of them go through painful treatments. I make it as easy as possible for them. I don't want them to get depressed. We can fight cancer.

I help them strengthen their spirits. I make sure they understand all about the disease and all the treatments available. I want them to know they have choices. Sometimes I suggest support groups they can join. It helps some patients to talk with other people who have the same illness. I work hard at my job. Every day is a challenge. I deal with each person individually. Nobody reacts the same way to being sick.

I'm good at what I do because I really care about people. Helping others is important to me. Sometimes my job can be very sad. I've learned to deal with it. I look forward to the times when a patient becomes healthy again and no longer needs treatment.

SALARY

= $50,001 or more

JOB GROWTH

= 21% or more

EDUCATION

Four-year degree or more

SCHOOL SUBJECTS

science

reading

social studies

math

computers

Heating and Cooling Systems Mechanics

SALARY

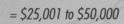

= $25,001 to $50,000

JOB GROWTH

= 21% or more

EDUCATION

Four-year degree or more

SCHOOL SUBJECTS

math

reading

industrial arts

It's hot in here! I feel like butter in a frying pan. I'll have that fixed in just a minute, though. I'm a heating and cooling systems mechanic. Let me translate that for you. I fix heaters and air conditioners.

Nobody likes to be too hot or too cold. That's why they have me. I make the temperature in houses and offices comfortable. Think of your house as a big refrigerator. A machine inside makes a refrigerator stay cool. Your air conditioner and heater work the same way.

I know a lot about machines. I fix furnaces and thermostats every day. I use tools like screwdrivers and wrenches. The equipment I work with has a lot of parts. I know about every part in an air conditioner or heater. I can't fix things if I don't know how they work. People call me when they are having a problem. I go to their home or office to help. Most calls are on the hottest day in the summer or when the temperature drops low in the winter.

I get really busy sometimes. Nobody likes to be uncomfortable. I work with my hands all day. I'm good at fixing things.

Heavy Equipment Operators

I work for a construction company. I make land flat with a bulldozer. I use an excavator to dig out earth, trees, and rocks from construction sites. Sometimes I use a dump truck to take what I dig up away.

Right now I'm digging out a piece of land for a lake. My construction company is going to build houses around the shore. They'll fill it with water once I'm done digging. My bulldozer has a blade in front. I raise or lower the blade with switches by the steering wheel. An excavator uses a big bucket to lift earth.

I use equipment to dig foundations for buildings and move rocks. Imagine trying to dig up rocks with shovels. Equipment like bulldozers makes building things much easier and quicker.

Working outside is great. I'm always in the fresh air. In really bad weather I don't work at all.

• SALARY

= $25,001 to $50,000

• JOB GROWTH

= 10% or less

• EDUCATION

Training after high school

SCHOOL SUBJECTS

math	physical education
reading	
industrial arts	

© JIST Works

Horticultural Workers

SALARY

= $25,000 or less

JOB GROWTH

= 10% or less

EDUCATION

High school diploma

SCHOOL SUBJECTS

reading   computers

math

science

I can answer any questions you may have about plants. I'm a horticultural worker at Shady Lane Plants. We supply plants to gardening stores around the state. I know everything about growing plants. I take seed and saplings and turn them into beautiful flowers and trees.

I know the perfect soil for each plant. Some plants prefer sandy soil. Others grow better in rocky earth. I spend a lot of time in our greenhouses. I nurse the plants as they grow. I fertilize and water them. I make sure they get the right amount of light. I get rid of weeds and bugs.

Sometimes I feel like a parent. I take care of them until we sell them. I like to talk to plants. I believe that helps them grow. Sometimes I even play music for them. They seem to grow faster when I play classical music and hip-hop. I put plants into new pots. I prune the trees and shrubs.

I stay busy around here. I help people from nurseries buy plants to sell to their customers. I tell them how to take care of the plants so they will stay nice and healthy. This is the perfect job for me. I get to work with both plants and people.

NATURAL RESOURCES

Hospice Workers

I work for Mr. Wilson. He's very sick with cancer. He is no longer able to work. He spends most of his time in bed. He doesn't have anyone who can stay with him during the day. His daughter went to my organization to get somebody to care for him. My name is Billie. I'm a home health aide for a local hospice. We're a lot like nurses, except we work in people's homes.

Mr. Wilson is not sick enough to be in the hospital. But he needs a lot of attention. I help him get out of bed in the morning and get him dressed. Then I bring him breakfast. I bring him the newspaper so he has something to read. I run errands for him while he reads. I may go to the post office or to pick up some groceries.

I carry a beeper and a cell phone. He can reach me if he needs any help. I make lunch for him when I get back. I make sure that he takes his medicine. I check his blood pressure and temperature. I write information about him on a chart for his doctor. I know first aid in case he has a problem.

Mr. Wilson is very nice. I like to see him smile. He always thanks me for the work I do. I go home to my family when his daughter comes home from work. Taking care of a sick person is a full-time job.

SALARY

= $25,000 or less

JOB GROWTH

= 21% or more

EDUCATION

Training after high school

SCHOOL SUBJECTS

science   computers

math

reading

Hospital Administrators

SALARY

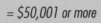

= $50,001 or more

JOB GROWTH

= 21% or more

EDUCATION

Four-year degree or more

SCHOOL SUBJECTS

math	computers
reading	writing
social studies	

I run a hospital for a living. I'm not a doctor. I'm a business person. Hospital administrators organize all of the business activities for a hospital. We let the doctors take care of the patients.

I make budgets for the hospital. I make sure we have all the medical equipment and supplies we need. I have a large staff of department heads to help me keep everything straight. They make recommendations for my approval. Think of all the details that go into running a hospital.

The main part of my job is making sure that the hospital runs smoothly. I hire doctors. I hire nurses and aides. A lot of other people work at the hospital, too. I hire janitors and managers and food servers. I oversee the orders for everything from medicine to paper for our copy machines. I also have a lot of administrative duties. I set policies for the hospital. Policies are rules that my staff must follow.

I walk around the hospital to make sure that things are okay. I spend most of my time sitting at my desk and in meetings. Many nights I have to stay late. I barely get home in time to tuck my kids into bed. My business helps to save lives and improve health care. That's worth working long and hard for.

Hospitality Managers

Welcome to the Palm Gardens Hotel and Resort! We have one of the nicest hotels in this area. I'm the manager here.

Being a hotel manager is a lot of work. I'm responsible for everything that goes on at this resort. I want our guests to have a fabulous stay. I have a huge staff to help me. I talk with the head of the housekeeping department about keeping the rooms clean and attractive. I meet with the restaurant manager about the food we are serving. I make sure the gardeners keep the grounds mowed.

I'm in charge of the budget. I look over our accounting figures to set room rates and give money to each department. I approve the payment of all of the bills. Hotels have huge electrical and water bills.

I talk to our guests about the hotel. I want everyone to have a great time. Happy guests will come back to stay with us and recommend us to others. Hotel managers work hard to keep guests satisfied.

This week was busy because we're building a new pool. I meet with contractors and bankers. This job has lots of variety. I like it.

BUSINESS

SALARY

= $25,001 to $50,000

JOB GROWTH

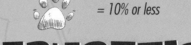

= 10% or less

EDUCATION
Two-year degree

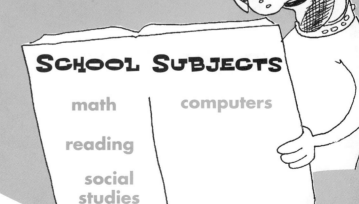

SCHOOL SUBJECTS

math   computers

reading

social
studies

Housekeeping Staff

SALARY

 = $25,000 or less

JOB GROWTH

 = 10% or less

EDUCATION

High school diploma

SCHOOL SUBJECTS

reading

math

physical education

I work at the Sea View Inn. I keep this motel clean. I clean the rooms after the guests leave.

I change the sheets and clean the bathroom. I put fresh towels in the bathroom. I fluff the pillows. I vacuum and dust. I take out the trash. I put any belongings people leave behind in the lost and found. I find the weirdest things in people's rooms. Usually they forget a sweater or leave shampoo in the shower. Once I found a six-foot-tall statue of a giraffe.

I have twenty rooms to clean by 2 p.m. every day. That's a lot of work. I also clean the lobby. The lobby is filled with brass furniture. I keep everything polished. I want it to be shiny for our guests. If people need things like extra soap or towels, I take it to their rooms.

I work hard to make this place nice for our guests. I'm glad to have this job. It's easy for me. I've always liked to clean.

Human Resource Workers

Hello! My name's Bobbie. I'm a human resource worker for a large company. I'm the people person of the company. I have to be good at talking with people.

I work with employees. I'm in charge of finding the right person for job openings. I set up policies for hiring people. I interview people to find the perfect applicant.

I decide on salaries based on what similar positions pay at other companies. I make sure the employees of this company get paid fairly. I plan what benefits employees will receive. Our company offers health and life insurance and stock in the company for its employees. Sometimes I meet with union representatives to talk about benefits and wages.

I manage new employee training. Sometimes I help employees work out problems with their supervisors. I want everyone at this company to have good working conditions.

Human resource workers are an important part of a company. We make sure the company's work gets done right and that the employees get what they deserve.

SALARY

 = $25,001 to $50,000

JOB GROWTH

 = 11% to 20%

EDUCATION
Two-year degree

SCHOOL SUBJECTS

math	computers
reading	writing
social studies	

Image Consultants

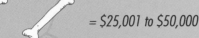

- ## SALARY

  = $25,001 to $50,000

- ## JOB GROWTH
  = 21% or more

- ## EDUCATION
  ### Four-year degree or more

SCHOOL SUBJECTS

art	social studies
reading	
writing	

BUSINESS

Do you realize that everybody and everything has an image? An image is what people think you are. People can look successful or shabby. Companies can appear to be powerful or caring. I'm an image consultant. I help clients to create the image they want people to have of them.

Sometimes executives going on television hire me to consult about the clothes they wear. Companies also hire me to do change their public image. A luxury car company wanted to change the image of their cars from expensive to safe. I helped them. I did a survey to see what their customers thought of them. I suggested that they change their advertising. I talked to car designers. I worked with their public relations person to change their image.

Some people refer to a company image as branding. I help clients create a brand. Think of your favorite clothing. Do you buy it because it seems cool or inexpensive or young? I may have helped to create that image.

Immigration Inspectors

America is called the "great melting pot." That means the many citizens of our country came here from other countries all over the world. People who come to our country from another country are called immigrants. We are a country made up of people from many different nations.

I'm an immigration inspector. I work for the government. People from foreign countries have to register when they come to America. They have to show identification like visas, passports, and green cards. Identification has people's pictures on it and tells what country they are from. I check people's passports and visas when they come to America.

Foreigners must register with our government to get an alien identification card. That is a way for us to control our population. If someone does not register with our government, they are sent back to their own country. We call that being deported. I work with people from all over the world. I can speak several languages.

My job allows other people to become citizens here. Immigration inspectors help thousands of people every year move to this country. That makes my job worthwhile.

SALARY = $25,001 to $50,000

JOB GROWTH = 21% or more

EDUCATION Two-year degree

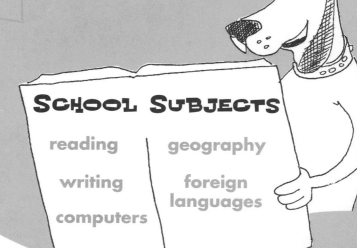

SCHOOL SUBJECTS

reading	geography
writing	foreign languages
computers	

Importers and Exporters

• SALARY

 = $25,001 to $50,000

• JOB GROWTH

 = 10% or less

• EDUCATION
Two-year degree

SCHOOL SUBJECTS

math

reading

foreign languages

computers

social studies

Shipping things into our country is called importing. Shipping things out of our country is called exporting. I work as an importer and exporter.

I help companies in China import their products to America. Look around your home. You probably own many things that were made in China or other countries. An importer had to arrange to have them shipped here. I know the shipping rules of many countries. Every country has its own rules. I also have to know about shipping taxes called tariffs. The government taxes many of the things I import.

Sometimes I work with American companies to ship their products overseas. I tell them the best ways to get their products into another country. I have a huge warehouse staff that helps me. They receive freight, assess charges, and collect fees for shipping. I make sure they do their jobs correctly.

Importing and exporting can be tricky. I am fortunate that I speak several languages. That helps me straighten out problems. I learn new things on the job every day. I like working with people from other cultures. I help bring people and businesses together.

Industrial Designers

I create products that will make lots of money for my company. I'm an industrial designer for a camping equipment manufacturer. I combine my artistic talent and my knowledge of business to design new products.

I keep up with people's needs and wants. I talk to our marketing department to find out what our customers are looking for. I just finished a design for a tent. This new tent fits easily into a backpack. I consider a lot of different things when I make a design. The new product has to be affordable. People won't buy the tent if it is too expensive. I have to think about our factories. I don't make designs that we won't be able to manufacture.

I pass my ideas to a design committee. The committee lets me know if I should make any changes. Sometimes I make a full-scale model so the committee can see what the finished product will look like. I create instructions so our factories can make thousands of our latest tent. I drew blueprints with all the little details.

I design camping equipment that people need and want. My products sell as soon as they appear on the store shelves. Giving people what they want is what business is all about.

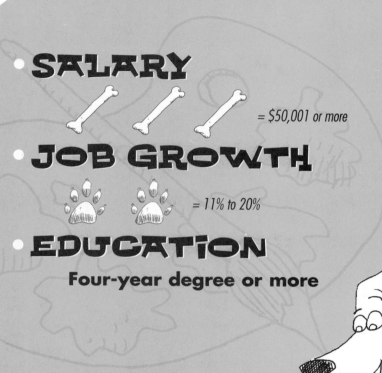

- **SALARY** = $50,001 or more
- **JOB GROWTH** = 11% to 20%
- **EDUCATION** Four-year degree or more

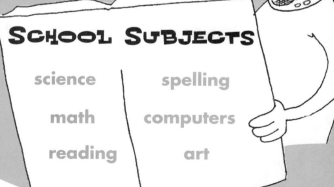

SCHOOL SUBJECTS

science	spelling
math	computers
reading	art

Industrial Engineers

SALARY

= $50,001 or more

JOB GROWTH

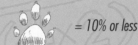 = 10% or less

EDUCATION

Four-year degree or more

SCHOOL SUBJECTS

science	reading
math	computers
art	

Working together is very important. Think about team sports. The players have to cooperate to win. Teams suffer when even one member isn't doing a good job. Factories are like a team. The machines and the workers have to work well together. Industrial engineers are like coaches for factories. We make sure that factories operate as best they can.

I travel to different factories around the country. I observe the way they work. I watch the employees. I check all of the machines. I look at the materials the factory uses and the goods it produces. Then I write a plan. I make suggestions on how the factory can work better. I tell factory owners how they can improve their production. I want everything to run smoothly.

My reports help workers do better jobs. They are able to produce more by following my comments. That makes their jobs easier. I look at a lot of charts and data. I calculate big numbers to make my suggestions. Math is very important. My report has to be technical and scientific. My data must be perfect. I work long hours. I spend many late nights going over figures at my computer. I want companies to be successful.

Information Abstractors and Indexers

I'm in charge of updating the database at the city library. I work as an information indexer. Everything we have in the library is listed in this computer. Our computer is an electronic card catalog.

I read newspapers, magazines, and journals. I list articles in our computer files based on subject matter. I try to list them in many different ways. That makes it easier for people to find the information. I just finished entering a story about watercolor paintings. I listed it in our computer under "watercolors." Then I listed it under "painting" and "art." I also listed it under "Liz Smith," the name of the artist.

I think carefully about everything I index. I wouldn't want someone to have a hard time finding the information. The information is useless if people can't find it. I like to help people do research at the library. I can tell them where to find just about anything. I think of myself as an information traffic director. I lead people in the right direction.

SALARY

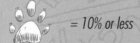

= $25,000 or less

JOB GROWTH

= 10% or less

EDUCATION

Training after high school

SCHOOL SUBJECTS

reading	science
math	computers
social studies	writing

Information Technology (IT) Managers

- ## SALARY

  = $50,001 or more

- ## JOB GROWTH
  = 21% or more

- ## EDUCATION
  Four-year degree or more

SCHOOL SUBJECTS

math	science
reading	computers
social studies	

I spend most of my day in cyberspace. I'm an IT manager. IT stands for information technology. I'm the manager of a computer system for a large accounting firm.

I keep the computers running. That's not easy. We have a huge staff here. Lots of things can go wrong. I have employees who go into the network to find a problem. Sometimes they have to do some reprogramming. I bought this system and managed its installation. My job depends on how well it runs.

I spend most of my day making decisions. My staff often calls me to find out how to do things. I can usually tell them what to look for. They solve the problem. Sometimes I buy new computers and software to help us do more things.

Offices can't function without computers. IT managers make sure the technology we have runs smoothly.

BUSINESS

Instrument Mechanics

I'm not a scientist, but I help with important scientific research. I keep sensitive measuring devices working properly. I work with NASA as an instrument mechanic. I adjust the equipment that they use to do space research.

I take the machines apart to find problems. Most of the equipment has lots of small parts. The parts have to work together to perform a function. If one part isn't working the right way, the entire machine will be off. I use special machines to test the instruments and their circuits for defects. The machine can help me find where a problem is occurring. I replace defective parts. These machines are very complex. Finding a problem can be very challenging.

I work with the scientists to make sure the instrument is working properly. It can't be off by even a tiny amount. Scientists need their instruments to measure things by really small amounts. I like working with details and solving problems.

SALARY

= $25,001 to $50,000

JOB GROWTH

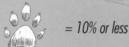

= 10% or less

EDUCATION

Four-year degree or more

SCHOOL SUBJECTS

math	industrial arts
reading	
computers	

Insurance Adjusters

- ## SALARY

= $25,001 to $50,000

- ## JOB GROWTH

= 11% to 20%

- ## EDUCATION

Two-year degree

SCHOOL SUBJECTS

math	computers
reading	
social studies	

I work for an insurance company as an adjuster. I investigate auto accidents. I figure out how much money we need to pay people who have been in an accident.

I try to be fair. I have to look at many details. I read the police report. I talk with everyone who was involved in the accident. I talk with any witnesses. I read over our client's policy. I check to see exactly what it covers.

Sometimes I help to settle lawsuits. I try to settle the case out of court for less money. If the case goes to court, I may have to testify. I help people as much as possible. Insurance adjusters help people get the money they deserve for medical bills and auto repairs. We try to save our companies money.

BUSINESS

Insurance Salespeople

I sell protection. I work for an insurance company as a salesperson. I sell insurance policies to people and businesses to protect them. Our policies protect people from possible losses from fire, theft, disease, death, accidents, or lawsuits.

I meet with customers to find out their needs. Not everyone needs the same kind of insurance. I create a policy especially for you. I help customers fill out applications. I tell you how much you will have to pay. I explain what the policy covers. It is important that people understand their insurance policies.

I received a license from the state to sell insurance. That lets people know that I am an honest salesperson. I get paid a commission for every new policy I sell. A commission is a percentage of the amount the customer pays.

Insurance helps people feel safer about their future. I make sure customers have what they need to feel safe.

- ## SALARY
  = $25,001 to $50,000

- ## JOB GROWTH
  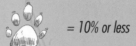 = 10% or less

- ## EDUCATION
  Two-year degree

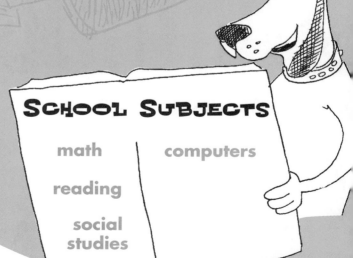

SCHOOL SUBJECTS

math computers

reading

social studies

Interior Designers

- ## SALARY
  = $25,001 to $50,000

- ## JOB GROWTH
  = 21% or more

- ## EDUCATION
  ### Four-year degree or more

SCHOOL SUBJECTS

art

math

reading

I design the inside of buildings. I'm an interior designer. I make places like houses and offices beautiful.

I talk to people to find out what they like. I want their buildings to be nice and comfortable. Some people want a house full of antiques. Offices usually have modern furniture. We talk about colors and paint. I show them fabrics for furniture and curtains. I pick out carpets and lamps. I tell them how much the project will cost. Then I place orders for the furnishings.

I help decorate when everything arrives. I work with painters and wallpaper hangers to get the rooms ready. I keep track of many details. I have a computer in my office. It lets me draw a model of a room. The model helps me decide where to place furniture. I make printouts to show people. I spend a lot of time on the phone placing orders. Sometimes I have meetings at night.

Interior designers have to know about color and style. I know the best places to buy things. I have a special store where I buy lamps. I buy carpet at another store. I talk with other designers to get ideas. I'm very lucky. I get paid to make places beautiful.

Interpreters and Translators

I can speak and write in four different languages. I know Japanese, Spanish, French, and English. I work as an interpreter and translator for the United Nations. I help people from different countries communicate with each other. I explain to people what has been said or written in one language in another language.

People speak very quickly in their own language. I have to be able to understand them and explain to someone else what they are saying. That can be tricky sometimes. I have to know about a country's customs as well as its language. I have to understand slang expressions. Not every word means exactly what it seems to. Sometimes I translate written documents. I have even translated entire books. I translated a great Japanese novel into English.

Languages fascinate me. People say the same things in very different ways. I feel like I make it easier for people from different countries to understand each other. Communication is very important in the modern world. We have to be able to deal with people from every country in the world. Translators and interpreters make that easier.

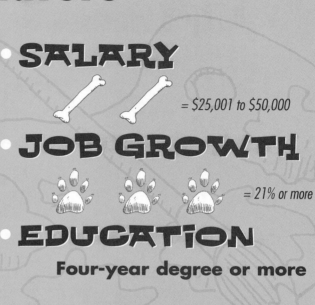

- ## SALARY
  = $25,001 to $50,000

- ## JOB GROWTH
  = 21% or more

- ## EDUCATION
  Four-year degree or more

SCHOOL SUBJECTS

reading	computers
spelling	writing
speech	foreign languages

Investigators

- ## SALARY

= $50,001 or more

- ## JOB GROWTH

= 21% or more

- ## EDUCATION

Training after high school

SCHOOL SUBJECTS

reading

math

computers

social studies

I'm a private investigator. People hire me to find other people or get information. I charge a fee and expenses for my work.

I do a lot of my work on the computer. I find people who are missing by searching records. The rest of my day I spend out around town. Sometimes I follow someone to see where he goes and report back to my client. Other times I go around asking questions to get information.

Usually my work isn't dangerous. Sometimes people get angry when I follow them, so I have to be careful not to be seen. When I get the information, I write a report for my customer. I include all the facts.

There is a lot of variety in my work. I don't sit behind a desk all day. I help people find answers.

Jewelers

I have a whole safe full of diamonds and rubies and gold. No, I'm not a pirate. I'm a jeweler. Jewelers make and repair jewelry for a living. I work for a large jewelry store in the city.

Jewelers know all about stones and metals. I can tell the quality of a diamond just by looking at it. I spend my day making beautiful sapphire earrings and stunning opal bracelets. I make lots of rings. I make a model for each ring out of wax. The model looks exactly like the finished ring will look. I use the model to make a mold. I melt down some gold or silver and pour it into the mold. I let the metal cool and become solid again.

Sometimes I place precious stones like diamonds or emeralds in metal settings. It all depends on what the customer wants. I've made some fabulous jewelry. Sometimes I repair things that people bring in. I may have to tighten a stone in a ring or fix a clasp. I can make rings bigger or smaller so they will fit people's fingers better.

I dress up at work so I'll look nice when I deal with customers. I want them to know that I have good taste. I love to make really fancy jewelry. People get very excited when they buy something I have made.

SALARY
= $25,001 to $50,000

JOB GROWTH

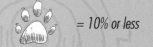

= 10% or less

EDUCATION
Training after high school

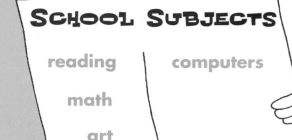

SCHOOL SUBJECTS

reading

math

art

computers

Journalists

- ## SALARY

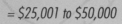 = $25,001 to $50,000

- ## JOB GROWTH

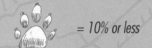 = 10% or less

- ## EDUCATION

Four-year degree or more

SCHOOL SUBJECTS

reading

spelling

social studies

computers

math

ARTS AND ENTERTAINMENT

I write stories for a large city newspaper. It's a tough job. Look through a newspaper. People write every story inside. Imagine writing that many school reports in one day!

My editor gives me assignments. It's like when your teacher gives you homework. I write stories to tell people about important events. I write about fires and accidents. I have to find the important details. I talk to people and look up information. I have to get all the facts right. I write the story on my computer. Then I give it to my editor. The editor looks it over and makes changes. Editors are like teachers grading papers. Sometimes I need to make changes.

I work late at night to cover important stories. Journalists must be good writers. I know how to use and spell big words in my stories. I have to be able to talk with people to get information. I always get my stories to the editor on time. I can't be late.

Journalists get to talk to very interesting people. Sometimes I write about sad things. I know that it is important to let people know about the news.

Kitchen Helpers

Think about all the food that restaurants serve. Imagine trying to cook all of it yourself. The vegetables have to be cleaned and chopped. Salads have to be made. Dishes have to be washed. Chefs can't do all of the work themselves. I'm here to save the day. I'm a kitchen helper.

I do a little bit of everything. I wash and cut vegetables and fruit. I bring pots and pans to the chef from our back storeroom. I get food out of the coolers. Kitchen helpers do whatever the chef wants. I make sure the waiters get the right plates for their tables. Sometimes I add parsley or fruit to the plates. That's called a garnish. I sometimes help unload delivery trucks.

I stay pretty busy. I'm exhausted at the end of the day. Helping in the kitchen is hard work.

- **SALARY**

= $25,000 or less

- **JOB GROWTH**
= 11% to 20%

- **EDUCATION**
High school diploma

SCHOOL SUBJECTS

reading

math

Landscape Architects

SALARY

= $50,001 or more

JOB GROWTH

= 21% or more

EDUCATION

Four-year degree or more

SCHOOL SUBJECTS

science	reading
art	computers
math	

Take a good look at the land the next time you're at the park. I bet you never thought that someone drew plans to design the flower beds. I'm a landscape architect. I design outdoor areas. I take a piece of land and turn it into a beautiful park or a walking trail. Building a park isn't as easy as you would think. I carefully examine the land. I plan around rocks or hills. If there is a lake, I like to put a sidewalk around it so people can take nice walks.

The park I am working on now will have docks that go into the water. People will be able to sail boats. The lake will be full of ducks and geese. There will be a fountain in the middle of the park. I'll have the gardener plant beautiful flowers around it. I draw my ideas on paper. My plans tell the construction people what to do. I plan every foot of the park from the monkey bars to the park benches.

I have to be good at art. I know a lot about plants and land. If I want to put a basketball court in the park, I make sure that it is the right size. I pick the right kind of stone to make the sidewalks sturdy. I want people to enjoy my parks for many years. Last year I designed a park that stretched along a river. Old, falling-down buildings were there before. Now people walk dogs and play Frisbee on the land. There's even a good spot with trees to have a picnic or take a catnap.

NATURAL RESOURCES

Laser Technicians

How much do you know about lasers? Lasers are used for much more than guns in science fiction movies. We use lasers for a lot of different things today. I know all about lasers. I work as a laser technician. I work mainly with medical equipment.

Doctors use lasers to do some kinds of surgery. I build and repair the machines that they use. I have instructions that I use to build the machines. I follow a blueprint. A blueprint tells me exactly where each part should go and how the finished machine will look. I pay attention to many details. These machines are very sensitive.

I talk with the engineers who designed the equipment. They explain exactly how the machine operates. I work with the production team to build the machine. The lasers we use have mirrors and lots of metal parts. I give them instructions based on the blueprint and the information I got from the engineers. Each machine has to be made exactly right. I wouldn't want a doctor to have problems with a machine during surgery.

The machines I help to make are at the cutting edge of technology.

- **SALARY** = $25,001 to $50,000
- **JOB GROWTH** = 11% to 20%
- **EDUCATION** Two-year degree

SCHOOL SUBJECTS

reading   computers

math

science

Lawyers

- ## SALARY

= $50,001 or more

- ## JOB GROWTH

= 11% to 20%

- ## EDUCATION
Four-year degree or more

SCHOOL SUBJECTS

science	reading
math	computers
social studies	

I'm sure you've seen lawyers on TV before. TV usually shows us arguing in court. That is only a small part of what we do. Most of our time is spent in an office.

People write agreements when they buy or sell something to each other. These agreements are called contracts. A contract describes in writing exactly what they are buying or selling. People use contracts for buying or selling things like cars and houses. Contracts are good protection. Contracts prevent people from claiming they agreed to something else. People come to me to help them write contracts. I write contracts so a judge will understand what the people agreed to.

Lawyers work in many different areas of law. Some lawyers argue cases in front of a judge. Other lawyers represent the government and enforce laws. Criminal lawyers represent people who are accused of crimes. Lawyers use law books and databases to make decisions. I look up information so I know how to defend my client. I spend a lot of time helping my clients. I like helping people get what is legally theirs.

I never leave work on time. Sometimes I stay at the office past midnight. I always wear nice clothes. You can't go to court wearing jeans.

Legal Secretaries

I'm a secretary in a lawyers' office. I have duties that are more specialized than most secretaries. I prepare many legal documents. I have to be careful with the wording on the papers. Legal papers have to be phrased exactly. A lawyer tells me what needs to be done. I may have to create a summons, a motion, or a subpoena. I use my computer to create the documents. I have a standard form set up in the system to make my job easier. I add the specific information.

Lawyers file many papers with the courts. The law requires that those papers follow a specific format. I do most of the paperwork. I fill out forms and send them to the right place. My boss and his client would be in big trouble if I made a mistake.

Sometimes I look up information online or in books. A lawyer may need me to find out the details of a past case. I can look up the decision to save the lawyer some time.

BUSINESS

SALARY

 = $25,001 to $50,000

JOB GROWTH

= 11% to 20%

EDUCATION

Two-year degree

SCHOOL SUBJECTS

computers	math
reading	writing
social studies	

Liberal Arts Teachers

- ## SALARY
  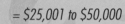
  = $25,001 to $50,000

- ## JOB GROWTH
  = 11% to 20%

- ## EDUCATION
  ### Four-year degree or more

SCHOOL SUBJECTS

reading	computers
writing	history
social studies	

I teach English at Wintergreen High School. English is considered a liberal art. Drama, foreign languages, history, government, art, music, health, and physical education are also considered liberal arts. Liberal art classes teach students to think creatively

In my English class I ask students to read and analyze literature. I get them to write essays covering major themes. I want to hear their ideas about these great books. Literature is supposed to make us think about our place in the world. I meet with my students' parents a couple of times a year. I let them know about their child's work in my class. Parents are important to their kids' education.

I grade homework and tests almost every night. I keep track of grades. We issue report cards every six weeks. Totaling up grades is a lot of work. I love my job. I hope that I am teaching students to think as well as teaching them about wonderful books.

Librarians

What's your favorite book? Maybe you like to read about animals or famous explorers. I can help you find a book that you will like. I'm your school librarian.

Look at all these books. I ordered all of them. I decide which books to buy. I buy books that people want to read. I make sure we store all of our books in order. I'm a very organized person. Each book has its own special place. I don't like misplaced books. I can tell you how to find a book by using the computer card catalog and the Dewey decimal system.

I know my library inside out. I can tell you where to look up information you need. I do have one favor to ask. Please don't talk in the library. People come here to study and read. They need quiet to think.

I always liked to read. My Mom had a huge collection of books. I read all of them at least once. I think they helped me in my studies. I spend almost all of my time with books. I can learn about anything I want by looking it up. I like getting students interested in books. Reading makes you smart.

SALARY
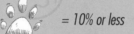
= $25,001 to $50,000

JOB GROWTH
= 10% or less

EDUCATION
Four-year degree or more

SCHOOL SUBJECTS

reading	science
writing	computers
social studies	

Licensed Practical Nurses

- ## SALARY
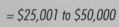
= $25,001 to $50,000

- ## JOB GROWTH

= 11% to 20%

- ## EDUCATION
Two-year degree

SCHOOL SUBJECTS

science	computers
reading	
writing	

I do all the little things to help patients in hospitals. I work as a licensed practical nurse. I don't handle emergencies or stitch up wounds. I take care of the details.

I bathe and dress patients and help them comb their hair. I change the sheets on their beds. I record their temperature, pulse, and breathing. I go on rounds and give medicine according to the doctors' orders. The patients at the hospital see me more than anyone else. I check on them. I make sure they stay comfortable. I bring them food and help them eat.

Licensed practical nurses help make your hospital stay more comfortable. I know that hospitals can be scary. I want to be a friendly face to make your recovery easier.

Loan Officers

I work at a local bank. I can help you borrow money to build a house or buy a new car. I'm a loan officer. Just come into the bank and talk with me.

First, I'll need you to fill out a loan application. I need to know information about your age, your employer, and how much money you make. I also need to know if you own any property. Then I like to talk with you to find out about you. I have a credit analyst look up your credit history. That will tell me if you are good about paying your bills. We don't like to loan money to people who don't pay.

If I approve the loan, we'll work out a plan for you to pay it back. You can make a payment each month until you've paid the entire amount back with interest. Interest is the amount we charge to make the loan. I talk with lots of people every day. I've helped finance vacations and weddings.

It doesn't cost anything to talk to me. I'm here to help. Loaning money is my business.

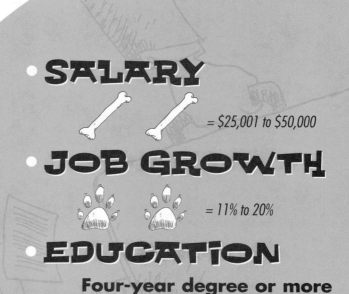

- **SALARY** = $25,001 to $50,000

- **JOB GROWTH** = 11% to 20%

- **EDUCATION**
  Four-year degree or more

SCHOOL SUBJECTS

math	science
reading	computers
social studies	

Locksmiths

- ## SALARY

= $25,001 to $50,000

- ## JOB GROWTH

= 21% or more

- ## EDUCATION
Training after high school

SCHOOL SUBJECTS

reading

math

industrial arts

I like to help people keep their houses secure. I'm a locksmith. I fix the locks on doors and windows.

Most of the time I put in new locks. I may drill a hole in the door to insert the lock. I may be able to fix the old lock on your door. I'll have to take it apart to look at the inside. It may just have a worn tumbler or spring. I can make extra keys for you. I have a special machine to cut duplicate keys. I just need one of your keys to copy. I can open your lock if you have lost your key. I have a special tool that I use to pick the lock. I make sure that you really do live at the address. I wouldn't want to help someone break into a house.

I keep track of all the work I do on our computer at the office. I type in every customer and the service we performed. Locksmiths are very important. We help people feel safe and secure.

Loggers

I work in large pine forests. I'm a logger. I work for the lumber company that owns this property. I cut down the trees to make lumber and paper.

My supervisor tells me which trees to cut. I use a big, gas-powered chainsaw to make the cuts. A chainsaw is much easier to use than a regular saw. I'm an expert at making cuts. I know where to saw to make the tree fall in the right direction. I wouldn't want it to land on our equipment. I cut the tree into log lengths so it will fit on our trucks.

Sometimes we go deep into the woods. Then we attach chains to the logs and drag them with a tractor. The other loggers help me load the trucks. We cut and load all day long. We only cut certain trees. We have to leave some of the forest here. My company plants new trees to replace the ones it cuts down. We'd run out of wood if we didn't replant. At the end of the day, we drive our trucks to a mill. We unload the logs so they can be used to make lumber or paper.

Being a logger requires hard work. I have strong muscles. Chainsaws are heavy and can be very dangerous. I have to be careful. I like working out in the woods. Nothing beats the smell of fresh pine.

SALARY

= $25,001 to $50,000

JOB GROWTH
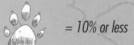
= 10% or less

EDUCATION
High school diploma

SCHOOL SUBJECTS

reading

math

physical education

industrial arts

Machine Tool Operators

- ## SALARY
  = $25,001 to $50,000

- ## JOB GROWTH
  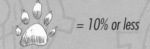
  = 10% or less

- ## EDUCATION
  Training after high school

SCHOOL SUBJECTS

reading

math

industrial arts

PRODUCTION

I make screwdrivers for a living. I work in a factory as a machine tool operator. Machine tool operators shape metal into tools, parts, or instruments. I follow a blueprint to get the heads the right size. I make adjustments to my machine so the pieces will match the handles.

I have to pay attention. These machines are dangerous if you aren't careful. I make sure they are working properly. I keep them lubricated so the parts run smoothly. I make hundreds of screwdrivers every day. I have to work at a set pace. I can't slack off. My supervisor tells me how many I should be able to make in a day. Sometimes I have to rush to meet my quota. We work hard to fill the big orders.

I like working in a factory. I don't have to sit in an office all day. When the whistle blows, I can leave work and head for home. I don't worry about taking my work home with me.

Machinists

I'm sure you've seen pictures of factories with big assembly lines. Have you ever noticed how many different machines a factory has? Well, each machine is made of lots of parts. All the parts work together to keep the machine running. Now, think for a minute. Each one of those parts has to be made. I'm a machinist. I make metal parts for machines.

I use tools like metal cutters and welding torches to shape pieces of metal into working parts. I wear a safety helmet with eye protection and thick gloves. I wouldn't want to cut or burn myself. I look at blueprints to make sure that I have every piece exactly right. A blueprint shows the exact size and shape of every part in the machine. If I am off by even the slightest amount, the piece will keep the machine from working. I cut and weld the piece with a blowtorch. I use a grinder to get the surface smooth and even.

I have to be very careful. The equipment can be dangerous. I think machinists are the most important people at factories. Without us, factories wouldn't have all the machines that make the products they sell.

SALARY

= $25,001 to $50,000

JOB GROWTH

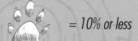

= 10% or less

EDUCATION

Training after high school

SCHOOL SUBJECTS

reading

math

Mail Carriers

- ## SALARY

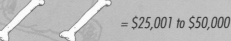 = $25,001 to $50,000

- ## JOB GROWTH

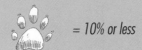 = 10% or less

- ## EDUCATION

High school diploma

SCHOOL SUBJECTS

reading

math

computers

I'm a mail carrier. I work for the U.S. Postal Service. I deliver mail to houses and businesses.

I go to work at the post office early in the morning. I sort the mail for my delivery area. I work in one neighborhood. I load the mail in my car and drive to my route. I park and walk around delivering the mail for several blocks. I go back to my car and get more mail to deliver. I move the car as I go along the route. I know the name of every family in the neighborhood. I deliver to a lot of different places.

I know all the rules of the post office. I have to know how much postage belongs on letters and packages. Sometimes I collect money from people for their packages. I work every day, except Sunday. People have all different sizes and colors of mailboxes. Some just have a slot in their door for the mail. I have to watch for dogs. Some dogs like to attack mail carriers. I carry a can of spray to keep them away. I wear a uniform to work.

Most of the people along my route are very friendly. Mr. Cooper always gives me a drink of water when I get to his house.

Manufacturing Workers

I build airplanes for a living. I work as an aerospace assembly worker at an airplane factory. I'm in charge of building the windshields for every plane we manufacture.

I work with other assembly workers. We work together to make an airplane. Some of us work on the tail or the wings. Another crew works on the engine and the landing gear. It's a lot like putting together a car. We just have a much bigger machine to build.

Airplanes have many parts. We have to work as a team and pay attention to what we are doing. The airplanes we build would be unsafe if we didn't do a good job.

People who work in manufacturing work in factories doing repetitive work. They might work in a steel mill or assembling cars. Even the toys you play with are manufactured somewhere. We have to be safe in the factory. It has many tools and parts that could hurt you.

PRODUCTION

SALARY
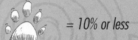 = $25,001 to $50,000

JOB GROWTH
= 10% or less

EDUCATION
Training after high school

SCHOOL SUBJECTS

reading	science
math	computers
physical education	industrial arts

Marketing Directors

SALARY

 = $50,001 or more

JOB GROWTH

 = 21% or more

EDUCATION

Four-year degree or more

SCHOOL SUBJECTS

math	reading
reading	writing
social studies	computers

BUSINESS

Businesses sell products or ideas. This company relies on me to get our products sold. I'm the marketing director. I plan strategies for selling our products and services.

I work closely with our advertising director and our sales manager. I tell the advertising manager what kinds of ads we need. We talk about the audience we would like to reach. I make suggestions to the sales manager. I tell her about any stores or magazines where I would like to see our products.

Marketing directors develop a company's sales campaign. I use research to help me make decisions. I analyze sales figures from the past year and look at what the competition is doing. I keep up with trends in my market. Businesses can't fall behind. I have a staff to help me with my work. I get them to do research. They help develop our marketing strategies.

My job is very important to this company. I am under a lot of stress. I work really hard. I spend many extra hours in my office. I have to be competitive. My decisions and ideas help the company make money. I want us to be the best.

Market Researchers

Hi there! I am a market researcher for the Scrub-A-Dub detergent company. I study customer buying habits and attitudes to predict the success of our new products. Have you heard of EverClean dishwashing detergent? Our scientists have just developed it. It will change the way people do dishes.

I'm traveling around the country to test our new product. I let people sample it to see what they think about the way it cleans. I ask them to fill out a survey. I ask them what they think about the scent and the color. I want their opinions. I also ask them about the detergent they usually use. I have to know about the competition.

I put all the answers I get in a marketing report. I give the information to the managers at the Scrub-A-Dub headquarters. They use the information to decide how to sell the new product. They may want to run advertisements on TV or send free samples.

Market researchers give managers the information they need to make good decisions. We're an important part of the product selling team.

SALARY

= $50,001 or more

JOB GROWTH

= 21% or more

EDUCATION

Four-year degree or more

SCHOOL SUBJECTS

math	reading
science	writing
computers	

Massage Therapists

SALARY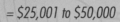

= $25,001 to $50,000

JOB GROWTH

= 21% or more

EDUCATION

Two-year degree

SCHOOL SUBJECTS

reading

math

science

Have you ever woken up with a stiff neck? I could make you feel better. I work as a massage therapist. Maybe you should make an appointment with me.

I see lots of different people every day. Many clients come back at least once a week. Sometimes I bring a massage table to a client's office or home. I help people relax. Nothing feels better than a good massage. My office has a comfortable table for you to lie on. I play soothing music during the session. I have expert fingers. Your muscles tighten when you are under a lot of stress. I rub your back and neck to help relax stiff muscles. Tell me if you have any aches or pains.

I use special oils. I can rub a mixture on your back that feels tingly and smells like peppermint. I can give you a full body massage. I can rub your feet and ankles. I can even massage your face. Sometimes I use steam or water treatments.

Massage therapists are trained professionals. I went to school to learn how to help you relax. I believe that people should be pampered. We would all get along much better if we could just relax.

Materials Engineers

I can tell you the best metal to use on a satellite. I'm a materials engineer. I work for a company that develops new satellite technology. I'm an expert at materials. I find the best materials for my company to use on the equipment we manufacture.

I did a lot of work on our latest satellite. I met with different companies to discuss the new metal alloys they are creating. Scientists have found that they can make metals better by altering their chemical compounds. I had to find a metal that was sturdy but didn't weigh a lot. I had to analyze the satellite design to see which metals would work with the plan.

My company relies on me to make a sound recommendation. I have to consider the strength, the weight, and the cost. Some of the metals were perfect for this satellite but were too expensive for us. I found other metals that would work just as well but were less expensive.

I do a lot of shopping around. I'm a technology bargain hunter. My company wants to make the best satellites for the least cost. They rely on me as a materials engineer to do that.

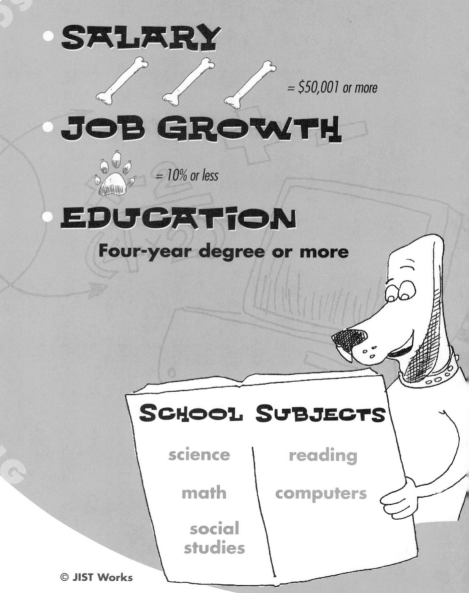

- **SALARY**
  = $50,001 or more

- **JOB GROWTH**
  = 10% or less

- **EDUCATION**
  Four-year degree or more

SCHOOL SUBJECTS

science	reading
math	computers
social studies	

Math and Science Teachers

SALARY

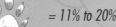 = $25,001 to $50,000

JOB GROWTH

 = 11% to 20%

EDUCATION

Four-year degree or more

SCHOOL SUBJECTS

science	reading
math	writing
computers	

Have you ever cut open a frog? You may when you get into my class. I teach biology. Biology is the science of plants and animals. I teach students all about life on the earth. We cover everything from single cells to humans. We even talk about plants.

Sometimes we do lab experiments to support the textbook readings and lectures. We cut open dead frogs to see what the insides look like. I know, that sounds a little disgusting. I show students the large intestine and the heart. Some of a frog's organs look similar to humans. Students learn a lot from it. I assign chapters in the book for my students to read. Then I talk about the information the next day in class. I give tests every two weeks. I record grades so I can put them on report cards.

I want my students to know all about the different plants and animals by the time they leave my class. Some of my students will go on to be veterinarians, surgeons, botanists, and zoologists. That makes me very proud.

Mathematicians

I love math! I have all my life. Now I use it to study stars. My name is Dr. Oberman. I work as a mathematician for a research company. We are studying stars using advanced telescopes.

I use math to calculate light years. I figure out how long it takes light to reach our planet from distant stars. I know that sounds complicated. The speed of light is very fast. I use long, technical formulas. It takes a lot of work. The math you do now in your classes can prepare you for the kind of math I do. Each year you'll take more complicated classes. The more math you do, the easier it gets. I'm sure you know that from your homework.

Math takes practice. I don't mind the practice. To me, math is a challenge.

SALARY
= $50,001 or more

JOB GROWTH
= 10% or less

EDUCATION
Four-year degree or more

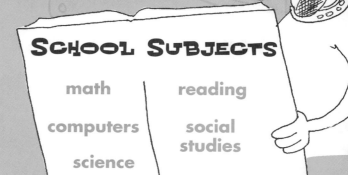

SCHOOL SUBJECTS

math	reading
computers	social studies
science	

Meat Cutters

- ## SALARY

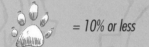 = $25,001 to $50,000

- ## JOB GROWTH

= 10% or less

- ## EDUCATION

Training after high school

SCHOOL SUBJECTS

reading

math

PRODUCTION

I work at the Food Chain Supermarket in the meat department. I prepare meat, fish, and poultry to sell. I'm a meat cutter. I package meat into those little plastic-wrapped packages.

I cut the meat with big power saws. I start with a huge side of beef or an entire pig. I separate it into the different cuts of meat. I turn the beef into steaks, ribs, and hamburger. Each cut comes from a different part of the animal's body. I keep the work area clean. Working with meat can be pretty messy. You get used to it.

I wear a uniform to work. I keep it washed and sanitary. I have to be careful about germs because I am working with food.

Look in the meat department the next time you go to the grocery store. People like me put together those packages.

Mechanical Engineers

I'm a mechanical engineer. Mechanical engineers design machines. I design cars for an automobile manufacturer. A lot goes into designing a car.

I start with a rough sketch. I decide if I want the car to be a sports model or a family sedan. The car I am working on now is very sporty. I designed the outside so it can travel really fast. I planned the engine so it can reach high speeds quickly. Mechanical engineers have to know about electronics and engines. I chose tires to grip the road when it is raining. I don't want it to skid.

I want the car to be safe. I designed air bags that pop out of the dashboard if the car gets in an accident. I think about every part of a car from the engine to the trunk. I spend a lot of time on my designs. Sometimes I stay late at work and sit in front of my computer for hours. I send the finished designs to the factory. I must make sure they understand my technical instructions. Factories have to build them exactly right.

SALARY

= $50,001 or more

JOB GROWTH

= 10% or less

EDUCATION

Four-year degree or more

SCHOOL SUBJECTS

science	reading
art	computers
math	

Medical Assistants

SALARY

= $25,000 or less

JOB GROWTH

= 21% or more

EDUCATION

Two-year degree

SCHOOL SUBJECTS

reading

math

computers

I work as a medical assistant in a large clinic. My name is Robbie. I work with the doctors and nurses to take care of the many patients we see every day.

I get the examining rooms ready for the doctors. I clean up after the last patient and make sure the instruments are sterilized. You wouldn't want to use a thermometer that had someone else's germs. I talk with the patients about their health. I weigh them on a scale and take their temperatures. Sometimes I help the doctor during the exam.

I also work a lot in the front office. I help with all the paperwork. I keep track of X rays, medical files, and insurance papers. I help to schedule appointments. It's tricky to make an appointment schedule. The doctors at this clinic stay very busy.

I like working here. I am an important part of our team. We work hard to make people well again. Doctors appreciate the work that medical assistants do.

Medical Equipment Repairers

I go to the hospital all the time, but I'm hardly ever sick. I work as a medical equipment repairer. I fix broken X-ray machines and heart monitors.

I'm a specialist. I can look at a piece of equipment and figure out how to fix it. I keep spare parts in my truck. I take the equipment apart to find out what is wrong. Sometimes I solder a part into place. I use a soldering gun to join metal together with a material called solder. It melts a piece of metal in between the other two metals. The solder works like glue.

Sometimes the equipment just needs to be cleaned to work the right way. The parts can get pretty dirty. Most of the time I can fix a machine just by cleaning the parts. Then it will operate as it is supposed to.

SALARY

= $25,001 to $50,000

JOB GROWTH

= 11% to 20%

EDUCATION

Two-year degree

SCHOOL SUBJECTS

reading	industrial arts
math	
computers	

Medical Laboratory Assistants

SALARY

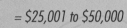 = $25,001 to $50,000

JOB GROWTH

 = 11% to 20%

EDUCATION

Training after high school

SCHOOL SUBJECTS

science   computers

reading

math

I look at things under a microscope all day long. I work in a hospital as a medical laboratory assistant. I work with pathologists and medical technologists. They give me instructions on how to run medical tests.

I look at body fluid samples under a microscope. I put the sample on a glass slide. I do tests on blood. I check for diseases and illnesses. A lot of diseases affect the way blood looks under a microscope. Blood cells change when you are sick. I look for small details under the microscope.

I keep track of hundreds of samples every day. I can't get them mixed up. I give the information to the pathologist or the medical technologist. They look over everything and confirm my report. The tests I run help doctors find out what is wrong with people.

Our blood and body fluids tell us about our health. My work helps us discover illnesses more quickly. That means we can make patients better much sooner.

Medical Records Administrators

I'm the medical records administrator at City Hospital. I'm in charge of our records.

Every patient who comes through these doors has a file. We have to include their medical histories. The file can tell us if they are allergic to any medicines. It lets us know if they have had surgery before. I created this system. I keep it organized. Our files are on computer. I make sure the system is updated. Medical information is very important.

I also manage legal documents and insurance information. I make sure that we provide information to insurance companies. They need to know what services their clients have received. Insurance companies pay most of our patients' medical bills. I train the hospital staff to use our computer system. They have to know how to find patient files. We want all the information to be up-to-date.

The law requires that our files be accurate. Our database is huge. Every file is important. I have to be very responsible. People's lives depend on the information I manage.

SALARY

= $50,001 or more

JOB GROWTH

= 21% or more

EDUCATION

Four-year degree or more

SCHOOL SUBJECTS

reading	math
spelling	computers
science	

Medical Records Clerks

SALARY

 = $25,000 or less

JOB GROWTH

= 21% or more

EDUCATION

Two-year degree

SCHOOL SUBJECTS

math

reading

computers

I'm sure you've been in offices with filing cabinets full of information. Secretaries keep track of files in most offices. I keep track of medical files for a hospital. I'm a medical records clerk.

I prepare, update, and file patient medical records. This hospital has hundreds of files. When a patient comes in, I have to get complete medical information. I have them fill out the forms so we will know all about their health record. Doctors use this information to make important decisions.

I keep every file in our computer filing system up to date. We recently switched to keeping files on computer. The new computer allows me to run reports for the hospital administrator. I can give details on the number of patients we see every day or on how many operations we perform in a year. I set the guidelines and the computer does the busy work. With the computer, I can access any patient's file. It makes looking up medical information much quicker.

Medical records clerks are an important part of the hospital team. We're like hospital librarians. We keep track of information so other people can find it.

Medical Secretaries

I can make an appointment with the dentist if you'd like. I'm a medical secretary for Dr. Dunn.

I keep this office running efficiently. I process the paperwork. I schedule appointments for checkups. I help people get in to see the dentist when they have an emergency. I keep track of our patients. I have them fill out medical records when they come to the office. I put the information in a file. I let them know when the dentist is ready to see them. I show them to the examining room.

I talk with them when the dentist is finished working. I arrange a way for them to pay for the work. Sometimes people have their insurance company pay. I get the insurance information from them. Some people pay in the office. I can accept their check, money, or credit card. I send notices to our patients when they need to schedule an appointment. We recommend that they have a checkup every six months.

Dr. Dunn appreciates the work I do. I handle the business details so she can worry about the patients' health.

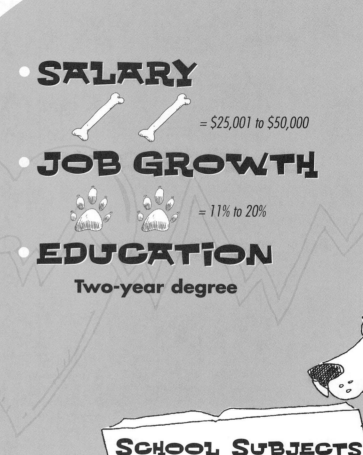

- **SALARY**
  = $25,001 to $50,000
- **JOB GROWTH**
  = 11% to 20%
- **EDUCATION**
  Two-year degree

SCHOOL SUBJECTS

computers

math

reading

Medical Technologists

SALARY

 = $25,001 to $50,000

JOB GROWTH

 = 11% to 20%

EDUCATION

Four-year degree or more

SCHOOL SUBJECTS

science   reading

math   computers

social
studies

Doctors can't always tell if you are sick just by looking at you. Sometimes they have to do a test. They may take a sample of your blood and send it to a lab. I am the person who checks the sample at the lab. I am a medical technologist.

I work in a lab in a large hospital. We have different ways to find out if your blood is healthy. My office is filled with test tubes and computer equipment. I may look at your blood sample under a microscope. Sometimes I mix chemicals together to see how they react with the blood sample. I let the doctors know if I find a problem. I tell them exactly what is wrong.

I have to be very careful. I don't want someone who is healthy to think they are sick. Many samples are sent to me every day. I have to keep them straight. Sometimes when people have an operation and lose too much blood, they need to use someone else's blood. This is called a blood transfusion. I must check to make sure the blood matches. The patient will get sick if it is not the right type. I have to know a lot about the human body's chemicals. I'm good at keeping everything in order. My attention to details helps people stay alive.

HEALTH

Mental Health Counselors

I help people deal with emotional and personal problems. I'm a mental health counselor. I talk with lots of people every day.

I get background information about them. I want to know about their families and health. I try to find out about their personalities. I work with many people who are overweight or smoke. They come to me because they want to change. I talk with them about their lives.

Other people have problems with relationships. They don't get along with other people or are very shy. Sometimes a group of patients get together with me to talk. This is called a support group. Sometimes people feel better if they can talk with someone who has similar problems.

My job is very important. I work hard to help people understand and change themselves.

- **SALARY**
  = $25,001 to $50,000

- **JOB GROWTH**
  = 21% or more

- **EDUCATION**
  Four-year degree **or more**

SCHOOL SUBJECTS

reading	science
writing	computers
social studies	

Metallographic Technicians

SALARY

= $25,001 to $50,000

JOB GROWTH

= 10% or less

EDUCATION

Two-year degree

SCHOOL SUBJECTS

math	writing
science	computers
reading	industrial arts

Metals are used for everything from building bridges to elevators. Metals used in these ways have to handle different amounts of stress. I can take a piece of metal and tell you everything about it. I work for a steel company as a metallographic technician.

I test metals and metal alloys to find out about their physical makeup. A metal alloy is a mixture of two different metals. I look at samples of the metal under a microscope. I can see if it is a pure metal or an alloy. I can tell how strong the metal is.

Sometimes I run chemical tests or use radiation to find out about a sample. I write my findings in a report. I like to use graphs and charts to point out the physical features.

Metal Refining Workers

It gets pretty hot around here. You can't do what I do if you don't like to sweat. This work is very physical. I work in a metal refining plant. They call me Nails, because I'm as tough as nails. I have to be. I get quite a workout every day.

I operate the furnaces that convert iron ore into iron. Ore is the natural form that iron is in when they dig it out of the ground. I heat the ore to separate the iron. These furnaces heat up to hundreds of degrees. I wear a special uniform to stay protected. I pour the molten iron into molds. The molds shape the iron into manageable sizes. This refinery sells the molded iron to other factories. The factories use the iron to make all kinds of products. But they couldn't do it without me.

If it weren't for metal refining workers, that iron would just be a pile of rocks. I go home at the end of the day mighty sore. But I'm happy to be doing something with my hands and muscles.

SALARY

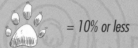 = $25,001 to $50,000

JOB GROWTH

 = 10% or less

EDUCATION

Training after high school

SCHOOL SUBJECTS

reading	industrial arts
math	
physical education	

Meteorologists

SALARY

= $50,001 or more

JOB GROWTH

= 11% to 20%

EDUCATION

Four-year degree or more

SCHOOL SUBJECTS

science	reading
math	computers
geography	

What's the weather going to be like tomorrow? Will you need an umbrella, or should you put on your swimming suit? Why don't you ask me? I'm a meteorologist. Some people call us weather people. We predict the weather by studying air and water patterns.

I work for a television station. I have science equipment to study weather fronts. Satellites send pictures to my computer to tell me if a storm is approaching. I follow the storms so I can tell you when it will snow in your area. People really listen to my reports. I'm sure you've checked the weather report to see if you have to go to school in bad weather. I predict the weather by guessing what will happen based on weather patterns.

But weather constantly changes. Many times storms die down before they reach you. I warn people about serious weather like hurricanes and tornadoes. That is the most important part of my job. I wouldn't want someone to get injured in a storm. I have to know the science of weather.

I like predicting the weather. I think it's amazing how cloud patterns sweep across the country and affect the temperature. My forecasts help people plan their days. Nobody wants to have a coat on when it's 90 degrees outside.

*M*icrobiologists

Have you ever looked at something under a microscope? Microscopes allow people to see organisms that can't be seen with our eyes alone. I'm a microbiologist. Microbiologists help find pollutants in the air or water and the causes of illnesses. We are biologists who specialize in studying microorganisms.

I'm doing research on cancer cells. I look at blood under the microscope to see the cells. They are very different from normal cells. I do experiments to see how they react to certain chemicals. I hope that my research will help find a cure for cancer.

Microbiologists also do a lot of work with the environment. They can check water samples for impurities. Microbiologists work with many other scientists on research projects. We are specialists at analyzing tiny organisms. The work I do could help save a lot of lives.

SALARY
= $50,001 or more

JOB GROWTH
= 11% to 20%

EDUCATION
Four-year degree or more

SCHOOL SUBJECTS

science	reading
math	writing
computers	

Midwives

- ## SALARY

  = $25,001 to $50,000

- ## JOB GROWTH

  = 21% or more

- ## EDUCATION
  Two-year degree

SCHOOL SUBJECTS

science   computers

math

reading

I'm a special kind of nurse who helps deliver babies. They call me a midwife. I work with obstetricians. Obstetricians are doctors who deliver babies. We help mothers throughout their pregnancy.

I examine a woman when she is pregnant. I check on the health of both her and her baby. I work with the doctor to give her special tests. I give the patient information about staying healthy. I recommend special diets. Nutrition is very important when you are pregnant. I tell her not to smoke cigarettes or drink alcohol or caffeine.

I deliver the baby. I get the doctor to help me if there are any medical problems. I let the mother choose where she wants the baby to be born. Some mothers want us to deliver the baby at home. Others prefer to have it done at the hospital. Many times the father is in the birthing room with us. We work together as a team to help the mother.

Some deliveries take many hours. It's amazing to see a baby being born. I've delivered hundreds of babies, but I get excited every time. I bring new life into the world.

Military Enlisted Personnel

I defend my country for a living. I'm a soldier. My name is Private Harris. I'm a member of the U.S. Armed Forces. My job is very important. I am trained to protect the United States and our allies during war and other emergencies. I've been through months of training. The military is very strict. We wear uniforms all the time. We also have to be in top physical condition. We get quite a workout. They wake us up early in the morning to go on long jogs and hikes. We even have to do it if it's raining!

We're always exercising. I think having to do push-ups is the worst. Training is pretty tough. Our sergeants have all the soldiers march together in a line to get us ready for combat. We have to work as a team. They teach us how to fire guns and rifles. We only use our guns when it is necessary. I also know how to drive a jeep and a tank. Soldiers must obey orders. We cannot talk back.

The military is training me to become a communications specialist. I've learned to work with computer equipment and important new technology. Many people in the military have special jobs they do. The military even hires doctors and nurses! America is very important to me. I work to protect it. Military enlisted personnel keep the United States safe.

SALARY
= $25,001 to $50,000

JOB GROWTH
= 11% to 20%

EDUCATION
Training after high school

SCHOOL SUBJECTS
reading

computers

math

physical education

Military Officers

SALARY

= $50,001 or more

JOB GROWTH

= 11% to 20%

EDUCATION

Four-year degree or more

SCHOOL SUBJECTS

reading

math

social studies

science

computers

writing

TECHNOLOGY

You're a lucky kid. It's not easy to get clearance to enter a military base. You've got good credentials. I'm the commander of this United States military base. I'm in charge of everything that goes on here. I'm kind of like the mayor of a city.

I make sure that everything on the base runs smoothly. I maintain security. I let only certain people on or off the base. I make sure the guards are doing their jobs. I also make sure all the other employees on the base do their jobs. I check on everyone from the cooks in the mess hall to the pilots of the planes. I'm the top boss on this base.

I make sure we have plenty of supplies. I don't want us to run out of anything. I approve the ordering of food and office supplies. I keep stock of our weapons. I keep track of many details. The base has its own police and fire departments. I make sure they do their jobs. The base has many planes, jeeps, and tanks. I make sure they are all operational. Being base commander is a lot of work. I have to be very organized. I have a staff to help me with my work. They all report to me.

I keep records of our activities. Much of the information is top secret. I can't let anyone know about military information. Telling secrets could threaten our national security. My job is very important. I help protect our country.

Millwrights

Hey there! My name is Lane. I work as a millwright at a big factory. Factories use huge machines to make the same item over and over again. Each machine has its own special job. I know a lot about machines. Millwrights set up the machines that are used in factories.

I read a blueprint to set the machine up properly. The blueprint is a detailed drawing of the machine and all of its parts. I build a foundation for the machine. The foundation is what holds the machine in place. Sometimes I use wood and sometimes steel. I like to set the foundation in cement. I don't want the machines to wobble around. These machines are so big that I can't move them by myself. I place them on the foundation using dollies and trucks. Some of this equipment is pretty heavy!

Other workers and I put the machine together and fasten it to the foundation. We follow the blueprints closely. We make sure the machine is sturdy. These machines get a tough workout every day. They have to be installed perfectly.

I've even learned about computers. New machines are really technical. I have become a microchip expert. Millwrights do important work. Factories couldn't operate without the machines we install.

SALARY

= $25,001 to $50,000

JOB GROWTH

= 10% or less

EDUCATION

Training after high school

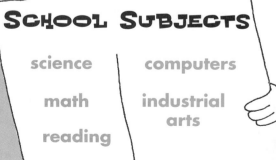

SCHOOL SUBJECTS

science	computers
math	industrial arts
reading	

Mining Engineers

- ## SALARY

  = $50,001 or more

- ## JOB GROWTH

  = 10% or less

- ## EDUCATION

  Four-year degree or more

SCHOOL SUBJECTS

science	geography
math	computers
reading	

My name is Digger. I'm a mining engineer. Right now I am in South Africa checking out a new mine location. I work for a company that mines diamonds and gold. Mining engineers look at maps to find good places to dig for coal, iron ore, diamonds, and other minerals.

I know a lot about geology. It is the science of the composition of the earth. Once I have found a good spot, I plan the best way to reach the gems. The diamonds we are mining now are far below the earth's surface. I am designing mine shafts to reach the precious stones. I plan very carefully. The tunnels have to be sturdy and safe. The crew must check them for poisonous gas. I wouldn't want any workers to get hurt.

In a few days I will travel to another mine to check on our progress there. My job takes me all over the world to many exotic places. I get to use my knowledge of science to find diamonds and gold.

Models

I'm a model. When you think of models, you probably imagine glamorous people in fancy clothes. Some models are like that. Others are not. You'll never see my face in a single TV commercial or magazine ad, but I do modeling all the time.

I'm a hand model. Hand models are chosen because we have perfect hands. It's rare for someone to have a hand that is the ideal size and shape. I just did a TV commercial for a line of watches. Once my hands appeared on a billboard. They were huge. I'm talking the size of minivans. That was a little weird.

All models have to stay in very good shape. Nobody wants to look bad in front of the camera. As a hand model, I don't have to worry about my hair or waistline. I have to worry about my hands. They always have to look good. I eat healthy food so they won't swell. I pamper them so they look nice and smooth. I spend more time taking care of my hands than you probably spend on your entire body.

I think the hardest part about being a model is the odd hours I work. It's fun to have your picture taken, but it can be very tiring. Some models get lots of money for the work they do. Most of us don't make very much. It's hard to become a star.

SALARY

= $25,000 or less

JOB GROWTH

= 11% to 20%

EDUCATION

High school diploma

SCHOOL SUBJECTS

reading

drama

physical education

196 Jobs A–Z

Molders

SALARY

= $25,001 to $50,000

JOB GROWTH

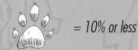

= 10% or less

EDUCATION

Training after high school

SCHOOL SUBJECTS

reading

math

science

My name is Charlie. I'm an expert sculptor. I don't make museum pieces. I make engines. I work for an automobile manufacturer as a molder.

I use a mold based on a pattern to cast the engine. I pour hot metal into the mold. I use a ladle to help me. Then I use a special machine to shape the engine parts. Each part has a special shape. I have to get it exactly right. Each piece has to fit together with the other pieces. Using molds makes that a lot easier. A mold guarantees that each part I make comes out the right size. By using a mold, I am able to make the same part over and over. Every car this factory manufactures has to have an engine.

My molded parts are used for each and every car. That's a lot of engines! The auto workers rely on me to make perfect parts every time. My job is very important to this factory. You wouldn't want to drive a car without an engine.

PRODUCTION

Musicians

Do you listen to music? Think about what you hear. Every song is a series of notes. Musicians use instruments to play each note. I play the violin in an orchestra.

I learn new music each season. I have to play all the songs perfectly. I rehearse with the entire group. We want to sound good together. People come to hear us play in a concert hall. Sometimes we give concerts in parks. People have picnics on blankets all around us. Our orchestra performs at schools. We play for ballets and operas. The orchestra plays in front of hundreds of people.

I get paid to play. Most musicians don't make a lot of money. Some musicians work at other jobs to get by. I give music lessons to a few students for extra money. When I was your age I started lessons after school. I learned to read notes and make my fingers touch the right strings. I wasn't very good at first. I made some awful noises. I didn't like to practice every day. But I got better.

I went to music school. I learned to play other styles of music like classical and jazz. I had to practice for many hours. Now I can play a note without even thinking about it. People like to hear me play. I can't imagine my life without music.

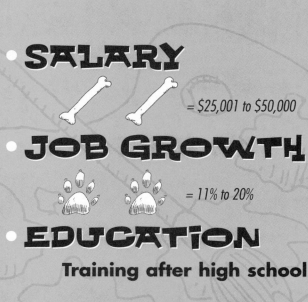

- **SALARY**
  = $25,001 to $50,000

- **JOB GROWTH**
  = 11% to 20%

- **EDUCATION**
  Training after high school

SCHOOL SUBJECTS

music

reading

math

Network Administrators

SALARY

 = $50,001 or more

JOB GROWTH

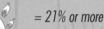 = 21% or more

EDUCATION

Four-year degree or more

SCHOOL SUBJECTS

computers

reading

math

science

I make computers get along. I'm a network administrator. I hook computers up to a network so they get the same information and services. Computer networks make it easier for several people to get the same information at one time.

Businesses use computer networks to keep track of their files. Employees can look up a customer's information from any computer at any office branch. It would be difficult for people to go to a main computer away from their office to print a report. Networks save people a lot of time.

I updated the network at City Hospital. They needed to add more terminals and servers. I did an upgrade for their network. The new network makes the hospital much more efficient. The doctors can now look at someone's file in seconds. You have to love to tinker with computers in this job. People call on you all the time to help with computer problems.

TECHNOLOGY

Novelists

I'm a novelist. Maybe you would like to read one of my books. I write mysteries.

I use a computer to do my writing. I have an office in my house. I get up early in the morning and start to write. I like to get up early so I have some quiet time. I look up facts and plan the whole story before I start to write. I have to know what the book is about. My new book takes place during the Civil War. I looked up information about the clothing people wore back then. The facts have to be right.

I write for many hours every day. That can be very hard. Sometimes I have a hard time writing when I am staring at the computer screen. Some days I can't think of anything to write. Other times I write late into the night. I even try to write on Saturdays and Sundays.

I sell my novels to companies that make books. It is easier to sell a book once you have already sold one. It is very hard at first. Many writers never get a book published. I used to have another job so I could afford to buy groceries. I tried to write before I went to work and when I got home. You really have to want to be a writer to be successful.

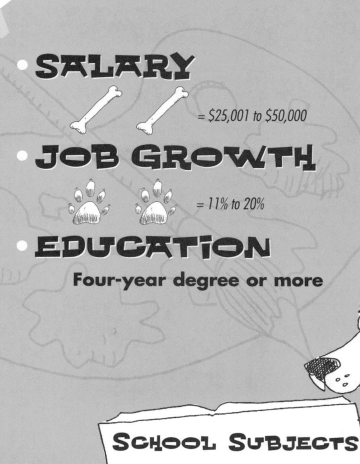

SALARY

= $25,001 to $50,000

JOB GROWTH

= 11% to 20%

EDUCATION

Four-year degree or more

SCHOOL SUBJECTS

reading   writing

spelling   computers

social studies

Nuclear Engineers

- ## SALARY

  = $50,001 or more

- ## JOB GROWTH
  = 10% or less

- ## EDUCATION
  Four-year degree or more

SCHOOL SUBJECTS

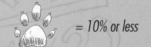

science	computers
math	reading
social studies	writing

I'm doing research on nuclear energy. I'm a nuclear engineer. I'm working to develop ways to prevent dangerous radiation leaks. Many people are concerned about the safety of nuclear power plants.

I'm designing shields for the outside of reactors. My shields will make power plants much safer. I have a computer in my lab. I use it to do tests. I can gauge how my shields will hold up to exposure to radiation. The shields will prevent harm to the environment. I'm also working with the power plant to find safe ways to get rid of the radioactive waste they create. I'm doing research to recycle the material back into energy production. It will be years before this is possible.

I document the findings of my tests in technical papers. I include complicated mathematical equations. This helps other scientists understand my ideas. My work must be very accurate. Small mistakes could create dangerous situations.

Nuclear engineers are an important part of technology. The United States has many nuclear power plants. We work hard to ensure the safety of the people and wildlife that live around them.

Nuclear Technicians

Welcome to the Watertown Nuclear Power Plant. We're Alonso and Rita, two of the nuclear technicians that work here. We help to create energy for the entire surrounding area. The next time you plug in your toaster, think of us.

We bring electricity into your home. Well, actually it's more work than that. We control the machines that run the nuclear reactor. The nuclear reactor turns atoms into energy. We monitor it very carefully. We watch our meters and gauges to make sure that the radiation stays at a safe level. Nuclear energy can be very dangerous if the people who run power plants aren't careful. This plant is very careful about the employees it hires. It makes sure that each employee gets trained. We had to take classes to learn how to run this equipment.

Most of our time is spent checking the operation of the reactor. We check the temperature and the power flow. The safety of this community depends on us. Nuclear power plants are an amazing source of energy. Hiring qualified employees like us is a good way to help keep nuclear energy safe.

SALARY
= $50,001 or more

JOB GROWTH
= 10% or less

EDUCATION
Two-year degree

SCHOOL SUBJECTS

science
math
reading

writing
computers

SCIENCE AND ENGINEERING

Nurse Practitioners

SALARY

 = $25,001 to $50,000

JOB GROWTH

 = 21% or more

EDUCATION

Four-year degree or more

SCHOOL SUBJECTS

science	reading
math	computers
social studies	

I work for a large medical clinic as a nurse practitioner. We help lots of people every day. The doctors don't have enough time to see everyone. As a nurse practitioner, I do many of the doctors' normal duties.

I'm a registered nurse with special training in the diagnosis and treatment of illnesses and disease. I examine patients when they come to the clinic. I may order tests to check on the patient's condition. I analyze the results when they come back from the lab. I prescribe medication or therapy to some patients.

I discuss my work with the doctors. They review my work to make sure I have made the right decision. A second opinion is very important in medicine. I ask the doctors any questions that I have. Sometimes I have a doctor examine the patient if I find something seriously wrong.

Nurse practitioners help people get medical attention more quickly. I have the knowledge and training to help people with minor illnesses. I get them feeling better a little sooner.

HEALTH

Nurses Aides and Orderlies

Hi! My name is Raven. I work as a nurses aide at Community Hospital. Nurses aides are also called nursing assistants or orderlies. We play an important part in running a hospital. We spend a lot of time taking care of the patients.

Many people in the hospital need special care. I help them get dressed and undressed. I give them sponge baths. It is important that our patients stay clean. I change the sheets on their beds and make sure they are comfortable. I deliver meals to the patients. I help some people eat. Mr. Redgrave has two broken arms. He couldn't eat without my help. I make sure that the patients are able to get around the hospital. I take them in a wheelchair to see the doctor. They may need to go to another room to have X rays or special tests done. I do minor medical procedures. Sometimes I change a bandage or check someone's temperature. The doctors and nurses do most of the medical tasks.

Like most people who work in a hospital, I have to wear a uniform. My uniform keeps me from ruining my favorite clothes. If you like helping people, you might enjoy working as a nurses aide. The only bad thing about my job is the weird hours. Hospitals have people working around the clock.

- **SALARY**
  = $25,000 or less

- **JOB GROWTH**
  = 21% or more

- **EDUCATION**
  Training after high school

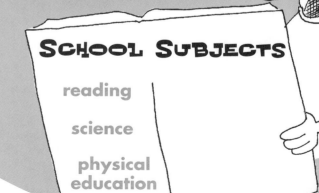

SCHOOL SUBJECTS

reading

science

physical education

Occupational Therapists

- ## SALARY

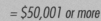

= $50,001 or more

- ## JOB GROWTH

= 21% or more

- ## EDUCATION

Four-year degree or more

SCHOOL SUBJECTS

science	computers
math	physical education
reading	

I help people with disabilities become independent again. Occupational therapists help people do activities to treat physical or mental disabilities.

I work with people who are in wheelchairs. I work out a plan to make their lives normal. My goal is to help them live comfortably and get a job that they like. I talk with them about their needs. I find out about their interests. We work together to help them become independent.

One of my patients, Becky, just moved into her own apartment. She likes to cook. I helped her get a kitchen designed so she can get around easily in her wheelchair. Everything is within her reach. Becky is a writer. She will work at home on her computer. At first Becky was worried about living on her own. Now she likes her independence.

I work hard to help people with disabilities lead a normal life. These people are just like everyone else. We all need to have our independence and freedom.

HEALTH

Oceanographers

Have you ever seen a shark up close? I have. I've seen hundreds of them. I'm an oceanographer. Oceanographers study the ocean floors, shores, and the air above them. I specialize in aquatic biology. That's the study of the plants and animals that live in the water.

I'm doing research to see the effects of pollution on sand sharks in the Gulf of Mexico. We had an oil spill in the gulf last year. I am checking to see how the sharks are adapting. I check the water every day. I measure the amounts of salt and oxygen in the water. It affects the sharks' health. I run tests to look for chemicals.

I analyze the tests on special machines. I record very small numbers. I keep track of the numbers in my computer. It's very complicated. I do most of my work on the ocean. I take the results back to my lab. I use biology, chemistry, and geology every day. I understand how the water, land, and animals work together.

Studying the ocean is fascinating. We don't know very much about it. Oceanographers examine everything in the ocean. We look at the geology, plants, fish, and animals. My work tells us lots of new information. One day students will read about my research.

SALARY
= $50,001 or more

JOB GROWTH
= 11% to 20%

EDUCATION
Four-year degree or more

SCHOOL SUBJECTS

science	geography
math	computers
reading	writing

Office Managers

SCHOOL SUBJECTS

math	science
reading	computers
social studies	writing

This company keeps me really busy. I'm the manager of the New York office. I'm in charge of everything that goes on around the office.

The owners of the company expect me to run a top-notch operation. I make sure we do our work efficiently. I supervise a big staff. I make sure our administrative assistants answer all of our correspondence. I check on the clerks and update them on our new filing system. I meet with my employees to discuss projects. I make sure new employees have the supplies to get started in their jobs. I want everyone to do a good job.

We use a lot of office supplies. I reorder paper and ink for our laser printers almost every week. I keep up on the latest technology. I look through magazines and reports to look for new equipment. I save the company money when I can. Good office managers get the most for the least amount of money.

I do many different things at once. I spend a lot of time in my office on the phone and in front of my computer. I make sure our office machines get serviced when they need it. I like knowing that I am responsible for making everything around here run smoothly.

BUSINESS

Operations Research Analysts

People hire me to suggest ways to improve their workflow. Operations research analysts use math and computers to find better ways of doing things. I meet with managers to find out their problem areas. I get as much information from them as I can. My goal is to develop a plan to help the company make lots of money efficiently.

I use my computer to develop a mathematical equation. The math equation stands for the workflow at the company. I run tests on my computer to find ways to make improvements. I develop many different equations until I find the best one. Then I give the information to the managers in a report.

I explain the data so they understand how to use it. I tell them what they need to change. They may need to add more workers or machines. Sometimes they need to close down factories that aren't efficient. I'm the suggestion person. I help businesses get back on track.

- **SALARY**
  = $50,001 or more

- **JOB GROWTH**
  = 10% or less

- **EDUCATION**
  Four-year degree or more

SCHOOL SUBJECTS

math	reading
science	writing
social studies	computers

Optical Technicians

SALARY

= $25,000 or less

JOB GROWTH

= 10% or less

EDUCATION

Training after high school

SCHOOL SUBJECTS

reading

math

I help people see better. No, I'm not an eye doctor. I'm an optical technician. I make eyeglasses for a living. If you go to the eye doctor and find out that you need glasses, he or she will write you a prescription. A prescription is like a recipe that tells optical technicians how to make your glasses.

Glasses are like magnifying lenses. The strength depends on the thickness of the glass. Thicker glass corrects poorer eyesight. I work with an optician. An optician helps you pick the frames for the glasses. It is important that you find a comfortable pair that you like. Nobody wants to look bad. Then I do my work.

I use a grinder to make the glass the right thickness. I have to be very careful to follow the prescription. If I am not exact, you could get a headache when you wear your glasses. I put the glass into the frames you picked. The optician lets you try them on so I know that they are a good fit. I want them to be perfect. I know that the little details are very important. People rely on glasses. I have to do a good job.

Optometrists

If you can read this page, you have pretty good eyesight. If everything looks fuzzy to you, you may need to come to my office. I'm an optometrist. Optometrists help people see better.

I know all about the eye. I check people's vision. I run tests to see if you need glasses. I have a chart hanging on my wall with rows of letters on it. I have you read it to learn how well you see. I figure out exactly how thick the glass should be. I can prescribe contact lenses if you don't like glasses.

I help many people see every day. I keep information about your eyes in my computer and filing cabinets so I know how to make your glasses. You should come back to see me once a year to make sure your vision hasn't changed. Sometimes people need more than glasses. Then I may send them to an ophthalmologist to get medicine or for an operation. Helping you see more clearly is very important to me.

SALARY

= $50,001 or more

JOB GROWTH

= 11% to 20%

EDUCATION

Four-year degree or more

SCHOOL SUBJECTS

science	reading
math	computers
social studies	

Painters

- ## SALARY
  = $25,001 to $50,000

- ## JOB GROWTH
  = 11% to 20%

- ## EDUCATION
  Training after high school

SCHOOL SUBJECTS

reading

math

CONSTRUCTION

Do you like to paint? I mean really paint. I'm a painter. I paint beautiful things every day. I paint walls and buildings for a living.

I mix colors together to get the right shade. I just painted a purple house. I painted another one bright yellow. In two days I am supposed to paint Ms. Jordan's office walls the color of strawberries. It's great to see the finished color. I use a different paint for the outside of a building than I use for a bedroom wall. My customers tell me what they want. I make that happen. That's not always easy.

Sometimes the old paint is in bad shape. I scrape it with a metal tool and go over the wall with a sander. Sometimes I put a coat of primer on before I put on the color. Primer makes the paint stick to the walls better. I put the paint on with a brush or roller after I mix it. I have to be careful not to splatter the floor or furniture. Sometimes I use a spray gun for big surfaces. I paint most things twice to get a nice, even finish. I spend a lot of time on a ladder or standing on metal scaffolds. I like to paint a nice straight line with just my brush.

I remember every room and house I have painted. My work makes people happy. I've painted buildings all over town.

Paralegal Assistants

I do all the paperwork for lawyers. I work in a lawyer's office as a paralegal assistant. I help my boss prepare cases for court.

Judges decide cases based on the way decisions have been made before. I do research to find information about similar cases in the past. I look for articles in law journals and databases. I find copies of all necessary legal documents. Lawyers need papers like wills, contracts, and deeds to argue their case in court. Lawyers know a lot about laws. Some laws are very technical. I look up specific information about laws to save my boss time.

I create contracts and file legal papers with the court. Paralegal assistants handle the details for lawyers so they have more time to actually work on cases. My job is very interesting and fast-paced.

- **SALARY**
= $25,001 to $50,000

- **JOB GROWTH**
= 21% or more

- **EDUCATION**
Four-year degree or more

SCHOOL SUBJECTS

reading	social studies
writing	
computers	

Park Rangers

- ## SALARY

  = $50,001 or more

- ## JOB GROWTH

  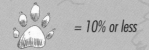
  = 10% or less

- ## EDUCATION

  Four-year degree or more

SCHOOL SUBJECTS

science	math
reading	social studies
writing	

My name is Ranger Roberts. I manage and patrol a public park. Some park rangers work in national parks like the famous Grand Canyon in Arizona. Others work in smaller state or county parks.

Park rangers stay very busy. I greet visitors. I tell them what is going on in the park. I explain the park rules. I plan and put on programs about safety, history, wildlife, and first aid. I keep track of the number of people who visit the park. I make sure that everyone obeys the rules. I know many rules and laws about parks. We have rules to keep the park safe and nice.

Sometimes I rescue visitors. I stop whatever I am doing to handle emergencies. Wild animals and bad weather can be dangerous in a park. I work with other park rangers to make sure the park stays clean. We repair equipment that breaks. We keep everything in good shape.

Park rangers spend most of their time outdoors. I also have an office where I write reports and train new rangers. My job is great. I get to work with both people and nature. I like teaching people about wildlife and the earth. It's fun to see them learn. I make this park a wonderful place to visit. That makes me very proud.

Parole and Probation Officers

People meet with me when they get out of prison. I work as a probation officer. I help people who have been in prison to get their lives in order. I help them get an education and find a job. They can talk to me about what is bothering them. I will listen and help them.

They report to me. I must know where they are every day. They come to see me at my office. I make sure that they follow rules. They are not allowed to carry a gun or leave the state. They can be arrested again and put back in prison if they try to run away.

I am in charge of many people. It is not easy keeping track of everyone. Some people lie to me. I check up to see who is telling me the truth. I have to know a lot about people. I have to be able to talk with someone and figure out how to help them. I have to know about our legal system and how the law works.

I like to make people's lives better. It is hard for people who have been in prison to adjust to a regular life. I want them to be able to find a job and live a normal life.

SALARY
= $25,001 to $50,000

JOB GROWTH
= 11% to 20%

EDUCATION
Two-year degree

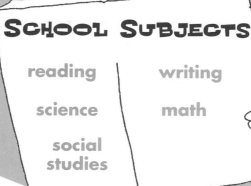

SCHOOL SUBJECTS

reading   writing

science   math

social
studies

Parts Managers

SALARY

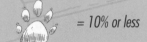

= $25,000 or less

JOB GROWTH

= 10% or less

EDUCATION

Training after high school

SCHOOL SUBJECTS

reading	industrial arts
computers	
math	

I order carburetors, fuel pumps, and brake pads. I'm the parts manager of Autopia Repair Shop. We fix cars and trucks. I keep all the parts in stock.

I work closely with our mechanics. We have a great computer system here. I keep track of the entire inventory. Every part is in the system. I know exactly when to order new parts by looking at my computer screen. I fill out the paperwork for the parts I order. I talk with our customers about which parts they need.

Don't think that I can't do repairs myself. I understand what mechanics do with the parts I supply. I can fix anything you put in front of me. Parts managers keep repair shops operating smoothly. It would take a lot longer to get your car fixed if we didn't have the parts in stock.

I like working at Autopia. I've always liked working with cars and engines. I think of myself as a maintenance mechanic. I maintain this business so the mechanics can do a good job.

MECHANICS AND REPAIRERS

Pathologists

I help other doctors find diseases. My name is Dr. Homer. I work at a large hospital as a pathologist. Pathologists study human tissue and fluids to find the causes and effects of diseases on the human body.

I work in a big lab. Doctors send samples to me to check for disease. I look at them under a microscope. I may run tests on them to analyze the content. I look for dangerous levels of chemicals. Doing sample work is very complicated. I know a lot about different diseases to know what I am looking for.

Sometimes I help doctors find out why someone has died. I perform surgery on the body to look for disease. This is called an autopsy. Pathologists are very important doctors. We help doctors in many different fields of medicine. We take some of the mystery out of illnesses. Our work makes it easier for doctors to treat their patients.

 **SALARY**

= $25,001 to $50,000

JOB GROWTH

= 11% to 20%

EDUCATION

Two-year degree

 **SCHOOL SUBJECTS**

science	reading
math	computers
social studies	

Patient Account Representatives

SALARY

= $25,000 or less

JOB GROWTH

= 21% or more

EDUCATION

Two-year degree

SCHOOL SUBJECTS

reading

math

computers

I work for a hospital. I'm not a nurse or a doctor. I don't work with medicine at all. I work with money. Hospitals are businesses. I collect payment for the services we provide. I'm a patient account representative. I work with patients to develop a payment plan. I find out what kind of insurance the patient has. I talk with the insurance company to find out how much it will pay the hospital. I bill the patient for the rest.

I can set up a payment plan. Hospital bills are very expensive. I can work out a monthly payment schedule. I'm here to help patients. I make paying your bill easy. I have a computer that I use to look up accounts. I can see exactly how much money people owe. I fill out a lot of forms. Insurance claims take a lot of paperwork.

My job can be very hectic. I deal with many people every day. Some of them can be grumpy. I try to calm them down and work with them.

Personal Trainers

I work hard to help people feel better about themselves. I'm a personal trainer for a health spa. I work with people who want to lose weight or get in better shape. I meet with them to find out their goals.

Most of customers come to me because they want to look thin. I explain that being thin and being healthy are not always the same thing. Losing weight quickly can be dangerous. The best way to lose weight is to change bad habits. I work with my customers to develop an exercise program. Everyone needs to exercise. Walking is a good aerobic activity.

I talk with them about the kinds of food they eat. I try to get them to cut their fat intake. I encourage them to drink lots of water. We need water to stay healthy.

Liking the way you are on the inside is the first step to being beautiful. Not all of my customers become thin, but most of them do become healthier. They feel better about themselves because they start eating good food and getting exercise. I am glad to know that I can make a difference in people's lives.

- **SALARY**
  = $25,001 to $50,000

- **JOB GROWTH**
  = 21% or more

- **EDUCATION**
  Four-year degree or more

SCHOOL SUBJECTS

science

math

reading

physical education

Pest Control Workers

I get rid of vermin. I'm the exterminator. I'm a pest control worker for the Scram Extermination Service. I can clear your house of almost any pest.

I use chemicals and traps to kill insects, roaches, spiders, mice, and rats. I come once a month to offices, homes, and restaurants. I spend a lot of my time in my truck. I drive around the city from building to building.

I spray around the baseboard to keep out insects. I answer special calls. One man called me because he had termites in his attic. Termites can ruin a house. They feed on the wood structure of buildings. Getting rid of termites is a difficult job.

I am trained to use dangerous chemicals. I have to be very careful when I work. The chemicals I use are poisonous. I could get very sick if I did not use them correctly.

Give me a call if you're having a problem with a pest. Sorry! I can't do anything about brothers or sisters.

Petroleum Field Workers

Welcome to our crew. We've been working on this oil rig for the past three days. My name is Smith. I'm a petroleum field worker. My job is to work the machinery that pumps oil and gas out of the ground.

This rig is three miles offshore in the Gulf of Mexico. We get here by helicopter. The workers stay busy all day. We keep those pumps running. We use wrenches and power tools to repair the equipment when it breaks down. We connect flow lines to tanks to collect the oil. It's a hard workday with lots of physical labor.

I wear clothes that can get dirty and thick gloves to protect my hands. An oil rig can be a dangerous place. You can't goof off here. You have to be careful around the big machines. People can get hurt. My boss tells us exactly what to do. He makes sure that we do a good, safe job. It's important that we work together.

My job is never boring. We work long hours for several days in a row. Then I get several days off. That gives me some time to catch up on my sleep.

- **SALARY**
  = $25,001 to $50,000

- **JOB GROWTH**
  = 10% or less

- **EDUCATION**
  Two-year degree

SCHOOL SUBJECTS

reading

math

Pharmacist Assistants

- ## SALARY
   = $25,000 or less

- ## JOB GROWTH
     = 21% or more

- ## EDUCATION
  Two-year degree

SCHOOL SUBJECTS

science	computers
math	
reading	

I can help you get well again when you're sick. I work in a drug store as a pharmacist assistant. I work with the pharmacist to fill the prescription from your doctor. Doctors write a prescription so I will know exactly what medicine to give to you.

The pharmacist I work with checks every prescription that I fill. She tells me exactly what to put in the bottles. I have to know about different medicines. I keep track of our inventory. We have hundreds of different kinds of pills. We can't get them mixed up. We have them filed in order much like a library has its books. Every medicine has its own place. Taking the wrong medicine can be very dangerous.

I record every prescription on our computer. It keeps a record of all of our customers. I label the bottles for customers. I make sure the doctor's orders are on every bottle. People have to know exactly how much medicine to take and how often to take it.

The pharmacist and I work together as a team. Getting people healthy again is our main concern.

Pharmacists

I give you medicine when a doctor prescribes it. I work in a drugstore. I'm a pharmacist.

Doctors examine patients and then decide what medicine they need to take to feel better. The doctor writes a prescription. It's a note telling me what kind of medicine you need and how much you should take. I read the note and then find the right pills. Sometimes I mix different ingredients together to make your medicine. I check to make sure that the pills won't make you sicker. I check that you don't take two medicines that cause a reaction when you use them together.

It is important that I don't get the medicine wrong. Mistakes can be very dangerous. I must be very responsible. I like to talk with you to make sure you understand exactly how to take the medicine. It is important that you follow directions if you want to get better. I keep records of all the medicine you take.

SALARY

= $50,001 or more

JOB GROWTH

= 21% or more

EDUCATION

Four-year degree or more

SCHOOL SUBJECTS

science	reading
math	computers
social studies	

Photographers

- ## SALARY
  = $25,001 to $50,000

- ## JOB GROWTH

  = 11% to 20%

- ## EDUCATION
  Training after high school

SCHOOL SUBJECTS

art

math

reading

I can make anything look good. I'm a photographer. Photographers make pictures with cameras and film. We don't just press a button on a camera. Photography is like painting.

First, we choose a subject for the picture. Then we set up the equipment. Sometimes I shoot with a camera on the streets. I may get up early in the morning or stay out late at night to get the right shot. For fashion shoots, I may take hundreds of pictures of the same thing to get one that looks perfect.

I have a special lab filled with chemicals to develop the film into prints or slides. I keep it dark inside except for a red light bulb. Film gets ruined if it is exposed to regular light. I transfer the picture from a negative to special paper. Developing film is really neat. The pictures suddenly appear on the paper. It's like magic every time! I also use digital cameras with no film.

Professional cameras are very complicated. Photographers have to know how to focus and which lens to use. I started taking pictures when I was your age. I'd keep the photos in an album so my friends could look at them. I love taking pictures. I feel like I am creating art out of everyday people and things.

Physical Therapists

Three weeks ago Michael got in a car accident and injured his legs. I'm a physical therapist. I'm helping him learn to walk again. Physical therapists know all about bones and muscles and nerves.

Michael broke several bones. He damaged some of his nerves. His parents were afraid that he would not get better. Right now he has to get around in a wheelchair. I taught him how to use it. I am teaching him how to walk with crutches. It will take a couple of weeks. He has braces on his legs. I work with a doctor to plan activities for him. He has to do special exercises every day. Some of them hurt. I help Michael with his workout. I encourage him along the way. The exercises help strengthen his muscles. He is doing very well.

Sometimes people's injuries are so bad that they do not recover. I help them adjust to life in a wheelchair. People in wheelchairs are like everyone else. It is just a little more difficult for them to do things. I show them how to use special equipment. We work on strengthening muscles. You have to have strong arm muscles to operate a wheelchair. I don't like making people do painful exercises. But I know that I am helping to make them better. Otherwise they would be sick much longer. I have helped some very nice people.

SALARY

= $50,001 or more

JOB GROWTH

= 21% or more

EDUCATION

Four-year degree or more

SCHOOL SUBJECTS

science	reading
math	computers
social studies	

Physical Therapy Aides

SALARY

 = $25,000 or less

JOB GROWTH

 = 21% or more

EDUCATION

Two-year degree

SCHOOL SUBJECTS

reading

science

physical education

Hello! My name is Nickie. I'm a physical therapist's best friend. I work for a medical clinic as a physical therapy aide. I help people recover from automobile accidents.

Many people who have been in automobile accidents need to go to physical therapy to get well again. A physical therapist makes them do exercises to strengthen their muscles. It can be painful, but it is very important. I work closely with the physical therapist and the patients. I help the patients get ready for their session. I may help them change clothes. Sometimes I take their arms out of slings or their legs out of splints. I have to be very careful when I do this. I try not to make them too uncomfortable.

I work with the therapist on their exercises. The therapist may have me help them do some of the repetitions. I help them get from the waiting room to the treatment area. I stay with them during most of the session. We really get to know each other. I also help the physical therapist by keeping the treatment area clean and ordering supplies.

We work really hard at this clinic to help people get better. It is very rewarding to see our patients get well enough that they don't have to come back. We want them to live independent lives.

HEALTH

Physician Assistants

I'm a physician's best friend. I work closely with a doctor to help treat patients. Physician assistants examine patients and write information in their medical files.

I include important information about their medical history. I also write down what I find in the physical exam. I write down their heart rate and their blood pressure. Sometimes I need to order more tests. They may need to have an X ray or have some blood work done. I always talk with the doctor about my exams. The doctor helps me by giving me medical advice.

I do a lot of the basic medical care for the physician I work with. My job changes with every patient. I do whatever needs to be done to make someone healthy again. I give shots and vaccines. Sometimes I even give people stitches. I can handle anything that isn't too serious.

SALARY

= $50,001 or more

JOB GROWTH

= 21% or more

EDUCATION

Four-year degree or more

SCHOOL SUBJECTS

science	math
reading	computers
social studies	

HEALTH

Physicians

- ## SALARY
   = $50,001 or more

- ## JOB GROWTH
   = 11% to 20%

- ## EDUCATION
  Four-year degree or more

SCHOOL SUBJECTS

science	reading
math	computers
social studies	

I'm a doctor in a small country town. The people in my town come to see me when they are sick. Sometimes they call me at home late at night. I see people before they go to a special doctor. I am called a primary care physician.

I try to figure out what is wrong with my patients. I know all about the human body. I do everything from bandaging cuts and bruises to delivering babies. I have to be very careful. It is important that I do not make mistakes. People trust me to make them feel better. I have many tools to help me make decisions. I have an X-ray machine to see if your arm is broken. I use a stethoscope to listen to your heart beat.

I have to be able to explain why you are sick. That can be hard. Medical words are often long and complicated. I make you feel better and get well. Most of the time I can give you some medicine to take. I send people to the hospital or to a special doctor if they are very sick. Doctors keep information on everyone we see.

I love my job. I get to help people. Nothing makes me happier than knowing that I have made someone healthy again.

Physicists

I'm a physicist. I study matter, energy, motion, and force. Think of how magical our universe is. Take gravity for example. Gravity holds us to this planet. It keeps planets in orbit. I use science to understand concepts like gravity.

The earth continually spins. It does it on its own. Physics can explain why. Physicists have developed long math equations to use in their work. These equations represent forces like gravity. Many physicists teach and do research at large universities.

I work for NASA. I help the people in the space program understand all about gravity. I simulate gravity by using a computer. I have my computer programmed to show how things will react to different levels of gravity. We wouldn't be able to travel into space without understanding the effects of gravity.

Physics has made it possible to predict forces in nature like gravity. I think that's amazing! I am working to understand our universe.

SALARY

= $50,001 or more

JOB GROWTH

= 10% or less

EDUCATION

Four-year degree or more

SCHOOL SUBJECTS

science	writing
math	computers
reading	

SCIENCE AND ENGINEERING

Piano Tuners

SALARY

= $25,001 to $50,000

JOB GROWTH

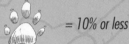

= 10% or less

EDUCATION

Training after high school

SCHOOL SUBJECTS

music

reading

math

science

Piano teachers call me when they need advice. I work as a musical instrument repairer. I tune and repair pianos. I can make pianos sound brand new again.

I know all about piano parts. Pianos are machines. Pianos have many different parts. Each one has its own function. You strike the keys to control little hammers that strike the strings inside. I know how each part of the instrument operates. I come to people's homes or concert halls to repair the pianos. I wouldn't want people to have to bring a piano to me!

I play the piano to hear the problem. That usually gives me a pretty good clue. I make an adjustment or replace the strings or pads inside. Sometimes the parts need to be cleaned and tightened. I have tools just like any other mechanic. I use a small metal tool called a tuning fork to check the sound. I compare the sound quality of the piano to the pitch of the fork. I match the sound the fork makes.

I like being a piano tuner. I make beautiful music possible. I love to hear the ringing of a perfect note.

© JIST Works

Pilots

Hi! I'm a pilot for a major airline. I travel all over the world. It's a fun job, but it's not very easy. I am responsible for the safety of hundreds of people on every flight.

I had to pass a strict physical exam to get this job. I have to be in good health. I must have perfect eyesight. I had to get a commercial pilot's license.

Pilots check over many details before planes take off. I get the crew to look over the plane and refuel it. I check out the weather conditions. I make sure I know my flight schedule and pattern. I look over the control panel. I taxi to the runway when everything looks clear. I contact the control tower by radio. I get their permission before I can go. I release the brake and move the throttles and controls to take off. Then we're in the air. I keep checking the gauges to stay on course.

When we've reached our destination, I get an okay from the control tower to land. Landing is the most difficult part of my job. It always feels good to get my feet back on the ground again.

Flying is my life. I like working for an airline. Sometimes I fly at weird hours and am away from home for several days, but it's worth it.

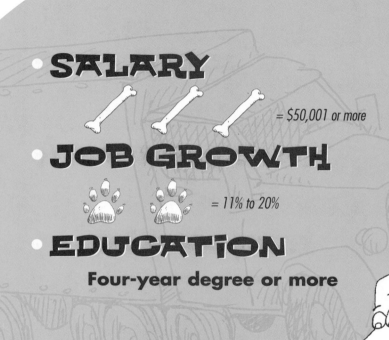

- **SALARY**
  = $50,001 or more
- **JOB GROWTH**
  = 11% to 20%
- **EDUCATION**
  Four-year degree or more

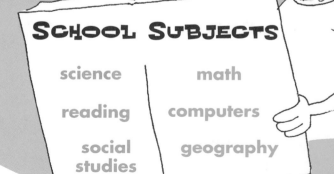

SCHOOL SUBJECTS

science	math
reading	computers
social studies	geography

Plastic Molders

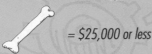
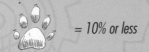
My name is Clem. I make laser guns and dinosaurs. I work in a plastic plant as a plastics fabricator. We specialize in making toys. I use our machines to shape plastic into all kinds of things.

I follow a blueprint for every toy. The blueprint is like a recipe for that toy. It tells me exactly what size each piece needs to be. It tells me how to fit the pieces together. I cut the plastic into different pieces. I glue them together to match the diagram in the blueprint. I must get all the measurements exact. Otherwise I could make a lopsided dinosaur.

Plastics fabricators make many important products. Think of all the things in your home that are made of plastic.

I like working in this factory. We make some great things for kids. I wouldn't mind having one of those dinosaurs myself.

Plumbers

Hand me that wrench. Oh, I'm sorry! You're not my assistant. You probably want to know what I do for a living. I'm a plumber. You could call me the pipe person. I work with pipes.

I bring water into houses and offices. I put in sinks and showers and toilets. If it needs water, call me to make it work. Sometimes I install pipes. Sometimes I fix them. I can fix your clogged sink. First, I'll try to use a plunger. I may run a long wire down the pipes if that doesn't work. Sometimes I take the pipes apart and rebuild them.

Plumbers are very important. You need us to have water in your house. I go to people's houses in the middle of the night to handle emergencies. I wouldn't want water leaking all over your house all night long. Nobody wants to live in a swimming pool.

I like my job because I get to travel around. I don't sit at a desk all day. I stay busy. That helps the time go by quickly.

SALARY

= $25,001 to $50,000

JOB GROWTH

= 11% to 20%

EDUCATION

Training after high school

SCHOOL SUBJECTS

reading

math

CONSTRUCTION

Podiatrists

SALARY

 = $50,001 or more

JOB GROWTH

 = 11% to 20%

EDUCATION

Four-year degree or more

SCHOOL SUBJECTS

science

math

social studies

reading

computers

How often do you think about your feet? Feet are important to us. They help us stand and walk. Have you ever stubbed your toe or dropped something on your foot? It can affect the way you walk.

I'm a podiatrist. I work only on feet. I see lots of feet every day. Sometimes I perform surgery to make people's feet better. I may remove painful growths. The surgery isn't very complicated. It really can help.

Many times I put casts on the feet to mend broken bones. The patients usually have to walk around on crutches for a while. I also give people therapy on their feet. Sometimes I have them soak in whirlpools. I may hook them to a machine that gives them small electrical shocks. The electricity gets the blood flowing into the feet. I work with children whose feet are not growing properly. I can give them special shoes to correct their problems.

Being a foot doctor probably sounds a little weird to you. But I love my job. We take walking for granted until we can't do it anymore. Podiatrists help people keep walking.

Police Commissioners

Hi there! I'm Commissioner Feltner. I'm in charge of the police force in this city. Police commissioners are the managers of the police department. I make sure every officer does a good job. That's a lot of police work in a big city.

I meet with the mayor and make a budget. I make sure the city gives us enough money. It takes a huge budget to keep everyone safe. I make sure that I have plenty of officers. I don't want people to wait for us in an emergency. I buy new police cars and equipment.

I make sure all of my people have the top training. I want them to know how to handle dangerous situations. I also want to keep my staff safe. I don't want my officers to get hurt. I make sure our police officers abide by the law. I care about this city.

I'm a good commissioner because I was an officer myself for many years. I know how this department operates. The mayor appointed me because I had the most experience. My job is very stressful. Keeping the city safe is a big responsibility. I wouldn't trade my job for anything.

SALARY
= $50,001 or more

JOB GROWTH
= 11% to 20%

EDUCATION
Four-year degree or more

SCHOOL SUBJECTS

science	writing
math	computers
reading	social studies

Police Officers

- ## SALARY
  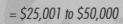
  = $25,001 to $50,000

- ## JOB GROWTH

  = 21% or more

- ## EDUCATION
  Two-year degree

SCHOOL SUBJECTS

reading	writing
math	computers
social studies	

My name's Officer Arizona. I work for the city police. I'm sure you've seen me around. I'm here to protect you. That's the main job of a police officer.

People think we spend all day giving out speeding tickets. We don't. We spend most of our time on our beats. Sometimes I work the night shift. We protect you 24 hours a day. My beat is an area I patrol to protect people who live and work there. We get calls over our car radios. We go to the address to make sure things are okay. I would much rather talk someone out of committing a crime than take them to jail.

My job is dangerous. I am trained in self-defense. I carry a gun. I try not to use it. I wouldn't want to hurt anyone. I always wear my uniform. I want people to know that I am a police officer.

We write reports for every crime we investigate. We need a record of everything we do. Sometimes I give people tickets. Please remember that I am only doing my job. I am here to enforce the law. Laws are made for your protection.

Political Aides

I work for Senator Featherston as a political aide. I help the senator make important decisions. I help prepare legislation, gather opinions from voters, and answer questions.

I do a lot of research. I find out all the specifics of laws by reading information in journals and reviews. I help the senator draft bills and legislation. I go to meetings that Senator Featherston cannot attend. I write reports so the senator will know important information for doing his job.

I help the senator write speeches. I ask the senator about the important points. Then I write the speech. I'm a very good writer. I'm known as the senator's right-hand person. Sometimes I even speak at functions and give the senator's view.

One day I would like to be a senator myself. I like working for Senator Featherston. We believe in the same things.

SALARY

= $25,001 to $50,000

JOB GROWTH

= 21% or more

EDUCATION

Four-year degree or more

SCHOOL SUBJECTS

reading   computers

math   geography

social
studies

Political Scientists

SALARY

 = $50,001 or more

JOB GROWTH

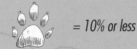 = 10% or less

EDUCATION

Four-year degree or more

SCHOOL SUBJECTS

history	geography
reading	social studies
writing	foreign languages
computers	

I am an expert on the governments of the world. I teach political science at a small college. Political science is the science of politics. Political scientists study the way people and governments gain and use power.

Governments are different all over the world. Every country has its own laws. I know about places in the world where one person controls what everyone else does. We call that a dictatorship. Our country is a democracy. The people of the United States elect our leaders. Our leaders make decisions based on what we say.

Government is an interesting thing to study. I try to figure out why countries are set up the way they are. Political scientists think about the relationships of societies in the world. We combine philosophy and history. Right now I am writing a book about President Taft. He was a fascinating man.

If you like to ask yourself why our country is the way it is, you might like to study political science. Political scientists like to ask a lot of questions.

Politicians

I'm the governor of this great state. I was elected by the people. I help enforce laws that govern this state and its people. I had to work hard to become governor. I was in the state legislature for many years before I was governor.

The residents of this state count on me. They know that I have to make decisions that will help our state run. I have a staff of people who work for me. They help me make sure that I am doing what needs to be done. I work with many people and groups. I work very hard to attract new business here. Business brings new jobs. I want every resident to have a good job.

I work on the budget for the state government. I find funding for schools, libraries, highways, and state police. I budget carefully. We get our most of our money from taxes and the federal government.

I work many hours every day. I make very important decisions. My plans affect everyone in this state. Being governor is my life. I don't have a lot of free time, but the work I do is very interesting and important.

SALARY
= $50,001 or more

JOB GROWTH
= 10% or less

EDUCATION
Four-year degree or more

SCHOOL SUBJECTS

math   writing

reading   computers

social
studies

Postal Clerks

SALARY

 = $25,001 to $50,000

JOB GROWTH

= 10% or less

EDUCATION

Training after high school

SCHOOL SUBJECTS

math

reading

computers

I work at the counter at the post office. I'm Mo, the postal clerk. I can answer any questions you may have.

People wait in line to see me. I sell stamps and weigh packages. I make sure you use the right amount of postage. I have a computerized scale that tells me exactly how much to charge. I sort the mail every day. I put it in people's post office boxes. I know all about postal regulations. We have guidelines to follow.

I know about different postal rates. I figure out how much it would cost to ship a box to Singapore or Turkey. I talk to people all day long. I help people with problems with their mail service. I help them change their addresses when they move.

The U.S. Postal Service is an important part of our daily life. Post offices across America work hard to get your mail to you quickly. That people to keep in touch and businesses to operate.

Power Plant Operators

The entire city would go dark if it weren't for me. I operate the machinery that sends power to all the houses and businesses in a five-mile area. My name's Slim. I'm a power plant operator. This power plant is hydroelectric. That means we make electricity out of water pressure.

The plant is located near a large dam. Water runs through pipes and gets the turbines running.

The turbines create the electricity. I make sure all the equipment is operating correctly. I check the water pressure on gauges. Sometimes I make adjustments. We like to keep the plant operating at a certain level at all times. I use a computer system to monitor the operations. It signals us when there is a problem. Most problems we can fix by making a minor repair. A major problem might make me shut down the system. I am trained to handle emergencies. I know all about the machinery at this plant. People could get injured if I made a mistake reading one of the gauges. I also make sure we generate enough energy to supply the entire city.

I work with my supervisors and other crew members to get the job done right. I get to use my hands and work with gadgets. I like that.

SALARY

= $25,001 to $50,000

JOB GROWTH

= 10% or less

EDUCATION

Training after high school

SCHOOL SUBJECTS

math	computers
science	reading
industrial arts	

Prepress Workers

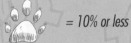
Welcome to the Prints Charming printing company. I handle the start of the printing process. This stage is called "prepress." I am a prepress worker.

I lay out the pages of a newsletter if the customer wants me to. Mostly I check electronic files that have been laid out by the customer. I create a proof for the customer to check. I look for mistakes. I make sure that the printing will be clear and sharp. I make sure that the photos will look good when printed. I use computers and other technology.

Then I use laser equipment to transfer the electronic images to printing plates. Other workers at Prints Charming handle printing and binding. Binding is when machines put the printed pages together to make a newsletter or magazine. That's fun to watch.

Everyone at Prints Charming works as a team. We have to learn about new equipment. We must meet deadlines. We know it is important to keep our customers happy. We make it possible for people to put ideas into print.

Preschool Teachers

I enjoy working with children. I spend every day with kids. I run a preschool day-care center. Day-care teachers take care of kids when their parents are at work. We teach kids before they go to kindergarten.

We do different activities. I teach them their colors, the alphabet, and how to tie their shoes. I make the learning fun. I teach them by playing games. I want my students to be smart when they go to school.

We run around to stay healthy. I help my kids learn to play well with other children. Kids should get along with each other. I also want them to have fun while they are staying with me. I don't want them to miss their parents too much. I make sure they eat healthy food. I have them take naps. Sometimes we go to the zoo or go for walks.

I know how kids grow and learn. I know about nutrition and first aid. My job is to keep everyone safe while they learn new things.

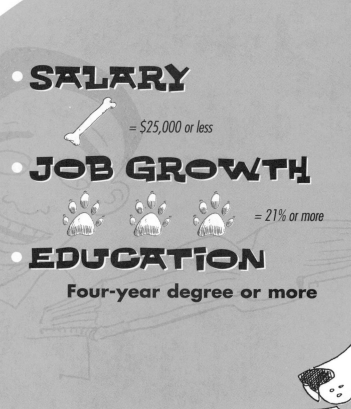

SALARY

= $25,000 or less

JOB GROWTH

= 21% or more

EDUCATION

Four-year degree or more

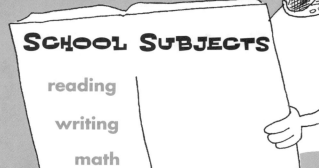

SCHOOL SUBJECTS

reading

writing

math

Production Assistants

SALARY

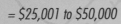 = $25,001 to $50,000

JOB GROWTH

 = 21% or more

EDUCATION

Four-year degree or more

SCHOOL SUBJECTS

writing	industrial
reading	arts
math	

I've probably worked on some of your favorite TV shows. You wouldn't recognize my face. I work behind the scenes. I'm a production assistant. I help set up and operate the equipment used to make TV shows.

I help with the lights, cameras, and microphones. I make sure the lights are angled right so you can see what the actors are doing. I help the camera operators set up their equipment. I do sound checks on the microphones so I know they are working properly. When scenes change I may move things around on the set. I may get everybody lunch.

Sometimes we shoot on location outside of the studio. I know where all of our cameras and lights are. The equipment is very expensive. Production assistants do odd jobs behind the scenes.

Production Planners

Our factory has to ship 3,000 birdfeeders to stores by the first week of next month. I make sure we can do it. I'm a production planner.

I look at our sales to see how many birdfeeders we need to make. I prepare a schedule for the factory. I let them know how many must be completed at the end of each day. I have the whole month planned out. I had to hire several new employees and buy a few new machines to get the project done on time. I know we can do it. We just have to stick to my schedules.

I meet with the production managers once a week to go over our production figures. I don't want us to get behind. Everyone is working hard to meet the deadline. Right now we're ahead of schedule. Production planners are important to factories. We set deadlines so factories produce efficiently. We make sure stores get the products they need on time.

By the end of this month our task will be complete. All 3,000 birdfeeders will be on trucks traveling across the United States. I'd better get back to work. I need to start planning schedules for the next few months.

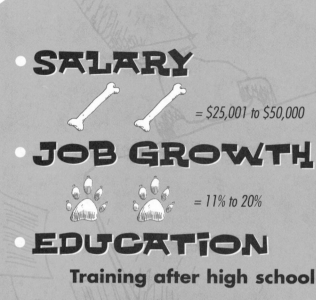

- ## SALARY
  = $25,001 to $50,000

- ## JOB GROWTH
  = 11% to 20%

- ## EDUCATION
  Training after high school

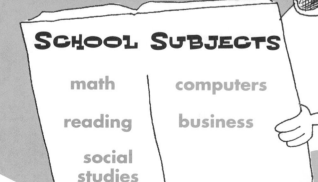

SCHOOL SUBJECTS

math	computers
reading	business
social studies	

Production Superintendents

SALARY

= $50,001 or more

JOB GROWTH

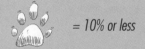

= 10% or less

EDUCATION

Four-year degree or more

SCHOOL SUBJECTS

reading	computers
math	science
writing	

I'm sure you like to get the best thing you can for the least amount of money. Well, factories are the same way. They like to make sure that they manufacture the best product they can for the least amount of money. I'm a production superintendent for a large company. I make sure that our factories make the best products they can.

I work with the factory managers to determine production and quality control standards. Then I develop a budget. I have to know everything about our products. I can't make recommendations unless I know exactly how they are made. Sometimes I have our engineers make changes to the machines in the factory. I record my ideas so the owners of the company can see exactly what we are doing. I pay attention to a lot of details.

Production superintendents help both the factory and the consumer. We keep costs down so factories can afford to produce more goods. We make it possible for the factories to charge less for our products. That means you won't spend as much when you buy them at the store.

Product Managers

You know that new toy you just bought? That was my idea. I'm a product manager. I suggest new products for my company to make.

I come up with ideas by seeing what people are buying. Sometimes I talk with lots of people or do surveys to get their ideas about new toys they would like to see. I look at production numbers to see if it is possible to make a toy. I have a computer to help me compare numbers. Sometimes I suggest that we make changes to one of our current toys. We like to keep everything modern and fun. We added laser sounds to our best-selling spaceship to meet customer demand. Now, it's even more fun to play with.

I meet with the people in our sales and marketing departments to talk about products. Sometimes we decide to stop making some of the older toys. We don't manufacture things people don't want to buy. I know a lot about toys. I know the kinds of things you would like to play with. Product managers make sure that a company's products match consumers' needs.

BUSINESS

SALARY

= $50,001 or more

JOB GROWTH

= 21% or more

EDUCATION

Four-year degree or more

SCHOOL SUBJECTS

math	computers
reading	science
social studies	writing

Professional Athletes

SALARY

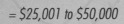 = $25,001 to $50,000

JOB GROWTH

 = 11% to 20%

EDUCATION

Training after high school

SCHOOL SUBJECTS

reading

math

physical
education

Do you like to play sports? Maybe you'll grow up to be like me. I'm a professional basketball player. Millions of kids dream about becoming a professional athlete. It's just a dream for most people.

Professional athletes get paid to play sports. That sounds like fun. Actually, it's very hard work. You have to be an excellent player. Recruiters pick only the best players to be professionals. I travel around the country playing games. I train all the time. I have to stay in shape. I have to practice with my team. I can't play any way I want. I follow all the rules. I have to listen to my coach. He tells me what to do.

You've probably never heard of me. Most professional athletes don't become big stars. I've never been in a TV commercial or made a rap video. I had to get good grades in school so I could go to college. Recruiters find athletes on college teams. I am lucky to be a professional. Most people don't make it.

Professionals don't play for many years. Athletes should have a backup plan. I'm glad I went to college.

Programmers

I designed some great computer programs for schools. I'm a computer programmer. Some computer programs are written in codes. Other programs are built using blocks of codes called objects. There are objects for everything that happens in the program. When you type something on a keyboard, my program tells the computer what to do. Some computer programs have hundreds of lines of code.

Making a program is very complicated. I have to be logical. I'm very good at math. Computer programs are like math problems. Programming takes a lot of thought. I can write a computer program to do just about anything.

Computers help make life much easier. But computers don't know what to do unless we tell them. That's where computer programmers come in. We give orders for computers to follow. I spend time looking for problems in my code. It has to run smoothly. Sometimes there are bugs that I fix.

TECHNOLOGY

- **SALARY**
  = $50,001 or more

- **JOB GROWTH**
  = 11% to 20%

- **EDUCATION**
  Four-year degree or more

SCHOOL SUBJECTS

computers	reading
math	
science	

Property Managers

SALARY

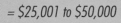 = $25,001 to $50,000

JOB GROWTH

 = 11% to 20%

EDUCATION

Four-year degree or more

SCHOOL SUBJECTS

math

reading

computers

social studies

I work at a property management company. We manage rental properties for people. We collect the rent, and make sure the properties are maintained. That means finding people to clean a place before a new tenant moves in. We make sure the land is kept clean and trimmed. If repairs have to be made, I arrange for that.

We advertise properties for rent and interview new tenants. We check the credit of applicants and make sure they can pay. We give tenants keys. Every month all the tenants pay the rent to us. We send the rent to the property owner.

If a tenant calls about a broken pipe, I find somebody to fix it. We keep a handyman on staff to do most things. Sometimes I call somebody to help like a plumber or electrician.

I help people find a place and make sure everything works right.

Prosthetists

Imagine what life would be like if you lost an arm or a leg. You would have to do things very differently. Sometimes people get sick or in an accident and have to have their limbs amputated. They suddenly learn new ways to do things. I help them make their lives more normal. I'm a prosthetist.

I design artificial arms and legs. I work with a doctor to help patients. I make limbs specifically for each person. I match the length and size to the person. I make sure they are comfortable. I try to make them look natural. Sometimes you can't even notice the difference unless you look closely. I show the patients how to get used to their new limbs. They learn how to adapt their behavior. Walking on an artificial leg is more difficult than walking on your natural leg. It takes a lot of practice to become comfortable.

I help people recover from tragedies. I offer them support and guidance when they really need it. That makes me feel important.

SALARY

= $25,001 to $50,000

JOB GROWTH

= 11% to 20%

EDUCATION

Two-year degree

SCHOOL SUBJECTS

science

math

reading

computers

social studies

HEALTH

Psychiatric Technicians

SALARY
= $25,001 to $50,000

JOB GROWTH
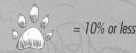
= 10% or less

EDUCATION
Two-year degree

SCHOOL SUBJECTS

reading

math

science

social studies

I bet you have someone who helps take care of you. Does your mom or dad or grandma or brother make sure that you clean your room, take a bath, and get up in the morning to go to school? A lot of people need a little help. I work in a hospital as a psychiatric technician. I help the patients at the hospital with the same tasks that your family helps you with.

Our hospital takes care of people who have mental and emotional problems. We help them learn how to live normal, healthy lives. They stay at the hospital until they feel comfortable living in the outside world. I work closely with the doctors at the hospital. I let them know all about the patients. I spend time with each one of them. I know when they are happy or sad or angry. I try to help them through their problems.

I make sure that my patients stay healthy. I check on them just like your family checks on you. I make sure they take a bath, keep their rooms clean, and eat healthy food. I make sure that they take the medicine that the doctors prescribe. I get to know them pretty well. I talk to them. We usually become good friends. They know that I really care.

My patients are just like anyone else. They need a little help overcoming their problems. We all need a little help from time to time.

Psychologists

I work all day listening to people talk about themselves. I'm a psychologist. I help people who are upset. You can talk to me. You can sit with me in my office and tell me what is bothering you. You can tell me anything. I won't tell it to anyone else. I can try to help you figure out what is wrong and what to do about it.

Psychologists work in schools, hospitals, clinics, and offices. We help people who have trouble learning or getting along with other people. I help people who have had something terrible happen to them. I talk to lots of people every day. Sometimes I have a group of people get together with me to talk. I can give tests to my patients to figure out how to help them. I feel like I'm always working. I think about how I can help my patients. I even think about them after I leave work.

Psychologists have to know all about people. I know how people grow and learn. I know about diseases people can get. I know what makes people unhappy or upset or angry. Sometimes people need to talk to someone they can trust. I am glad that they trust me and want me to help them.

SALARY

= $50,001 or more

JOB GROWTH

= 21% or more

EDUCATION

Four-year degree or more

SCHOOL SUBJECTS

reading math

science writing

social studies

Public Health Inspectors

SALARY

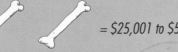 = $25,001 to $50,000

JOB GROWTH

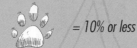 = 10% or less

EDUCATION

Two-year degree

SCHOOL SUBJECTS

science
math
social studies

reading
computers

I work for the city. I inspect restaurants to make sure they follow health codes. The government makes health laws to protect people. I am a public health inspector.

Public health inspectors enforce health laws for hospitals, water and sewage systems, hotels and apartments, and swimming pools. We make sure places are clean and safe. I look in restaurants to see if the kitchens are clean. I look for bugs and mice. I check to see if employees are washing the dishes in hot water. Hot water helps kill germs.

Kitchens have to be sanitary. I make sure that uncooked meat and poultry are stored properly and cooled to the right temperature in the refrigerator. I check how the food is cooked before it is served to customers. I don't want people getting sick. I talk with restaurant owners so they understand health laws. I tell them about any problems I find. Most places are happy to correct the problems. I can shut down any place that I don't think is safe.

I like to work with the community. I want this city to be a healthy place to live. Sometimes I arrange for training programs so people will know how to be safe. Being healthy is important.

Public Health Nurses

I'm a public health nurse in New York City. I work hard to help families who live in poor neighborhoods. Many of them cannot afford to take their children to see a doctor. I work for an agency that gives them free medical attention.

I work with women who are having babies to make sure they understand how to stay healthy. I give children the shots they need to get into school. Kids need vaccinations so they won't get sick. Sometimes I visit elderly people who can't leave their homes. I check on them to make sure they aren't sick.

I tell families about other free services they can find. The government has many programs to help people. Sometimes I work with church leaders and other people in the community. I try to get them to make the community aware of health care.

I think everyone deserves to live a healthy life. I work many hours every day helping people. Most of them would not get the help they need without me.

SALARY

= $25,001 to $50,000

JOB GROWTH

= 21% or more

EDUCATION

Four-year degree or more

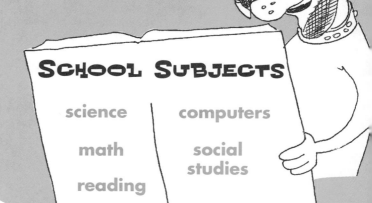

SCHOOL SUBJECTS

science

computers

math

social studies

reading

Public Relations Workers

SALARY

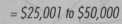 = $25,001 to $50,000

JOB GROWTH

 = 21% or more

EDUCATION

Four-year degree or more

SCHOOL SUBJECTS

reading	math
spelling	computers
writing	social studies

I know everything there is to know about my company. I have to. I'm a public relations person. I have to be able to tell people about our products and services. I work hard to give us a good name in the community. My job is to make sure this company keeps a positive image.

I write news releases to send out to newspapers, magazines, and radio and TV stations. I tell them about good things that are going on in our company. I give out brochures about our company to the public. I tell them about our history and the work we do. I write stories for our Web site. Sometimes I go to speak in front of community groups. I give tours of our offices to people who are interested. I tell them about our work and show them the equipment we use.

Public relations workers keep very busy. If people think our company is doing a good job, they may want to buy our products and services.

Purchasing Agents

I buy staples and paperclips and copiers for a living. I'm a purchasing agent. I work for a school district. I buy supplies for every school in this district.

I purchase the textbooks for classes. I buy fat pencils for kindergarteners to use. I buy computers. I find the best prices for everything. I deal with a lot of different companies. They send me samples to look at. I want to make sure I buy the best supplies at the lowest prices. Schools don't have money to waste. I make a contract with the company that has the best price. The contract states the quantity and how much our school district will pay for the supplies. Making contracts is an important part of my job.

Think about all the different things you have in a classroom. Each item had to be purchased. Desks and tables don't appear on their own. Sometimes we receive items that are damaged. I send them back to the supplier and get new ones. I just exchanged a computer that was damaged in shipping. The company was nice about replacing it. My job saves teachers from having to worry about buying supplies. They need to spend their time helping you learn.

BUSINESS

SALARY

= $25,001 to $50,000

JOB GROWTH

= 11% to 20%

EDUCATION

Four-year degree or more

SCHOOL SUBJECTS

math	science
reading	computers
social studies	

Quality Control Inspectors

SALARY

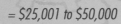

= $25,001 to $50,000

JOB GROWTH

= 10% or less

EDUCATION

High school diploma

SCHOOL SUBJECTS

reading	computers
math	writing
science	

PRODUCTION

Only the best pencils come out of this plant! I make sure of that. I'm a quality control inspector for the I. M. Wood pencil company. This company's reputation depends on me. I'm responsible for every pencil that comes off that line. That's a lot of responsibility. We manufacture thousands of pencils every day. Each one has to be perfect. Obviously, I can't test each one. It would slow things down too much.

I test the pencils by taking a sample. I check several samples from every batch that comes down the line. I have a checklist of standards that must be met. Each pencil has to be the right length and width. I examine the paint to make sure it is the right shade of yellow. I look at the eraser. It must be fastened securely to the end. Then I break the pencil in half to look at the lead. The lead has to fill the entire length of the wood. I write reports for every sample. The managers of this plant use my reports to operate the factory. If too many pencils are faulty, they may change the manufacturing process. My work can tell them if machines need to be replaced or if employees are slacking off.

Quality control inspectors are very important to factories. The company's reputation relies on our work. I leave work every day with a sense of pride.

Radio and Television Announcers

Hey, I'm a DJ on KHIP radio. In case you didn't know, DJ stands for disc jockey, because we play songs that come on discs.

Disc jockeys decide what songs to play on the radio. We can't just play any song. We play the kind of music our station is known for. If you work for a country music station, your boss won't allow you to play rap. I play the songs people want to hear. Sometimes people call in with requests. I try to play them if I can. I want the audience to enjoy my station.

In between songs I tell people what time it is and what the weather is like. I even get to tell funny jokes. Well, not everyone thinks they are funny. I also play commercials. I must write down everything that I play so my boss will know that I am not playing the same songs too much. DJs know how to work radio equipment. They have to be able to cue songs and play them over the airwaves.

When I was your age, I spent my allowance buying the latest songs. When I got older I even started my own band, but my dad didn't like my friend's drumming. I still like music. I get to listen to all day long. I think that's cool.

- **SALARY**

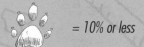 = $25,000 or less

- **JOB GROWTH**

 = 10% or less

- **EDUCATION**

Training after high school

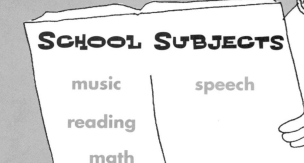

SCHOOL SUBJECTS

music	speech
reading	
math	

Railroad Engineers

SALARY

 = $25,001 to $50,000

JOB GROWTH

= 10% or less

EDUCATION

Two-year degree

SCHOOL SUBJECTS

reading

math

geography

I've seen this entire country. I travel across it every day. I'm a railroad engineer. I drive trains for a living.

I understand the mechanics of running a train. I control the train by using a throttle and air brakes in the locomotive. The locomotive is the front car of the train. I control it down a series of tracks. The tracks are like roads across the United States. I'm sure some are running through your town. I am in Michigan one day and Louisiana the next. Trains take things like grain and chemicals from one place to another. They also transport people.

Have you ever taken a train ride? My job is more than driving. I'm responsible for safety. Many people ride my train. I make sure they reach their destinations safely. I also make sure people along the tracks are safe. I watch intersections. I blow my whistle so people will know a train is coming. I wouldn't want to get in an accident. The train's brakes cannot stop it immediately. I know how to slow a train down.

I must obey many rules. Trains must follow speeding laws just like cars. I make sure the track is clear. Something blocking the track could cause us to derail. That would be very dangerous.

Range Managers

My name's Buddy. I'm the range manager at this cattle ranch. I find the best grazing areas for our livestock. We have several square miles of property. I direct the cattle to the best place for them to find food.

I have the crew seed areas so the cattle have plants to eat. I make sure I pick the right kind of plants. I know this ground pretty well. The soil is kind of rocky. Most plants don't grow very well. I also make sure the cattle get water. I had our crew build a watering hole for them. I had our workers fix the fence on the north side of the ranch. I didn't want the cattle wandering onto the highway.

I protect these cows. I'm careful to get rid of any poisonous plants. I don't want the cattle getting sick. I protect them from wild animals like mountain lions. There's nothing like being on a big, open piece of land.

SALARY
 = $50,001 or more

JOB GROWTH
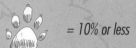 = 10% or less

EDUCATION
Four-year degree or more

SCHOOL SUBJECTS

science	geography
math	computers
reading	physical education

Real Estate Salespeople

SALARY

 = $25,001 to $50,000

JOB GROWTH

= 10% or less

EDUCATION

Training after high school

SCHOOL SUBJECTS

reading

math

social studies

computers

writing

I can find your dream house. Real estate salespeople, or realtors, help people sell and buy houses.

I study and write reports about how much houses are worth. I help people set a price for their houses. I write ads to advertise houses for sale. I show houses to people who are looking for a place to buy. The buyer and the seller both use me to make a deal. I work with banks, insurance companies, and appraisers. I get every sale approved.

Realtors know many laws. I help the buyer and seller obey the laws for buying and selling a house. Sometimes I work in an office. I use a computer to find and list properties. I use the phone to schedule meetings. I take people out in my car to show them houses that are for sale. I know about the different neighborhoods in my city. I can tell you about shopping malls and schools. I want people to find the perfect place to live.

I often work evenings, weekends, and holidays. I meet with people when they have free time. I enjoy seeing a happy family find a new home.

Receptionists

I'm a receptionist. I'm the first person a customer sees when he or she comes to our office. I answer the phone for the whole company.

I greet people in a friendly way. I direct them to the person in my company who can help them. People are usually very nice to me. They appreciate my help. Some people are grumpy. I'm still nice to them. Sometimes it is so busy that the phone won't stop ringing. On those days I keep track of a lot of calls. I remember who is out of town or away from the office.

I get back to people as soon as I can. I can't leave people on hold for long. I must have good phone manners. I help with filing, word processing, and sending out bills. I help keep things organized. I have my own desk in the front of the office. I keep track of all the calls and customers each day.

I dress nicely and keep my desk neat. I have to make a good impression. I am very important to my company.

BUSINESS

SALARY

= $25,000 or less

JOB GROWTH

= 21% or more

EDUCATION
High school diploma

SCHOOL SUBJECTS
math

reading

computers

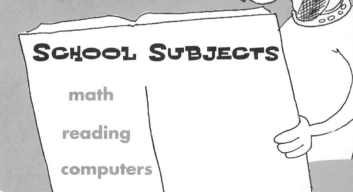

Recreation Aides

- ## SALARY

  = $25,000 or less

- ## JOB GROWTH

  = 11% to 20%

- ## EDUCATION
  Two-year degree

SCHOOL SUBJECTS

reading

physical education

social studies

I work for the city recreation department. I answer telephones and tell people about our summer programs. When kids come to play basketball on our courts, I check out the ball and make sure they know when it has to be returned. I also coach one of our softball teams every summer.

I help my boss organize great summer activities. We have swimming and soccer camps. We bring in college coaches to give kids expert advice. But mainly we have fun. Our program provides healthy ways for kids to keep entertained. We don't want you sitting in front of the TV all day long. During the school year we have a gymnastics program and flag football. We like to provide a good variety of activities. We even have a reading program.

I like being a recreation aide. I get to work with people and to be outdoors a lot.

Recruiters

When you get older and are looking for a job, you may deal with me. My job is finding good people to work for my company. I'm a recruiter for a large national company.

My boss is in charge of hiring our employees. I help her find great employees. I travel around the country looking for smart men and women to hire. I go to colleges and interview students who are about to graduate. I meet with them. I tell them about our company and why they might want to work for us. I know a lot about our company. I answer all sorts of questions. I have to be very polite. I want people to think the best of our company.

I also find out information about applicants. I look over their school records to see if they have done well in their classes. I only want to hire the most qualified people. If I think that we should hire them, I'll call them back a few days later to schedule a meeting with my boss. She makes the final decision.

I really like my job. I help people find good jobs. I help my boss find good people.

SALARY

= $25,001 to $50,000

JOB GROWTH

= 21% or more

EDUCATION

Two-year degree

SCHOOL SUBJECTS

math   computers

reading

social
studies

Registered Nurses

• SALARY

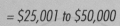 = $25,001 to $50,000

• JOB GROWTH

 = 21% or more

• EDUCATION

Four-year degree or more

SCHOOL SUBJECTS

science	math
reading	computers
social studies	

HEALTH

Hi! I'm Nurse Hammond. I work at City Hospital. Working as a nurse in a hospital is hard. Hospitals are always open to help sick people. Sometimes I work in the middle of the night.

I go to the nurses' station to see what the doctors need me to do. They keep us very busy. Today, I will give shots to four patients. Dr. Wagner wants me to make sure that Mr. Cronkite in room 103 takes his medicine. I go from room to room checking on patients. I wear a uniform so people will know that they can ask me for help. I take people's temperatures. I check their pulses and their blood pressures. I write the information on a chart. Doctors look at the charts to see how the patients are doing. It is important that I be very accurate.

Sometimes I see unpleasant things. I know how to handle emergencies. On Monday I had to help a man get stitches. It was very messy. It took me a while to get used to seeing people in pain. I know I am helping people.

Rehabilitation Counselors

Do you know anyone who has to use a wheelchair? Have you ever met someone who was visually impaired? If you know people who are physically challenged, you know that they are just like everyone else. They just have to do some things differently. I work hard to help people with physical disabilities. I work as a rehabilitation counselor. I help people who are physically challenged find jobs.

Many employers don't understand that people with physical disabilities can be very good employees. That's why a lot of them have a hard time finding a job. I talk with my clients to find out their interests. I just found a position for Margaret Talbot as an editor. She is in a wheelchair. The company she now works for bought her a special desk that her wheelchair fits under. It makes it much easier for her to do her job. Margaret is a very good employee.

Some of my clients are not as easy to help. I help them discover what their special skills are or help them learn new ones. I teach them how to find a job. Nothing makes me feel better than knowing that I have really helped someone. My clients are great!

- **SALARY**
  = $25,001 to $50,000

- **JOB GROWTH**
  = 21% or more

- **EDUCATION**
  Four-year degree or more

SCHOOL SUBJECTS

reading   computers

writing

social studies

266   Jobs A–Z

Respiratory Therapists

SALARY

= $25,001 to $50,000

JOB GROWTH

= 21% or more

EDUCATION

Two-year degree

SCHOOL SUBJECTS

science

math

social studies

reading

computers

Do you ever think about breathing? We breathe every second of the day. We never have to think about it. We would die if we didn't breathe. The body needs oxygen to work right.

Respiratory therapists treat patients who have problems breathing. I know all about the lungs and heart. I work in a large hospital. We have equipment that helps keep people alive and breathing. I deal with a lot of emergencies. I work with doctors and nurses. I must work very quickly. Doctors tell me who to help.

I hook patients up to breathing machines. I hook a hose to their nose and mouth that forces air into their lungs. I watch them very closely. I make sure they are breathing regularly. I record their progress on a chart. I must be very accurate. The doctor has to know exactly how the patients are doing. I make sure that their heart rates remain normal.

My job is very important. I save people's lives every day. Hospitals are always open. Sometimes I work late at night and on holidays.

HEALTH

Restaurant Managers

I'm the person who makes sure you have a nice time when you go out to eat. I'm a restaurant manager. Running a restaurant is more than just cooking a meal. If you think your parents have to buy a lot of groceries, try feeding 300 people every day.

I get my chefs to cook really good food. I hire waiters and waitresses to take your orders and serve your food quickly. I walk around the restaurant to see that things are okay. I have to know how to do every job. I like to talk to the customers. I want them to enjoy their food and be treated nicely. I want my restaurant to be a healthy and safe.

I count the money at the end of the night. I'm in charge of paying all the bills. I know everything that happens in my restaurant. Being the manager is a lot of work. Sometimes I stay late at night.

Having a nice restaurant is important to me. I like to hear that the food is delicious. Compliments make my job worthwhile.

SALARY
= $25,001 to $50,000

JOB GROWTH
= 11% to 20%

EDUCATION
Two-year degree

SCHOOL SUBJECTS

reading

math

social studies

computers

Retail Salespeople

SALARY

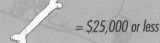

= $25,000 or less

JOB GROWTH

= 11% to 20%

EDUCATION

Training after high school

SCHOOL SUBJECTS

math

reading

computers

Thanks for dropping by Big Al's Surf Shop. My name is Terry. I work here as a salesperson. I know all about the products we sell. I should. When I'm not selling, I'm surfing.

You don't look like you've been surfing for very long. I can suggest the best products for a beginner. The boards in back would probably be just right for you. We carry everything a surfer might need. We even have sunblock. I stock the shelves. I set up displays when the store isn't busy. I answer questions for our customers. I like helping the people who shop here. Surfing is my life. I could talk about it 24 hours a day. It's easy for me to sell our products. I use most of them. I love getting people interested in surfing. Big Al says that I'm his best salesperson.

When people have finished shopping, I ring up their purchases at the register. Our entire inventory is on computer. Each product has its own code. The computer adjusts the inventory with the sales. I know how to work the credit card machines. Most of our sales are on credit cards. When people pay in cash, I make sure I give them the correct change. At the end of my workday, I go surfing.

Retail Store Managers

Hi! How are you today? My name is Mel. I'm the manager of Little Feet. We sell shoes to people with small feet.

I have different styles in hard-to-find sizes. I purchase stock from several different companies. I fill orders to keep everything in stock. I have several employees who work selling the shoes. I interviewed people for a long time before I found the right staff. I trained them to know all about our merchandise. Knowing the stock is important.

I coach the staff on selling shoes. I make the work schedules every week. I make sure I have employees working during every shift. I keep track of the money in the store. I make sure the money in the cash register balances with our sales. I make bank deposits and check our statements every month.

This business is very important to me. In our busy season I work six days a week. Taking care of our customers is very important.

- **SALARY**

  = $25,001 to $50,000

- **JOB GROWTH**

  = 10% or less

- **EDUCATION**

  Two-year degree

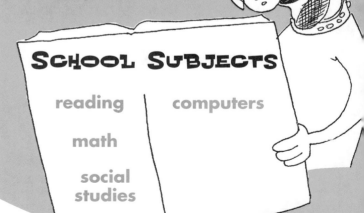

SCHOOL SUBJECTS

reading	computers
math	
social studies	

Robotics Technicians

- ## SALARY

  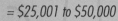 = $25,001 to $50,000

- ## JOB GROWTH

    = 11% to 20%

- ## EDUCATION

  ### Two-year degree

SCHOOL SUBJECTS

math	computers
science	writing
reading	

Robots are cool. They move almost like they are alive. I work with robots every day. No, I'm not the captain of a spaceship. I work as a robotics technician.

I set up and repair the robots that are used in factories. Many factories use robots to do repetitive tasks. They're not as advanced as the robots you see in science fiction movies. They are able to do a lot of work, though. The same robot can work all day and night. But robots get sick sometimes. They stop working the right way. When that happens, I take them apart to figure out what is wrong.

Robots are made of parts just like any other machine. I know a lot about electrical equipment and circuits. Usually, I just tighten a screw or replace a circuit. Sometimes I look at the blueprints and rebuild the robot. It's like being a surgeon. I like taking them apart and looking at their insides.

One day all factories will use robots. I think that's pretty neat.

TECHNOLOGY

Roofers

We all need a roof over our heads. Otherwise you would have to sleep in the rain or snow. A house without a roof is just a bunch of walls. Roofers put the finishing touch on houses and other buildings.

My name is P.J. I'm a roofer. I put on new roofs and fix old ones. Old roofs start to leak. I fix them. I patch holes using shingles and sealer. Sometimes leaks are so bad that I have to put on a new roof. I strip off the old roof and check the boards underneath for damage. I replace any wood that is rotten or has holes in it. Then I put on roofing paper and attach new shingles. I use a combination of glue and nails to keep them in place. I use hot tar and gravel to keep water from leaking through flat roofs. I know the right angle to slope a roof so water won't sit in puddles.

I spend most of my day climbing ladders and walking around on rooftops. It's a good thing that I am not afraid of heights.

CONSTRUCTION

SALARY
= $25,001 to $50,000

JOB GROWTH
= 11% to 20%

EDUCATION
Training after high school

SCHOOL SUBJECTS
reading

math

Route Salespeople

SALARY

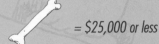

= $25,000 or less

JOB GROWTH

= 10% or less

EDUCATION

High school diploma

SCHOOL SUBJECTS

math

reading

computers

I'm the candy man. I supply candy to stores all around this city. I'm a route salesperson for the Choco-Lot Candy Company. I have a truck full of delicious chocolate candy. I have to keep up the stock in the stores on my route.

I talk with store managers to find out what they need. I fill out an order for whatever they want. I collect money for the candy and write a receipt. Sometimes they pay me in cash, and I make change. I record everything I sell. I go to stores that aren't our customers to ask the managers to sell our candy. I tell them about its creamy texture and rich flavor. I let them taste a sample. That gets them every time.

I drive from store to store. I unload the candy from my truck and bring it into the store. I work quickly to get to everyone on my route. I like being able to travel around all day instead of sitting at a desk. I like all the customer contact I have.

Sales and Service Managers

Hi! I'm Rusty. I'm the sales manager for a large toy company. I make sure our toys get in the best stores across the country. When we create a new talking robot or a dinosaur that walks and roars, I want you to find it in a store near you.

I have a staff of people who work for me. They are called sales representatives. I've divided the United States into four regions. Each representative has a region. I supervise their work for the entire country. I know all about our products. I meet with our marketing and advertising directors to find out about anything that's new. They tell me what the sales force should sell.

I pass the information to my staff. I show them how the new toys work. They know everything about our products to sell them. I make goals for our sales representatives. I tell them exactly how much they need to sell. They get paid based on what they sell.

Sometimes I go to trade shows for toy companies. I meet with owners of toy stores to tell them about our products. I report information about all our sales to my manager. I track our sales to see if we've met our goals.

- ## SALARY
= $50,001 or more

- ## JOB GROWTH
= 21% or more

- ## EDUCATION
Four-year degree or more

SCHOOL SUBJECTS

math	computers
reading	spelling
social studies	writing

BUSINESS

Sales Representatives

SALARY

= $50,001 or more

JOB GROWTH

= 11% to 20%

EDUCATION

Training after high school

SCHOOL SUBJECTS

reading   computers

math   writing

social
studies

They call me Stretch. That's because I sell rubber bands for a living. I work for the Elastico Rubber Band Company. I'm in charge of getting our rubber bands into stores throughout the South. I sell rubber bands to stores so they can sell them to you.

I have a long list of stores that call me when their supply is running low. I make sure my company ships to them so they don't run out. I travel from store to store. I let store managers know about the exciting new products my company is making. Elastico just started making rubber bands that glow in the dark. I think they'll be a really big seller.

I make sure my customers are happy. I want them to continue to buy from Elastico. I travel a lot. Sometimes I don't make it home for weeks at a time. It can be a rough life. You have to enjoy traveling and staying in motels. I don't have much time for sightseeing. I get paid by the number of rubber bands I sell. The more I sell, the more money I make.

School Counselors

I'm a school counselor. School counselors help kids with all kinds of things. Our main job is to be someone for students to talk to at school. You can talk to me about anything that is bothering you. I will try to help.

Maybe you are having a problem with a class. I can help you talk to your teacher so you understand each other better. Sometimes students are having a problem with another student. I help them straighten things out. I even talk with students about their problems at home. I am someone students can trust. I am here to help. Sometimes I do classes about feelings or how to be a good friend. Usually students come to my office to talk with me.

School counselors have to understand what makes people do what they do. We know how children grow and learn. I listen to a student's problems. I figure out how I can help. I deal with serious problems every day. I know all the laws about school and children.

I like my job because I help kids with their problems. I remember how difficult it was to be your age. I want to make life easier for you.

- **SALARY**
  = $25,001 to $50,000

- **JOB GROWTH**
  = 11% to 20%

- **EDUCATION**
  Four-year degree or more

SCHOOL SUBJECTS

reading · computers

writing

social studies

School Principals

- ## SALARY

 = $50,001 or more

- ## JOB GROWTH

 = 11% to 20%

- ## EDUCATION

Four-year degree or more

SCHOOL SUBJECTS

reading	science
math	computers
social studies	writing

I'm the principal at John F. Kennedy High School. I run the school. I make sure my school does not break any laws about classes, attendance, or safety. I hire the best teachers. I help them work with each other, the students, and parents.

I keep the building and playground clean and repaired. I can't spend more money than I have in the budget. Often, I stop what I'm doing to take care of a problem that comes up. I still have to get my work done on time. I study reports and go to meetings. I work in an office at the school. I use a computer to write letters and reports. Some days I talk on the phone for hours.

I work with all the people in and around my school. I hold meetings for parents and teachers. People turn to me to help them solve problems. I must work very hard and late to do my job well. I have to make decisions. I have to stand up to people who do not agree with me. I must know how children grow and learn, how to teach, how to manage money, and how to write reports.

I like my job because it is always changing. Every day there are new problems to solve. I like seeing my students grow and learn. I am very proud of them.

Securities Clerks

I work as a securities clerk for a large investment company downtown. Securities are things people invest money in, like stocks and bonds. I work with stockbrokers to keep track of the sales of securities. The stockbrokers make the investment decisions. I handle the paperwork and details.

I keep my company's files up-to-date. Stocks and bonds are constantly being sold and purchased. I keep track of many different transactions. I'm glad we have our files on a computer database. Changes are much easier that way. I use my computer to calculate cash balances and process online transactions. I have to be very careful. I am working with other people's money.

Accuracy and speed are very important. I make changes to accounts as soon as my bosses tell me. My job can be very stressful. I rarely sit around and chat with my coworkers. Being a securities clerk is never boring. I'm busy from the time I come in until I leave. Sometimes I have to skip lunch. Time is very important when you work with securities.

SALARY

= $25,001 to $50,000

JOB GROWTH

= 10% or less

EDUCATION

Training after high school

SCHOOL SUBJECTS

math

computers

reading

social studies

Security Guards

- ## SALARY
  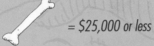
  = $25,000 or less

- ## JOB GROWTH

  = 21% or more

- ## EDUCATION
  High school diploma

SCHOOL SUBJECTS

reading

math

computers

I work late at night. My shift starts at midnight. I work until eight in the morning. I'm a security guard. Security guards protect property against fire, theft, vandalism, and illegal entry. I protect this entire factory when it's not operating. I have to be alert.

I walk around and make sure that everything is okay. I check the doors, windows, and gates to make sure they are locked. I look for fire hazards and problems like leaky pipes. I make sure no one is inside the factory who shouldn't be here. I sound an alarm and call the police if I see anyone. I have to be very careful. Intruders can be dangerous.

I have two guard dogs, Butch and Betsy. They help me patrol. They bark whenever they see something strange. They look very scary. They're sweet if you know them. I'm glad they know me. I also have video cameras that film the inside of the factory. I watch what is going on in several places at once by looking at my TV monitors. That makes my job easier.

Security System Technicians

I make people feel safe and secure. I work for an alarm company as a security system technician. I work with burglar alarms.

People hire my company to install alarms in their homes and businesses. My company uses an alarm system that will notify an operator if someone tries to break into your house. Our operator calls the police about the intruder. The alarm also sets off a signal to scare away the person trying to break in. Most burglars will leave if they know you have a security system.

I hook up all the wiring for people. This equipment is sensitive. I hook it up exactly right. I test the system to make sure it is working. Sometimes I make repairs to our systems. I take them apart to look for any problems. I check the wires and clean out any dirt. It is important that I keep the systems operating correctly. If they are not connected correctly, our office won't receive the alarm.

I am proud of my work. My alarms have prevented many break-ins and saved several people.

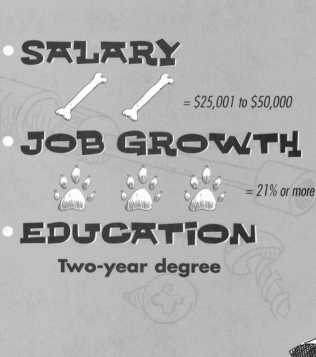

- **SALARY**
  = $25,001 to $50,000

- **JOB GROWTH**
  = 21% or more

- **EDUCATION**
  Two-year degree

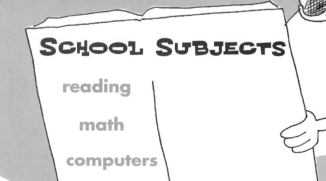

SCHOOL SUBJECTS

reading

math

computers

Seismologists

SALARY

= $25,001 to $50,000

JOB GROWTH

= 10% or less

EDUCATION

Four-year degree or more

SCHOOL SUBJECTS

science
math
geography

computers
reading

Earthquakes cause major destruction. I try to predict earthquakes. I'm a seismologist. Earthquakes are caused by pressure building up in the earth. This pressure has to be released. It's like when you are mad. You can't keep it all inside. The pressure is released at fault lines. Earthquakes usually happen near faults or volcanoes.

I'm studying the San Andreas Fault in California. I hope I can tell when an earthquake will strike. I do a lot of work outside. I look at the land and take measurements. I know every inch of the fault line. I watch it very closely. I look for the smallest changes. I know all about geology. Geology is the study of rocks and the earth. I have a lab with sensitive equipment. I use a Richter scale to measure the activity and movement of the earth. The ground is constantly moving. Most of the time, it is so slight that you can't feel it. Earthquakes cause the ground to move so much that you can feel it. Some are strong enough to damage buildings.

Seismologists have to be good at math. I use big numbers to make calculations. My information has to be very accurate. We can't stop earthquakes from happening. But the work I do might help us predict when and where they will happen. That could save many lives.

Sewing Machine Operators

I sew miles of fabric every day. I'm a sewing machine operator in a flag factory. I'm sure you've heard the tale of Betsy Ross stitching the first American flag. Well, she's a slowpoke as far as I'm concerned. I could stitch circles around her. Of course, I have machines to help me.

I sit at a big sewing machine all day long. We have an assembly line here. I stitch the stripes together on flags. Each worker stitches a different part of the flag. Mike down the line adds the stars.

I load thread onto the machine before I can get started. I use a lot of thread in a day. I loop the thread around the guides and then through the eye of the needle. Then I'm ready to sew. I control the machine with a foot pedal. I can start or stop it or make it slow down by moving my foot. I push the fabric under the needle with my hands. I have to pay attention. I wouldn't want a crooked seam. It would ruin the whole flag.

Sewing machine operators worked on a lot of things in your house. Look around to see how many things have thread and stitches. We make clothes, curtains, sheets, and lampshades. People use our products every day.

SALARY

 = $25,000 or less

JOB GROWTH

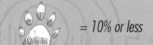 = 10% or less

EDUCATION

Training after high school

SCHOOL SUBJECTS

reading

math

industrial arts

Sheet Metal Workers

- ## SALARY
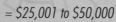
= $25,001 to $50,000

- ## JOB GROWTH

= 11% to 20%

- ## EDUCATION
Training after high school

SCHOOL SUBJECTS

reading

math

industrial
arts

I work in a factory that makes parts for the space station. I'm a sheet metal worker. My crew and I cut out and shape the large metal panels that go on the outside of a station.

We have a blueprint for every panel. The blueprint is an instruction that tells us exactly what size and shape to make each piece. We have to be accurate. We measure the piece on a large sheet of metal. Then we cut it using special shears. We use forming rolls to shape the metal into curves. We file and buff the metal to make it smooth. For really large pieces, we use welding torches to put several sheets of metal together. We wear protective goggles and gloves.

Our supervisor checks each part to make sure we made it exactly right. The parts we make will be sent to another factory where the space station is assembled. Workers will weld and rivet our parts to a metal frame. They can't do their jobs unless we have done ours.

Sheet metal workers make parts for everything from airplanes to filing cabinets. Products made from sheet metal are strong and tough.

Ship Fitters

I help build huge ships that travel the ocean. My creations travel to exotic ports like Madagascar and Oslo. I'm a ship fitter at a shipyard. I build and repair navy ships, oil tankers, and cargo and cruise ships.

I work with huge pieces of metal. I attach them to the ship frame. I make sure each piece fits exactly right. A welder rivets them into place. I align the metal sheets next to each other until we cover the entire ship. Think about how huge some ships are. A cruise ship may have thousands of sheets of metal covering its hull.

I follow the designer's blueprints to make sure I am fitting the pieces together correctly. I can't leave any gaps. I wouldn't want the ship to leak. My job is very strenuous. I get quite a workout. I work with other ship fitters on big jobs. It may take us weeks to finish an oil tanker.

I like working as a ship fitter. I keep physically fit. I imagine all the exciting places my ships will visit.

- **SALARY**

  = $25,001 to $50,000

- **JOB GROWTH**

  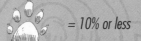 = 10% or less

- **EDUCATION**

  Four-year degree or more

SCHOOL SUBJECTS

reading

math

physical education

industrial arts

Shipping and Receiving Clerks

SALARY

= $25,000 or less

JOB GROWTH

= 10% or less

EDUCATION

High school diploma

SCHOOL SUBJECTS

math

reading

computers

Hand me that box. Thanks! I'm a shipping and receiving clerk for this company. I work in the warehouse. It's a large building full of shelves and boxes. All the things my company buys and sells come through here. It's my job to keep track of everything.

When a delivery is made, I fill out a report to the department that ordered it. I count everything to make sure nothing gets lost. I keep track of everything stored in the warehouse. I also fill the outgoing orders for my company. I get a printed list of what needs to go in the boxes I ship out. I make sure the correct mailing address is on the box. I am careful to use the right amount of postage. I write a report listing everything that is going out and where it is going. Sometimes customers don't get their orders. Then I track down the package for them. I use special software on a computer to see if the delivery company delivered it.

The thing I like most about my job is knowing that people depend on me. I keep the warehouse running smoothly.

Ship's Crew Members

I like to stay busy. There are a lot of different things for me to do on this boat. I'm a crew member on the Norma Rae. It's a big cargo ship. We carry shipments across the Atlantic Ocean. Crew members are the people who keep a boat running. We do a little bit of everything.

I follow a lot of orders. I do whatever the captain tells me. I do it the moment he asks. Crew members keep the equipment on board in good shape. We oil gears and repair cables and ropes. We check the lifeboats to make sure they will float. We wash and sweep the deck. Every so often I get to paint the ship. We like to keep it looking nice. When we get ready to dock at a wharf, I throw down the lines to tie the ship to the dock. Otherwise the ship would float back out to sea. I do a lot of tough, physical work.

We've docked in some great ports. I've seen the biggest cities in Europe. I get to spend days at a time out on the ocean. I find that very relaxing. I go to bed at night with the sound of the ocean in the background. The rolling waves rock me to sleep.

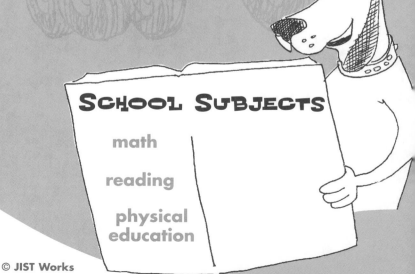

SALARY

= $25,001 to $50,000

JOB GROWTH

= 10% or less

EDUCATION

High school diploma

SCHOOL SUBJECTS

math

reading

physical education

Ship's Officers

- ## SALARY
  = $50,001 or more

- ## JOB GROWTH
   = 10% or less

- ## EDUCATION
  Four-year degree or more

SCHOOL SUBJECTS

reading	math
writing	geography
science	computers

TRANSPORTATION

I'm the captain of the Lenora. This ship transports bananas from South America to Canada. I'm in charge of everything that happens on this ship. Everyone on board has to answer to me. The owners of the ship trust me.

I make sure this ship travels safely. I set the course along with the ship's navigator. I make sure the pilot watches out for other ships and hazards in the ocean. We have radar devices to keep on course. They let us know about anything approaching. I give orders to my crew. I make sure all of them do their jobs. A ship's crew has to work together as a team. I keep this ship clean and safe. I have the crew check the life rafts on every voyage. I look over the entire ship for any safety hazards. I don't want any problems at sea.

At the dock, I supervise the loading and unloading of bananas. I'm the top banana on the Lenora. Then I supervise maintenance of the ship's systems before our next voyage. I am away from home for weeks, but I love the sea life.

Shoe Repairers

Welcome to the O-Sole-O-Mio Repair Shop! Let me introduce myself. My name is Jessie. I'm the head shoe repairer at this shop. Have you ever worn out a pair of shoes that you really liked? I bet you hated to throw them away. Our shop offers a solution. We make old shoes look new again.

O-Sole-O-Mio resoles your shoes or puts on new heels. We even work with tennis shoes made out of canvas and rubber. I put the shoe on a form called a last. It looks like a foot. I remove the old sole with pliers and a knife. The last holds the shoe so I can get the new sole on. I stitch the new sole in place. Sometimes I use cement and nails to fasten the heel. I work on lots of different pairs of shoes in a day.

I work with both men's and women's footwear. I also work on other things made of leather. I can fix purses, belts, and luggage. I hate seeing people throw away good things. With a little work, I can make most shoes look as good as ever. In my own way, I am helping to save the environment. The shoes I work on end up on people's feet instead of in a landfill.

I have a fun repairing shoes. I like being able to work with my hands. I listen to my favorite radio station and work away.

SALARY
= $25,000 or less

JOB GROWTH
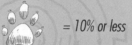 = 10% or less

EDUCATION
Training after high school

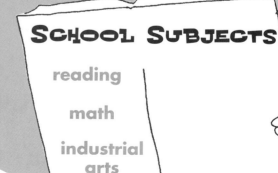

SCHOOL SUBJECTS

reading

math

industrial arts

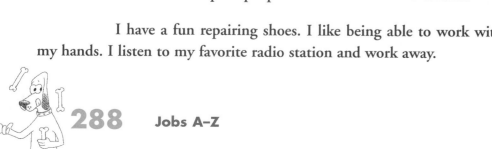

Short-Order Cooks

- ## SALARY
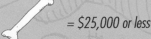
= $25,000 or less

- ## JOB GROWTH
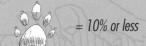
= 10% or less

- ## EDUCATION
High school diploma

SCHOOL SUBJECTS

reading

math

I'm a short-order cook at Penny's Pancake Palace. I cook breakfast and lunch. For breakfast, we specialize in pancakes. I make hundreds of pancakes every morning.

I cook side dishes like bacon, sausage, and hash brown potatoes. I work very quickly. We're really busy in the morning. I know what to cook by reading the waitresses' and waiters' orders. Some of them have awful handwriting!

We get a big lunch crowd. I make lots of hamburgers and french fries. I cook most of the food on a big griddle. I also use deep fryers. I keep the kitchen clean. You can't imagine how easy it is to dirty a restaurant kitchen when you're trying to get orders out.

The manager meets with me to find out what food we need. We order supplies together. Penny's Pancake Palace is a fun but busy place to work. The staff works together to get the customers served.

Small Business Owners

I'm the owner of this graphic design company. We design promotional products like T-shirts, coffee mugs, and calendars.

This is a small business. It's not part of a chain or a large company. I run it myself. I have one full-time worker and two part-time workers who help me stay organized. This business was a dream of mine for a long time. I used to work for a printing company. I wanted to be my own boss. I took out a loan from the bank to open it. I want my business to be successful.

I bought computers to keep track of my payroll, sales, and expenses. I read a lot of business magazines and Web sites to learn the best way to do things. I keep up with the competition. I know everything that goes on in this business. I help out with designing products and getting new customers. It's a labor of love.

I have a great job. I get to be my own boss. I talk with interesting people all the time. Starting my own business was really tough. I've had to work hard to make it a success. I'm proud of this place.

SALARY

= $50,001 or more

JOB GROWTH

= 11% to 20%

EDUCATION

Training after high school

SCHOOL SUBJECTS

math	science
reading	computers
social studies	writing

Social Directors

SALARY

= $25,000 or less

JOB GROWTH

= 11% to 20%

EDUCATION

Two-year degree

SCHOOL SUBJECTS

geography	foreign languages
reading	
social studies	

Hi! Welcome aboard the Pacific Pompadour! This is the finest cruise ship you can sail on. I'm the social director. I plan the fun activities on the ship.

I make sure our guests have a good time. Vacations should be relaxing. You can do different things on board. I teach aerobic classes in the morning. I don't want people to get out of shape because they're on a cruise. We have shuffleboard and volleyball games. For people who don't like sports and exercise, we have music playing most of the day. I hire bands to play music on the deck.

Sometimes I plan theme parties at night. I even teach dancing to our more adventurous passengers. You should see Mrs. Clutz dance! She's a natural! People take cruises to have fun. I work hard to make sure that they do. I enjoy working with people and traveling to new places.

Social Scientists

Do you ever sit and watch people? People are fascinating. I study people for a living. I gather information about people for the United States census. I'm a social scientist.

Social scientists study human societies. Anthropology, political science, geography, history, and sociology are all social sciences. The census includes information from all of these academic groups. Social science research provides insight that helps us understand individuals and groups. We learn how they make decisions. We can see how they respond to change.

The work I do is very important. The census gives us important information about the United States population. I work in an office most of the time with several other social scientists. We analyze the information from the census and find trends. We develop theories about why the population has changed since our last report.

The government uses our ideas and information to work on social and economic problems. My thoughts help shape new policies and laws.

SALARY

= $50,001 or more

JOB GROWTH

= 10% or less

EDUCATION

Four-year degree or more

SCHOOL SUBJECTS

reading   geography

math   computers

social
studies

EDUCATION AND SOCIAL SERVICES

Social Service Aides

- ## SALARY
  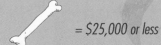
  = $25,000 or less

- ## JOB GROWTH
  = 21% or more

- ## EDUCATION
  Training after high school

SCHOOL SUBJECTS

reading   computers

math

social studies

I work for the Council on Aging as a social service aide. I work closely with the elderly people in this community. I want to help them live good lives.

Many of the people I work with have no family. They live by themselves. They have no one to take care of them. I check on them to make sure they are okay. I make sure they have rides to go to the doctor's office. I make sure they are taking their medication. I work with many people every day.

The agency I work for organizes activities for the elderly. We work hard to help them. We talked with local stores to create senior citizen discounts. We worked with the hospital to plan a day for the elderly. The hospital provided free medical exams to everyone who came. We also met with the mayor to let her know about our concerns. The Council on Aging got the city to buy a special bus for senior citizens. Now elderly people can get a ride just by calling us on the phone.

I work with nice people every day. I have become very close to many of my clients. I consider them my friends. They have worked hard all their lives. Now they need a little extra help. I am glad that I can be here for them.

Social Workers

I work with people who are having a bad time. I'm a social worker. I spend my day helping other people. Some social workers help people who want to adopt children. Others help people in hospitals get help when they get home. Social workers help people who lose their jobs. They help them get welfare to support their family until they can get another job. Social workers help people who are in trouble.

We specialize in many different areas. Sometimes people get hurt in bad accidents and can't work anymore. I help them get their lives in order. I help people find doctors. I arrange for them to go to physical therapy. I talk with them to find out what they need. I help them arrange their finances. They may qualify for money from the government if they are badly hurt. When they get better, I help them find a job again.

I know how to talk to people. I find out what problems people are having so I can help. That can be very difficult. A lot of people don't like talking about their problems. I want them to know that they can trust me. I am here to help. Social workers are very important. We help people out when they really need someone. I like making people happy again.

- **SALARY**
  = $25,001 to $50,000

- **JOB GROWTH**
  = 21% or more

- **EDUCATION**
  Four-year degree or more

SCHOOL SUBJECTS

reading	writing
math	computers
social studies	

Sociologists

SALARY

 = $50,001 or more

JOB GROWTH

= 11% to 20%

EDUCATION

Four-year degree or more

SCHOOL SUBJECTS

reading	geography
writing	computers
social studies	math

Sociologists study people's cultural patterns in families, cities, businesses, and schools. Do you think it's fair that many women make less money than men who do the exact same job? People's rights are very important to me. I'm a sociologist who specializes in gender issues.

I teach classes at the local university. When I'm not teaching, I'm doing research. I know quite a bit about the female population in the United States. I know how much money they make, how many women work outside of the home, and their marriage and divorce rates. To understand women's issues, I understand how women fit into American society. Do you know we've never had a woman president? I raise these issues in articles I write. I want to change the way women are treated.

Women's roles have changed a lot in the past 30 years. I hope my work will make our world even more fair in the next 30.

Soil Scientists

I spend my days studying ways to protect soil. I am a soil scientist.

Soil is an important part of farming. But farming can deplete soil of important nutrients. Different types of plants take certain minerals out of the soil. Soil can die if you don't farm it right. I suggest ways for farmers to rotate crops to keep the soil healthy. By planting different crops every few seasons, the farmers can keep the land productive.

I know the best kinds of plants to put in different soils. Some plants grow better in sand. Some grow better in rocky soil. Sometimes I run tests on the soil. I check the dirt for chemical content. I use my tests to find new fertilizers that work to replenish the soil. I write scientific reports explaining my work. I wrote a journal article about ways to renew damaged soil.

Soil scientists are an important part of modern farming. We help keep the land healthy.

SALARY

= $25,001 to $50,000

JOB GROWTH

= 10% or less

EDUCATION
Four-year degree or more

SCHOOL SUBJECTS

science	reading
math	computers
social studies	writing

Solar Energy System Installers

SALARY

 = $25,001 to $50,000

JOB GROWTH

 = 21% or more

EDUCATION

Two-year degree

SCHOOL SUBJECTS

math

reading

science

computers

I believe solar energy will be very important in the future. We can use the light of our sun to power our homes. Solar energy is a very clean source of fuel. We can use the heat from the sun instead of burning gas or oil. I install and repair solar energy systems.

I put big solar panels on rooftops and on the sides of buildings. I hook up collection tanks to store the energy. That allows you to use the solar electricity at night. Most of the systems I install are for hot water heaters. I hook up the plumbing for the water system. I test the electrical circuits and the plumbing to make sure it all works okay. I watch the system in operation for a while.

I make sure the solar panels are in the best position. I place them at an angle that will catch the most sunlight. Some solar systems are computerized. They will change position during the day to follow the path of the sun.

I'm proud of my work. Solar energy helps to protect the environment.

Sound Engineers

I can make thunder clap and lasers whir. I'm a sound engineer. Sound engineers control and mix sounds for music, TV, and movies. I do most of my work on movies. I add the sound effects to movies after they are filmed. I love movies. I read the script and watch the action to figure out where to put in a sound effect. I have to be very careful and get the timing exactly right. It would be weird if I put a camera clicking noise in where car brakes should be screeching. But I do more than add sound effects.

I take music and put it in the background to create a mood. In horror movies, I add creepy music to a scary scene. I add romantic music when people kiss. Sometimes I change the volume of people's voices. I can increase the sound to make people's voices louder. I want the audience to understand what the actors are saying. I do all of this by using a computer and music switcher.

Think about the sounds you hear when you are at the theater. I do each one of them. I have tight deadlines. I stay at my studio very late. Working with movies is interesting work. Going to the theater would be boring without me. The next time you watch a movie, think about what it would be like without any sound.

SALARY

= $25,001 to $50,000

JOB GROWTH

= 21% or more

EDUCATION

Two-year degree

SCHOOL SUBJECTS

music	science
reading	
math	

Special Education Teachers

- ## SALARY
 = $25,001 to $50,000

- ## JOB GROWTH
 = 21% or more

- ## EDUCATION
Four-year degree or more

SCHOOL SUBJECTS

math	computers
reading	science
social studies	writing

I am a special education teacher. I work with students who are blind. I teach them the same things you learn in your classes. My class is set up to make learning easier for these students because they have special needs. They cannot read the text in regular books. Everything they read is written in Braille.

Braille is a special alphabet. The letters are textures. Instead of reading with their eyes, my students read by feeling the textures with their fingers. Otherwise, my students spend their day the same way you do. I teach them math, science, and spelling. They learn how to use computers. They take tests and do homework, too. I'm sure they dislike homework just as much as you do.

I gear their lessons toward their needs. I present the information in a way they can understand. They learn through sound and touch. Sometimes we go on field trips.

Some special education teachers help students with learning disabilities that make it hard for them to read books. Special education is challenging but rewarding.

Speech Pathologists and Audiologists

Being able to communicate is very important. Most people take speaking and hearing for granted. I don't. I work as a speech pathologist and audiologist. Speech pathology deals with language and communication. I meet with people to see if I can improve their speech. Audiology has to do with hearing. I work in both areas.

I work with all kinds of people. Some are adults and some are children. One of my patients was a child who had trouble learning to speak. I tested his hearing. He needed hearing aids. I worked with him on his speech. Now he is able to talk normally.

I know the structure of the mouth, tongue, and teeth. The shape of our mouth affects the way we sound. I know how you shape your mouth to create different sounds. You hold your mouth in a different position when you say an "E" than you do when you say an "O." Communicating well is important to people.

SALARY

= $50,001 or more

JOB GROWTH

= 21% or more

EDUCATION

Four-year degree or more

SCHOOL SUBJECTS

science   math

reading   computers

social studies

Stagehands

SALARY

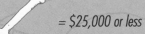

= $25,000 or less

JOB GROWTH

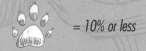

= 10% or less

EDUCATION

Training after high school

SCHOOL SUBJECTS

art

reading

math

I make trees and castles and sunsets for a living. I'm a stagehand. I work in the theater. Notice the sets and backdrops and props when you go to see a play. They're pretty nice, aren't they? I make them.

I talk with the director and producer of the play to see what they want. Then I plan the set and start building. I have to be good with tools. I cut things out of wood and nail them together. If they need a set that looks like a house, I may build an actual front porch. I paint everything so it looks real. Stagehands have to be good at art. We figure out clever ways to make props and sets.

I made a giant dragon for the last play. I joined a body out of old used tires. I painted it green. I made scales out of tennis shoe soles. I used red lightbulbs for the eyes. It looked fierce. I have to be very creative to do a good job. I want the audience to feel like they're somewhere else.

I work with lighting. I work with sound equipment. I love the theater. I know everything that goes on backstage. I'm too shy to get on the stage and act. Being a stagehand lets me be creative in a different way. The audience admires the great work I do behind the scenes.

CONSTRUCTION

Statisticians

Do you ever wonder how many other kids your age like chocolate ice cream? I can give you a good estimate. I'm a statistician. I work with statistics. I study information about groups of people to learn more about them.

I can find out information by asking people questions in a survey. To answer this question, let's ask 100 other kids your age. Out of 100, let's say more than 60 prefer chocolate. That means that two out of every three kids your age prefer chocolate. I use math and a computer to analyze the surveys. I find the answer to many questions by using percentages and ratios.

Sometimes I give the information to people in a graph or a table. That makes it easier to read. I'm sure some of your textbooks have graphs and charts. A statistician made them so you could understand the information better. I work with businesses. I help them find information about their customers. The information comes in handy. Businesses plan products based on the customers' needs. I make numbers mean something.

SALARY
= $50,001 or more

JOB GROWTH
= 10% or less

EDUCATION
Four-year degree or more

SCHOOL SUBJECTS

math	reading
computers	writing
science	

Steelworkers

SALARY

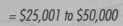

= $25,001 to $50,000

JOB GROWTH

= 11% to 20%

EDUCATION

Training after high school

SCHOOL SUBJECTS

reading

math

CONSTRUCTION

From where I work I have a great view of the city. I can see the park and downtown. I can see people running around. No, I don't have an office in a tall building. I'm a steelworker.

I build the metal framework for skyscrapers and bridges. I spend time high up in the air. It's my job to direct steel girders into place. Then they are welded together. Think about all the work that goes into a building or a bridge. Bridges are made of metal pieces welded together. Skyscrapers are made of metal beams. Each beam has to be put into place. I signal the crane operator and direct the beam to the right spot. I then fit it in so it lines up with the other beams. I do this all day long. I walk around from girder to girder.

I have to be careful since I'm high above the ground. I watch each step. You better not look down if you're new at the job. I like working in the sun all day. I wouldn't like my job if I had to sit in an office.

Stock Brokers

Have you ever heard of the stock market? People sell stocks and bonds on the stock market. Stocks are shares in a company. Most companies sell stocks to allow people to invest in their company.

I help people choose and buy stocks and bonds. I'm a stock broker. I work with a regular group of customers. I meet with them to find out their financial goals. I find out how much money they have to spend. I tell them what stocks I think they should buy. I arrange a sale based on what they tell me. Sometimes I call my customers to tell them about new investments. I work hard to make money for them.

I had to pass a state exam to sell securities. I am a licensed salesperson. I know all about business and economics. I read financial newspapers and magazines to find out new information. The stock market constantly changes. I like the challenge of this job. I use my intuition and knowledge to make money.

I make a commission from every sale. A commission is a percentage of what the customer pays. The more I sell, the more money I make.

SALARY
= $50,001 or more

JOB GROWTH
= 11% to 20%

EDUCATION
Four-year degree or more

SCHOOL SUBJECTS

math

computers

reading

social studies

Stock Clerks

- ## SALARY

   = $25,000 or less

- ## JOB GROWTH

   = 10% or less

- ## EDUCATION

  High school diploma

SCHOOL SUBJECTS

math

reading

computers

I work in the warehouse at a big department store as a stock clerk. I know everything this store sells. I keep track of our stock.

I look at the merchandise when they unload it off the trucks. I count and sort everything. I make sure what we receive matches what we ordered. I check to make sure nothing is damaged. We don't sell anything that's not in perfect shape. I fill out a report for damaged goods and send them back to the manufacturer.

I enter information about the items into our computer. We can look up the entire inventory of this store by typing in a few numbers. I put prices on the merchandise. I stock it on shelves in the store. I put everything in the right place. I put merchandise where people can find it. The shelves are labeled so I know where items should go.

Stock clerks keep merchandise in stores. This store is huge. We have several stock clerks to help out.

BUSINESS

Stunt Performers

I get into fights almost every day. Sometimes I get pushed off of buildings. I've even been set on fire. My name's Jamie. I'm a stunt performer. I make action scenes in movies, TV, and stage shows.

I make celebrities look brave. I film stunts for them so they won't get hurt. I do dangerous things every day. I work with the director and camera crew to plan the stunt. I make sure my action fits the script. I have special equipment set up for my safety. I fall into a net when I jump off a building. I wear padded suits to keep me from getting cuts and bruises. I have tricks to make my job a little safer. Don't get me wrong. I get hurt sometimes. I've been to the hospital many times. I've broken so many bones that I've lost count.

I rehearse to get a scene exactly right. I don't want to do dangerous stunts over too many times. Usually, several stunt people work together. We pretend to fight or do what the script tells us. My job is full of action. I have to be tough as nails. Think carefully about becoming a stunt performer. It's not as easy as we make it look.

SALARY

= $25,001 to $50,000

JOB GROWTH

= 11% to 20%

EDUCATION

Training after high school

SCHOOL SUBJECTS

reading

math

physical education

Surgical Technicians

SALARY
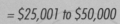
= $25,001 to $50,000

JOB GROWTH

= 21% or more

EDUCATION
Two-year degree

SCHOOL SUBJECTS

science

math

reading

HEALTH

I help doctors perform medical operations. I work in a hospital as a surgical technician. I set up the operating room for surgery.

The doctor tells me how to set up the equipment. I make sure the tools we need are neatly arranged. I sterilize everything. I make sure no germs are in the operating room. Everyone has to wear a uniform and a facial mask during surgery. I help the doctor and nurses put on their uniforms. They scrub their hands and put on gloves before surgery.

During the operation, I make sure the patient has enough fluids. I keep checking the blood level. I hand instruments to the surgeon. I know what each one is. I know the difference between forceps and a scalpel. After the surgery is over, I clean everything so the operating room can be used again.

Surgical technicians keep operating rooms clean and organized. We have to pay attention to the details.

Surveyors

Hi! I'm Dale. I'm a surveyor. I work for a civil engineer who designs bridges. My boss sends me to sites to do surveying. She needs information before she can begin designing.

I look at the land and take measurements. I calculate land areas and make drawings. I map everything for the engineer. I use math, science, and engineering in my work. I take notes at the building site. I write the information in a report when I get back to my office. I have a computer to help me keep everything organized.

My boss relies on me for all the details. I must be very accurate. She uses my report to help design the bridge. Surveyors don't always work for engineers. Some work for architects or building contractors.

I like being a surveyor. I'm a very organized person. I like looking at small details. I like working outdoors so much of the time.

SALARY

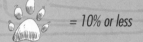 = $25,001 to $50,000

JOB GROWTH

= 10% or less

EDUCATION

Four-year degree or more

SCHOOL SUBJECTS

math	reading
science	writing
computers	

Tailors and Dressmakers

SALARY

= $25,000 or less

JOB GROWTH

= 10% or less

EDUCATION

Training after high school

SCHOOL SUBJECTS

reading

math

industrial arts

art

We make people look good. We're Sal and Al of Stevenson's Tailor Shop. Our customers are some of the best-dressed people in town. We make clothes. We alter clothes that are already made.

We fix the length of your pants so they fit you just right. We take them in if you lose weight. We want your clothes to fit you perfectly. Come in! We'll take your measurements. We measure sleeve length, waist size, hips, and inseam. Sometimes we even make clothes for people. We just finished making dresses for a wedding. We made 10 dresses for the bridesmaids. That was a lot of work.

We took each one's measurements. We used a sewing pattern the bride chose. We cut out the fabric for each dress. Each dress had to be made separately. They were all different sizes. We sewed the pieces together on a sewing machine. We had to hand-sew pearls onto the sleeves. We made them exactly like the bride wanted them. She was very happy with our work.

We can make just about anything. Sometimes we make suits or pants. We do exactly what our customers want. That's why we are so successful. We like being tailors and dressmakers. We get to work with beautiful fabric every day. Tailors and dressmakers turn fabric into fashion.

Talent Agents

You could be a star. I help entertainers find work. I'm a talent agent. Actors hire me to help them find roles in movies, TV shows, and plays.

I find out about auditions for them. If I'm working with a famous client, I may receive scripts for them to read. It's easier for me to get roles for famous clients, but I have other clients who also want acting jobs. Actors sign a contract with me. I get a percentage of the money they make from acting. I work hard to get them parts. If they make money, I make money.

Most of my clients play character parts. They may play police officers or cooks or school teachers. Once I find a part for my client, I handle the business arrangements. I discuss how much they will get paid. I work out travel arrangements. It's hard for an actor to find work without an agent. We know important people in show business. We are also very good with money. We know exactly how much our clients should be paid.

A good talent agent is an actor's best friend. I work hard to keep them working hard. We work as a team. They do the artistic side. I handle the business. After all, show business is a business.

SALARY

= $50,001 or more

JOB GROWTH

= 21% or more

EDUCATION

Two-year degree

SCHOOL SUBJECTS

reading   computers

math   writing

social studies

Taxi Drivers

SALARY

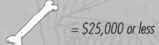

= $25,000 or less

JOB GROWTH

= 21% or more

EDUCATION

Training after high school

SCHOOL SUBJECTS

reading

math

TRANSPORTATION

I meet nice people all day long. I'm a taxi driver. I drive a cab around the city. I have a special radio in my car that receives messages from our headquarters. A dispatcher calls and tells me to pick someone up. I make sure I get the right address so I know where to find them.

Sometimes I get out of the cab and put their luggage in the trunk. A lot of my customers are tourists visiting the city. I ask them where they want to go. Then I set the meter. Taxis have meters that tell me how much to charge. The fare is based on how many miles I drive and how much time the trip took.

I know all the streets in the city without looking at a map. I know the quickest way to get to different places. Many people ask me questions about the city. I try to help them. When we reach their destination, I collect the amount of money on the meter. I usually have to make change. I must make sure that I get the money exactly right. People get mad if I'm wrong. Then I call the dispatcher and get a new assignment.

Sometimes I work during the day or all night long. Taxi companies never close. We are even open on holidays.

Tax Preparers

Every working citizen in this country has to pay taxes. We give the government a percentage of the money we make to help build roads, pay for schools, and defend the country. I help people figure out exactly how much tax they have to pay. I'm a tax preparer. I complete tax forms for people and companies.

I meet with my clients to find out exactly how much money they have earned in the last year. I need to know if they own a house or any land. I have to know if they have money invested in stocks or bonds. The government requires that we include this information on our taxes. I fill out tax forms so people don't have to. I know all the tax laws so it is much easier for me. I can save people money. Most people have some money taken out of each paycheck to help pay their taxes. By April 15, they file the tax forms with the government. Sometimes people have had too much money taken out of their paychecks. Then they get a refund from the government.

Taxes have to be done exactly right or the government might do an audit. An audit is a check on your financial information. I can help you if you get audited. I work hard to help people with their taxes. I make the paperwork less confusing. Tax preparers make paying taxes much less stressful.

- **SALARY** = $25,001 to $50,000

- **JOB GROWTH** = 21% or more

- **EDUCATION** Training after high school

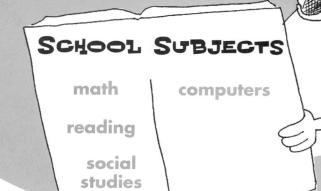

SCHOOL SUBJECTS

math	computers
reading	
social studies	

BUSINESS

Teacher Aides

SALARY

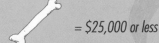
= $25,000 or less

JOB GROWTH

= 21% or more

EDUCATION

Two-year degree

SCHOOL SUBJECTS

reading	math
writing	science
social studies	

I work at Benbow High School. I'm a teacher aide for the science department. I help teachers in our chemistry and biology labs. I set the labs up for their classes.

I talk with the teachers to find out what they will be teaching that day. I make sure they have all the needed equipment. I put Bunsen burners and beakers in the chemistry lab. I get the right chemicals from storage. I help the teachers order supplies for the biology lab. I arrange for them to have frogs and earthworms to dissect. I put scalpels, pins, and forceps in the lab for the classes to use. Sometimes I help the teachers make charts to use while they are teaching.

I help the teachers as much as I can. They work hard to give students a good education. I work with the teachers in the lab. I may show students how to use the equipment safely. I make sure they wear safety goggles when they work with chemicals. I also help grade papers. It takes a long time for a teacher to grade 100 papers without any help.

Technical Illustrators

I'm an artist. I don't paint pictures of landscapes or flowers. I draw machines. I'm a technical illustrator. I make charts, graphs, and figures of mechanical and electrical parts.

My drawings appear in technical manuals, textbooks, and instruction books. I draw pictures so other people can visualize how a machine or process works. I have computer software I use to make my drawings. It's called CAD, which stands for computer-aided design. I draw the machines from several different angles. I have to include every part. I draw things like gears and pistons and rods. I like to add shading to my illustrations to emphasize certain parts. Sometimes I make drawings to illustrate directions for how to put a machine together.

I'm very good at what I do. I can see a machine and then put it on paper. I look at blueprints so I know every part inside. Technical illustrators make machines easier to understand.

Look at the pictures in an instruction manual the next time you put something together. Having a picture along with the words really helps. Illustrators save people a lot of time.

- **SALARY**

  = $25,001 to $50,000

- **JOB GROWTH**

  = 11% to 20%

- **EDUCATION**

  Two-year degree

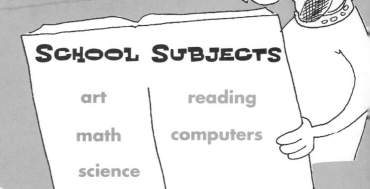

SCHOOL SUBJECTS

art	reading
math	computers
science	

Technical Support Specialists

- ## SALARY

= $25,001 to $50,000

- ## JOB GROWTH
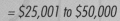
= 21% or more

- ## EDUCATION
Two-year degree

SCHOOL SUBJECTS

computers	writing
reading	
social studies	

I work on the phone all day. I'm a technical support specialist for a computer manufacturer. If people have a problem using one of our computers, they call me on the phone or send me an e-mail. I help them.

I know all about our computers. I know how to use the software that comes with the computers. I understand how computer hardware works. People have different models of our computer. I know how each model works.

When people have a problem with a computer, they may get upset. I calm them down and help them feel better. Most people are happy when they know I want to help. I ask them questions. I tell them to try different things. One of the things they try will fix the problem.

I really like my job because I work with computers and people. I get to play with the latest computers every day.

Technical Writers

I like to think of myself as a translator. Translators take documents written in foreign languages and rewrite them in English. But I don't work with foreign languages. I translate scientific and technical documents. I rewrite the information so the average person can understand it.

I work for a scientific research group as a technical writer. I write and edit reports, manuals, instruction books, and catalogs. I read a complicated scientific report and write a new document using the same information. I write the information for people who don't have a strong science background. Sometimes I write instructions from blueprints and technical drawings. That can be difficult.

My job is very challenging. I work hard to make sure other people can read my reports. I have to be logical. My writing has to be concise and clear. Technical writers are very important in the information age. We make science and technology much easier to understand.

- **SALARY** = $50,001 or more
- **JOB GROWTH** = 21% or more
- **EDUCATION** Four-year degree or more

SCHOOL SUBJECTS

reading	computers
math	social studies
science	

Telecommunications Analysts

SALARY

= $50,001 or more

JOB GROWTH

= 21% or more

EDUCATION

Four-year degree or more

SCHOOL SUBJECTS

reading

math

social studies

science

computers

industrial arts

Can you imagine life without TV? I can't. I work for an electronics company as a telecommunications analyst. I help the company develop new technology. My company wants to be a leader in television technology. I find out what products people need. I talk with people and analyze population statistics. I write detailed reports for my company about the products they want. We create new products based on consumer demand.

My surveys told me that people who lived in the country and mountains were not happy with their TV reception. Most of them could not get cable TV. Antennas gave them poor reception. Many people could pick up only a couple of stations. My company developed a new satellite TV system for them. Customers can buy a small satellite dish. They pay us a monthly fee, and we send a satellite signal to their homes. We provide hundreds of channels. We have movie channels and educational networks. We even have channels just for kids. It's amazing. Our customers are very happy with this service.

Telephone Installers and Repairers

Just give me a second to climb down from this pole. I work for the telephone company. My job is to install and repair phone lines. There are so many phones in this city that I stay pretty busy.

How many phones do you have in your house? I had to put in the lines and connect them to our main circuits. We have phone lines that connect all over the world. In fact, by using satellites, we can reach other countries. That's a lot of technology. Many things can go wrong.

Give my company a call if your phone isn't working. I'll come over to look at it. Small things I can fix quickly. I can get rid of that humming noise. Sometimes I check out the lines. I determine the problem when I get there. I spend my day traveling all over the city helping people just like you.

I like my job. I make my own decisions. I look at the lines and figure out what has to be done. People need telephones. I keep people in touch with the world.

SALARY
= $25,001 to $50,000

JOB GROWTH
= 11% to 20%

EDUCATION
Two-year degree

SCHOOL SUBJECTS

math

reading

Telephone Operators

- ## SALARY
  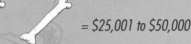
  = $25,001 to $50,000

- ## JOB GROWTH
  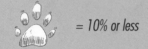
  = 10% or less

- ## EDUCATION
  High school diploma

SCHOOL SUBJECTS

computers

reading

BUSINESS

Hello! This is your operator Buzz. I work in a hotel. I sit in a telephone console. I help people make phone calls. Sometimes people call just to ask me questions about the hotel. I can ring another guest's room for them. I can also help them make a long-distance call. Sometimes people who call speak another language. I speak a little Spanish. I speak to them in Spanish if it will help. It's fun to see if they can understand me.

My job is important to the hotel. Someone has to answer the phone all night every night. My job can be very hectic. I answer a lot of calls quickly. I sometimes work the late-night shift. I can give people wake-up calls. I put their requests into the computer. The computer calls them the next morning to wake them up. I know how to operate all of the phone equipment. I have very good phone manners. Telephone operators like to help people. I represent the hotel I work for.

I like making people's stays in my hotel more pleasant. I meet some great people.

Textile Machine Operators

I work for the Bet-R Fabric Company. I'm a textile machine operator. I work on a machine that turns thread into cloth. First, we turn the fiber into thread. This company works mainly with cotton. We receive truckloads of freshly picked cotton. We have machines that clean the cotton. Other machines spin the fiber into yarn.

The yarn, or thread, is woven to make cloth. Have you ever woven strips of paper together? Our machines weave thread in the same way. The machine overlaps the thread until it makes a solid piece of fabric. The threads have to be woven together very tightly. I watch the machines to make sure they are working. I load new thread into the machine. I check the quality of the weave. Most machines in my factory are run by computers. I know how to operate the computer to get the machine working properly. Sometimes I make minor repairs. A lot of people work in this factory. We each have our own special job. We work as a team to make beautiful fabric to sell to clothing and furniture companies.

If you look closely at the clothes you are wearing, you can see that they are made of threads woven together. It took a whole team of machines and people to make that fabric.

PRODUCTION

SALARY
 = $25,000 or less

JOB GROWTH
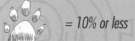 = 10% or less

EDUCATION
Training after high school

SCHOOL SUBJECTS

reading	industrial arts
math	
computers	

Ticket and Reservation Agents

SALARY

 = $25,001 to $50,000

JOB GROWTH

 = 11% to 20%

EDUCATION

High school diploma

SCHOOL SUBJECTS

math

reading

computers

Thank you for flying Happy Wings Airlines. I'm a ticket and reservations agent at the airport. I can help you book a flight. I have a computer to help me look up any information you may need.

Where do you need to go? I have our flights in my computer. I can check to see what time they leave this airport and when they land. I can look to see if we have available seats. Some flights fill up quickly. I can reserve a seat for you. I also help people who have paper or electronic tickets. I check their baggage so they don't have to carry it on the plane. I assign seats. Some people have special requests. Would you like an aisle or a window seat? Are you in a wheelchair? I check everybody's identification.

Once you're checked in, I'll tell you what gate your plane is leaving from. Airports are very big. They can be confusing if you don't know your way around.

Sometimes I talk with people who are upset because the flight they need is cancelled or full. I calm them down and help them find another plane. I have to be good at dealing with lots of people.

Title Examiners

I study the history of houses and land. I'm a title examiner. People come to me to find out about property and ownership.

Sometimes they need help because they want to buy a house. I find out the property's history. I look at mortgages, liens, and trust deeds. I can tell them if there are legal restrictions on the land. Some property can't be used for a store or a business because of zoning laws. I let them know who owns the property. I make sure the person selling the house has the right to sell it.

I do a lot of research. I usually find the information in the county courthouse or computer records. I look through old files and records. Title examiners make buying a house much easier. We answer any questions buyers may have. You should know all about the property before you sign a legal contract.

BUSINESS

SALARY
= $25,001 to $50,000

JOB GROWTH
 = 10% or less

EDUCATION
Two-year degree

SCHOOL SUBJECTS

math	computers
reading	
writing	

© JIST Works

Tool and Die Makers

SALARY

= $25,001 to $50,000

JOB GROWTH

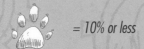 = 10% or less

EDUCATION

Training after high school

SCHOOL SUBJECTS

reading

math

industrial arts

Be careful! I work with a lot of dangerous equipment. I'm a tool and die maker. That sounds more complicated than it is. I make metal tools like saw blades and drill bits.

I work in a factory with a lot of other people. We use lathes and drill presses to make the parts. We watch our hands so we don't get cut. I wear thick gloves while I work. We look at blueprints to figure out what we need to do. We make the parts in many different sizes. There are hundreds of different drills.

My job is never boring. There's always something to do. When we finish one part, we go on to another one. I don't have time to sit around. My day goes by quickly. I like using my hands to make things. When the whistle blows, I head out the door. I don't worry about my job when I'm at home. I have a good life.

PRODUCTION

Tour Guides

I show people all the sights to see in New England. I'm a tour guide. Right now I'm planning an "Autumn Leaves" tour. I take tourists by bus to see interesting sights all over New England. The driver steers the bus. I tell about points of interest along the way. I have a microphone in the bus so everyone can hear me. We stop at beautiful inns and historic battle sites. New England is gorgeous in autumn. The leaves change to brilliant colors. I plan the entire trip.

People call my company to sign up for the tour. They pay one flat price. My company makes all the arrangements for them. They make reservations at hotels and restaurants. They decide which places we will see. Once the tour starts, I'm in charge of the details.

A lot of our customers are from other countries. I help them translate things as we go. I am fluent in Spanish and French. Knowing foreign languages helps me do my job.

Being a tour guide is great fun, but it's also a lot of work. I keep the trip organized. I fix problems that occur when we're on the road. Sometimes hotels mess up our reservations. Sometime a customer has an emergency and I help. I make sure my customers have a nice place to sleep. Tour guides can make vacations a lot of fun.

- **SALARY**

  = $25,000 or less

- **JOB GROWTH**

  = 11% to 20%

- **EDUCATION**

  Training after high school

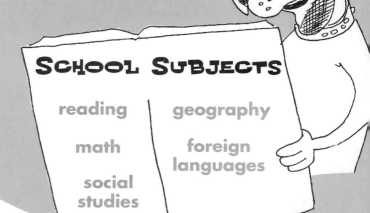

SCHOOL SUBJECTS

reading	geography
math	foreign languages
social studies	

Tourist Information Specialists

SALARY

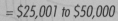 = $25,001 to $50,000

JOB GROWTH

 = 11% to 20%

EDUCATION

Training after high school

SCHOOL SUBJECTS

reading

geography

math

Hi! Welcome to the state office of tourism. My name is Jackie. I'm here to tell you anything you want to know about our state.

I know about the state's history and its cities. I can give you a map to help you get around. There are many great things to see. Have you been to the capitol? It's a beautiful building. We have a very nice zoo. Let me give you some information about things to see in our state. I have brochures on different places. I know some very nice hotels. I know one that has an indoor swimming pool. I can tell you about some great restaurants.

I help tourists plan where to go and what to see. Sometimes people write or e-mail us for information. I send them maps. I let them know about special events. I know a lot about places to see and things to do. I help people plan their vacations. I know a lot about highways and how to get to places.

The thing I like about working in a tourist information center is telling other people how they can have fun. I like talking with people about the great things to do here. I get to meet people from all over the world.

Trainers and Adult Education Teachers

People never stop learning. Even after you graduate from school, you still have many things to learn. I specialize in adult education. I help adults learn new job skills.

Many people are unhappy with their work. They can't get new jobs because they don't have the right skills. Adult education can give people the skills they need to get the jobs they want. I teach people office skills. I give classes on computers and word processing. I teach bookkeeping. I give tests and homework just like your teachers.

My students are eager to learn. They know how important these classes are. They can be successful in the business world once they learn the right skills. Many of them want to change jobs so they can make more money to support their families. Adult education gives people hope for a brighter future. People leave my classes and go on to the jobs they really want.

SALARY

= $25,001 to $50,000

JOB GROWTH

= 11% to 20%

EDUCATION

Four-year degree or more

SCHOOL SUBJECTS

reading	science
writing	computers
math	

Travel Agents

SALARY

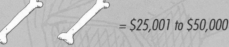 = $25,001 to $50,000

JOB GROWTH

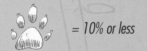 = 10% or less

EDUCATION

Training after high school

SCHOOL SUBJECTS

geography   math

reading   computers

social
studies

TRANSPORTATION

I can help you plan a vacation to an amusement park or a foreign country. I'm a travel agent. I plan vacations and business trips for people.

I shop around for the best airfares, car rentals, trains, tours, and hotels. I know how to write plane and train tickets. I have to read schedules so I know when flights take off. I find out about special events around the world. Do you like to go to festivals? I can tell you about concerts and parades. I plan what to see and where to go.

I'll give you all the information you need to know about your destination. You might have to get a shot to leave the United States. You'll need a passport. I keep track of how much everything will cost so you know how much money to bring. Every country uses its own money. I can tell you what you'll need for the place you're going.

I work in an office. I use a computer and phone almost all day. I talk to many different people every day. Some of them are from other parts of the world. I like to learn and read about travel spots. Sometimes I get to travel to places myself so I can tell you about them. That's my favorite part of the job.

Tree Surgeons

Howdy! We're with the Family Tree Service. We work as doctors. But we never see any blood. We're tree surgeons.

We do a lot of the same things that doctors do for people. We keep trees and shrubs healthy. A lot of our work is basic maintenance. Doctors recommend that their patients get regular checkups. We look the trees over for any problems. We prune them to keep them looking pretty. We cut out old limbs so new ones will grow. We check for bug problems. We have special sprays to make insects stay away. Certain insects will kill a tree if we don't spray it soon enough.

Sometimes people call us to nurse a sick tree back to health. We work with many farmers in their orchards. We help people with the trees in their yards. The Wyan family called us about the oak tree in front of their house. It was struck by lightning during that big storm. The tree is more than 200 years old. We added braces under the fallen branch. The tree would have lost its branch without our help.

If you like working around the yard and playing outside, you might enjoy being a tree surgeon. I understand all the things that make a tree grow. I sometimes get dirty cutting and cleaning up around them.

- **SALARY**

  = $25,001 to $50,000

- **JOB GROWTH**

  = 11% to 20%

- **EDUCATION**

  Training after high school

SCHOOL SUBJECTS

reading

math

science

computers

physical education

Truck Drivers

SALARY

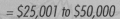 = $25,001 to $50,000

JOB GROWTH

= 11% to 20%

EDUCATION

Training after high school

SCHOOL SUBJECTS

reading	physical education
geography	
math	

I can't wait to get on the road again! I like to drive. That's what we truck drivers do. Drive and drive. I drive a big diesel truck for a living. My job is to take things from one part of the country to another. Sometimes I feel like I am on a vacation driving across the country. That's usually at the beginning of my trip. You see, I have to be able to meet tight deadlines. They need this truck full of lettuce on the other coast by tomorrow. It looks like I'll be driving all night. I'll get in the cab of my truck and take off.

There aren't too many miles of interstate highway that I haven't seen. Truck drivers know important laws about driving. We must obey speed limits and traffic regulations at all times. Driving a huge truck is much harder than driving a car. I have been trained to make turns and change lanes safely. I stop to eat a quick meal in a truck stop or diner. Some places even have showers I can use. I fuel up the truck. I stretch my legs for a minute. I may take a short nap. It's rare for me to get a good night's sleep when I'm on the road.

Being away from home all the time is rough. I get a little lonesome late at night. But I like the road. Traveling across the country is the best part of my job. I know people in every state. Some of the truck stop waiters and waitresses know me by name. I see interesting scenery.

Ultrasound Technologists

Did you know that bats can see things by sound instead of sight? Bats don't see well, but they find things by sending out sound waves. Doctors use sound waves, too. They can see the organs inside of your body by sending out sound waves. An ultrasound machine records the sound waves. It shows them on a monitor. The monitor shows how the sound waves bounce off your internal organs. These sounds can't be heard by a human ear.

I'm an ultrasound technologist. I operate the ultrasound equipment. I get the patient to sit in the right position. I move a transducer over the area we need to look at. The transducer sends the sound waves into the body. I can see the organs immediately on the monitor. I move the transducer around until I get the perfect angle. I can record the images on a photograph or videotape so the doctor can look at them later.

We use ultrasound machines to look at babies before they are born. We run the transducer across the mother's stomach. I get a picture of the baby on the video screen. It's amazing.

Ultrasounds are a safe way for us to look inside the body. We can see organs without having to do surgery or use X rays.

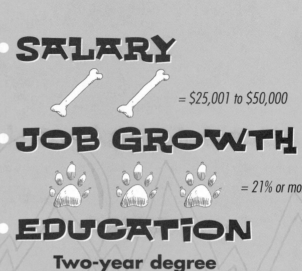

SALARY

= $25,001 to $50,000

JOB GROWTH

= 21% or more

EDUCATION

Two-year degree

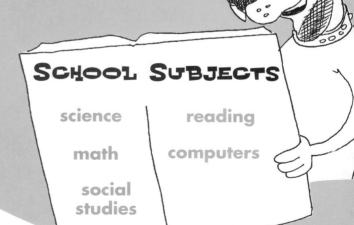

SCHOOL SUBJECTS

science   reading

math   computers

social
studies

Underwriters

- ## SALARY
   = $25,001 to $50,000

- ## JOB GROWTH
   = 10% or less

- ## EDUCATION
  Four-year degree or more

SCHOOL SUBJECTS

math	science
reading	computers
social studies	

BUSINESS

You can call me Jody. I'm an underwriter for the Farber Insurance Company. I study applications for insurance policies to see if they meet this company's guidelines. I decide whether or not we'll take someone on as a client.

I look at things like people's salary, age, occupation, and accident record to find out about them. When someone applies for car insurance, I have to see if he or she is a good driver. We don't insure people who have been in a lot of accidents. I check people's medical records if they apply for life insurance. We have to know if they are healthy. We also have to know how much a house is worth before we can insure it.

The Farber Insurance Company insures all kinds of things. I've approved policies on everything from apple farms to zoos. I even worked on an application for a rare pet bird named Chester. He was worth thousands of dollars!

I deal with numbers every day. I have to be very accurate. I make sure the things and people we insure are a good risk for us.

University and College Teachers

My name is Dr. Wilkins. I'm a college professor. Have you thought about what you want to do when you grow up? You have to go to college to hold certain jobs. You go to college after you graduate from high school. Doctors, lawyers, and scientists all go to college.

I teach Spanish at a large university. I'm an expert at the language. Como esta usted? That means "How are you?" in Spanish. Most college students have to take a foreign language to graduate. I teach my students to speak and write in Spanish. I ask the class questions. I only let them answer me in Spanish. I assign them homework to help them learn. They memorize vocabulary words. I give them tests to see how they are doing.

College students work very hard. So do college professors. We do a lot of research. I go to the library and look up information. I am writing an article on how the Spanish language has changed over the last 100 years. Writing is an important part of a professor's job.

College can teach you many important things. Going to college can make you really smart. Maybe I'll see you in one of my classes in a few years. Study hard. Adios!

- **SALARY**
  = $50,001 or more

- **JOB GROWTH**
  = 21% or more

- **EDUCATION**
  Four-year degree or more

SCHOOL SUBJECTS

reading	math
writing	science
social studies	computers

Upholsterers

SALARY

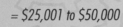

= $25,001 to $50,000

JOB GROWTH

= 10% or less

EDUCATION

Two-year degree

SCHOOL SUBJECTS

reading	industrial arts
math	
art	

I make chairs and sofas look new again. I own my own upholstery shop called Cover Ups. Cover Ups repairs and rebuilds padded furniture. I work with my customers to select a new fabric for their furniture. I carry hundreds of different patterns. I estimate how much the job will cost. Different fabrics cost different amounts.

Upholstering furniture is a lot of work. I don't mind. I consider myself an artist. I make old furniture look beautiful again. I remove the old fabric. Sometimes I replace the padding and parts of the frame. I may use a mallet or chisel to tear off the old material. Then I rebuild the furniture. I replace damaged wood or springs. I cut the new fabric to the right size. I sew it to the frame. I use a hand-held sewing machine. It would take me a long time to stitch those long seams by hand. I'm careful to make the seams nice and even.

I want the furniture to be perfect. Cover Ups does a good business. We help people make their favorite furniture look new again. Some customers say that I am a miracle worker.

PRODUCTION

Urban Planners

I work for the city as an urban planner. I know a lot about the economy of our town.

I know a lot about the land around here. One day that field will be a subdivision. I have surveyors look at the property. I know which spots would make good building sites. Some areas are too swampy.

I plan the growth of our town. In the next five years we will need more houses. People keep moving to this city. The houses will need streets leading to them. Electric lines will need to go up. We'll need to connect the houses to the sewage system. I meet with land owners and citizens to talk about the development. I check wildlife laws to make sure the subdivision won't cause any harm to nature. We want to keep the local environment intact.

This city is really growing. I think I'm one of the busiest people in this town.

- **SALARY**
  = $50,001 or more
- **JOB GROWTH**
  = 10% or less
- **EDUCATION**
  Four-year degree or more

SCHOOL SUBJECTS

reading	geography
writing	math
science	computers
social studies	

Utility Line Workers

- ## SALARY
  = $25,001 to $50,000

- ## JOB GROWTH
  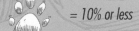
  = 10% or less

- ## EDUCATION
  Training after high school

SCHOOL SUBJECTS

math	physical education
reading	
science	

Sometimes big thunderstorms knock out the power in this city. It's usually because lightning struck a transformer or a tree limb fell across some wires. I work as a line worker for the electric company. I'm responsible for installing and repairing the power lines.

I replace circuits in the transformer or reattach the wires. I have to work outside in the rain. I also work on the lines when we aren't having an emergency. I help bring power to new neighborhoods and stores. I work with a crew to install power lines. We use augers and shovels to dig holes for poles. We hoist the poles upright in the holes by using a winch on our truck. Then we fill in the hole with dirt and cement. We climb the poles when they are set to add the wires. I attach the wires in a certain way.

I have to be very careful. These lines have a lot of power surging through them. I could get seriously hurt. Utility line workers bring people the electricity they need in their houses and offices.

CONSTRUCTION

Utilization-Review Coordinators

I'm the utilization-review coordinator for a nursing home. I know, my title sounds confusing. Actually, my job is very simple. I decide the best way for our nursing home to help people.

I look over people's medical records to determine what kind of care they need. Sometimes people need to go to a hospital instead of a nursing home. I tell our staff what kind of care to give to a patient. I want everyone to receive the best medical attention. I tell the nursing staff if a patient needs special attention. I made sure they were aware that Mrs. O'Brien is diabetic.

I help the patients pay for their medical care by working with their insurance companies and the government. The United States government helps older people pay for their medicine and their doctor bills. I process the paperwork so our patients and their families won't have to worry.

I want to help people at this nursing home. I see that everyone receives good care. I am on a committee that makes sure our nursing home provides care that meets state regulations.

SALARY
= $50,001 or more

JOB GROWTH
= 21% or more

EDUCATION
Four-year degree or more

SCHOOL SUBJECTS

science	math
reading	computers
social studies	

Vending Machine Mechanics

SALARY

= $25,001 to $50,000

JOB GROWTH

= 11% to 20%

EDUCATION

Training after high school

SCHOOL SUBJECTS

reading

math

industrial arts

You want a candy bar. You go to the snack machine and put in some change. You push the right button. Nothing happens. What do you do? You give me a call. I'm a vending machine mechanic.

I fix snack machines and keep them stocked with goodies. I work for the Vend-A-Friend Snack Company. I know all about the machines we use. I can get them working again in a jiffy. I may reconnect a wire or replace a part. I'll probably have to get inside to take a look.

I collect the money from the machines. I record everything we collect and bring it back to our main office. We have Vend-A-Friend machines in offices and factories all over town. I keep them full of stock and working properly.

I like to stay on the move and work outside of an office. But I can't eat my own snacks all day. I'd never get my job done.

Veterinarians

I'm a doctor. I don't help people. I help animals. I went to school to learn all about animals. I'm a veterinarian. You can call me a vet for short.

I help people take care of their pets. I spend my day working with animals. I know that pets are very special. I want them to live for a long time. I give shots to cats so they won't get sick. I can look at a dog to see if it needs to take medicine. I look at everything from mice to horses. I talk to their owners to let them know what is wrong. Sometimes I operate on animals if they are hurt.

People bring their pets in for checkups. I look them over to make sure they are okay. I check their teeth and their fur. I want them to be very healthy. I write the information in a file. I keep track of all of the animals I see. It is important that I let their owners know when the animals need a shot. Shots keep pets healthy.

I love animals. My job is great. I get to see weird dogs that look like sausages and big, fat cats. I don't even mind helping snakes. But please feed them before you bring them in.

SALARY
= $50,001 or more

JOB GROWTH
= 21% or more

EDUCATION
Four-year degree or more

SCHOOL SUBJECTS

science	reading
math	computers
social studies	

Vocalists

SALARY

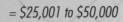 = $25,001 to $50,000

JOB GROWTH

 = 11% to 20%

EDUCATION

Training after high school

SCHOOL SUBJECTS

music

reading

spelling

drama

foreign languages

Do you like to sing along to the radio? I used to do that when I was your age. I liked singing so much that I decided to become a vocalist for a living. I took singing lessons and practice every day.

I sing with the Denim Jubilee. We put on Country and Western shows for tourists visiting Nashville, Tennessee. I sing in three shows every day. Sometimes I work on Saturday and Sunday. My schedule changes week to week. I also sing at clubs at night. It's not easy to make a living as a singer.

One day I want to become a famous recording star. I want to sell millions of CDs worldwide. Becoming a famous singer takes work. Most people never get to make a recording. The music industry is very competitive. Lots of people want to become famous.

Singers practice all the time. I sing songs over and over until I learn the melody and harmonies. I want to make sure that I give the songs lots of meaning. I like love songs the best. I can make people cry when I belt out a tune. I don't know if I'll ever become a big celebrity, but I like what I am doing. I make money while I am having a good time.

Wait Staff

Hi! My name is Arlin. I work at the Little Dragon Restaurant. I'm the person who takes your order and brings your food.

I know all about the food on our menu. I know the ingredients in every dish. I can tell you how anything tastes. People want more than just good food when they go out to eat. They want to have a nice time. I have to be friendly to everyone who walks in the door. Sometimes people are grouchy. I still have to be nice.

I make sure that you have plenty to drink. I don't want your glasses to get empty. I make sure you get your meal as soon as it is cooked. I know that you don't want your food to get cold. I check on people while they are eating to see if things are okay. I wear a uniform. It helps you find me in a big crowd. I bring you the check when you are finished. I don't want you to have to wait. You probably have other things to do.

I get to work with really nice people. I am friends with the chefs and other wait staff. I'm on my feet most of the day, but I enjoy meeting all the people.

- **SALARY**

  = $25,000 or less

- **JOB GROWTH**
  = 11% to 20%

- **EDUCATION**
  High school diploma

SCHOOL SUBJECTS

reading

math

Warehouse Workers

- ## SALARY

  = $25,000 or less

- ## JOB GROWTH

  = 10% or less

- ## EDUCATION
  Training after high school

SCHOOL SUBJECTS

reading   computers

math

physical education

I'm a warehouse worker. I make sure our products are organized in our warehouse so we can find them. I pack our products in boxes. I make sure they won't get damaged. I stuff the boxes with paper and foam. I tape the boxes so they are secure. I put the boxes in cartons. I store them on the shelf until they ship to customers.

I sometimes help our drivers load the boxes onto trucks. We have to be quick. We want our customers to get the products as soon as possible. Sometimes I find products that are damaged. I keep track of them so we can subtract them from our inventory.

I move around a lot. Warehouse workers work very hard. We lift heavy boxes and load trucks. I stay busy all day long. Sometimes I use a forklift to lift and move heavy cartons around. Twice a year I help take warehouse inventory to be sure we know what we have on hand.

Water and Sewage Plant Operators

My job helps keep the environment clean. Water is very important to us. We can't pollute it. We need clean water to drink. It's also nice to be able to go swimming every now and then. We couldn't do those things without clean water.

When you run water down your sink, take a shower, or flush your toilet, water runs down pipes through your house. The pipes carry the dirty water into the sewer system. Sewage treatment plants make the water clean again. I'm a water and sewage plant operator. I run the equipment that makes the water pure.

I start and stop pumps, engines, and generators to control the flow of the sewage. I check the equipment to make sure it is working right. I take samples of the water to check for problems. We want the water to be safe before we run it back into rivers and lakes. I keep a log of the work I do. I write down readings from the meters. I need to keep accurate records. My job involves many details.

Being a water and sewage plant operator isn't glamorous, but my job is important. The earth would be an awful place to live without us.

SALARY

= $25,001 to $50,000

JOB GROWTH

= 11% to 20%

EDUCATION
Training after high school

SCHOOL SUBJECTS

reading

math

computers

Web Designers

SALARY

= $25,001 to $50,000

JOB GROWTH

 = 11% to 20%

EDUCATION

Two-year degree

SCHOOL SUBJECTS

art	writing
reading	math
spelling	music
computers	

When you surf the Web and see all those cool Web sites and graphics, think of me. I'm a Web designer. I work with computers to create Web pages. Web pages contain text, graphics, music, and animation.

I work for many different companies. I design Web sites that show people things to buy. Many people shop online. I write computer code. I design pages with colors, text, and pictures.

I know about computers and design and business. The Web pages I build run online businesses. Online businesses are called e-commerce companies. Web pages have to change all the time. First I design a page. Then somebody changes what appears there every day.

When you visit your favorite site, look at the design. Can you find things easily? Is the site attractive? Then I have done a good job.

Webmasters

If you have a problem with our company Web site, you might e-mail me. I'm the Webmaster. I'm responsible for creating and maintaining the Web site.

I work with a team of Web designers who create graphics and text to go on the Web site. We change the contents almost every day so when you visit, you see new things. Posting the new content is part of my job.

Sometimes we do maintenance. I may solve a technical problem with the site. We make sure you can always get to our site. We sell things online, so our store is open 24 hours a day. If our site crashed, it could cost a lot of money. Our customers would be unhappy, too.

I understand Web design and how the Web works. I work with Web servers. These are computers that help run our site. There is a lot to juggle as a Webmaster. I like the fast pace. I help people get the most from our Web site.

- **SALARY**
  = $50,001 or more
- **JOB GROWTH**
  = 21% or more
- **EDUCATION**
  Two-year degree

SCHOOL SUBJECTS

computers	reading
art	writing
math	

TECHNOLOGY

Welders

- ## SALARY

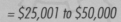

= $25,001 to $50,000

- ## JOB GROWTH

= 11% to 20%

- ## EDUCATION

Training after high school

SCHOOL SUBJECTS

reading	industrial arts
math	
physical education	

I make airplane wings for a living. My name's Lou. I'm a welder for a company that builds jets. Welders use torches to join metal together. The two pieces look like one piece when we are finished. We heat the metal to make the pieces stay together.

I adjust the gauge on my blowtorch to get it to the right temperature. It has to be really hot to melt the metal. When the metal dries it creates a joint. My job is like putting a model plane together. I put the pieces in place. I use my welding tools to fasten them, just like you would use glue on a model.

I wear a safety helmet with eye protection. I wear thick gloves so I won't get cut or burned. Welders have to be careful. We work with dangerous equipment. I move around a lot while I am working. I make sure the pieces on the outside airplane wing are secure. A welder never wants a weak joint.

I like not having to stand behind a counter or sit at a desk. It's neat to see my blowtorch shoot sparks as it melts metal together.

Wireless Technology Product Managers

I work for a manufacturer of wireless devices. You know our product. It's a cool handheld computer called a PDA, or personal digital assistant. You can use it as a phone or get your e-mail, but there are no wires at all. It's great for people on the go.

I manage the product line. I work with wireless software developers to create programs for our PDAs. I meet with the design department to talk about product improvements. I talk to our marketing manager about how to let people know about our PDA. I think it's the best one out there.

Wireless technology is the wave of the future. People can make phone calls, play games, make notes, and look up addresses at online map sites. They don't have to be at a desk. All they do is connect with a wireless service.

My day is fast-paced. I work with product design and marketing plans. I talk to people at trade shows about our products. I travel to tell people about what we do. Next month we come out with a new model. I'll be very busy then!

SALARY
= $50,001 or more

JOB GROWTH
= 11% to 20%

EDUCATION
Four-year degree or more

SCHOOL SUBJECTS
computers

math

science

reading

Woodworkers

SALARY

 = $25,000 or less

JOB GROWTH

= 10% or less

EDUCATION

Training after high school

SCHOOL SUBJECTS

reading

computers

math

industrial arts

I make doors for a living. I work for a lumber company as a woodworking machine operator. I turn pieces of wood into beautiful doors for offices and homes.

Making a door is a lot of work. I make doors in many sizes and styles. I have to plan each one. I choose the right saw blade to use for each cut. I cut the boards so they are the exact size I want. I can't be off by even a fraction of an inch. I use a plane to get the wood smooth. I get rid of knots or imperfections in the wood.

Sometimes I use special saw blades or routers to cut fancy decorations into the wood. I can add grooves to make a design or do a border of flowers. I drill a hole for the doorknob. I can't forget that. I sand each door until it is smooth to the touch. I get rid of any slivers or rough spots.

I love making doors. I add a special touch to each one. I love the smell of the wood as I cut it.

PRODUCTION

Writers

I'm a freelance writer. Freelance means that I work for myself. My name is Sue D. Nim. I work hard to find writing assignments. Most of my work is for magazines. I write to editors of magazines to sell them my story ideas. If they like my ideas, they may hire me to write for one of their issues. When I first started out as a writer, it was difficult to get assignments. Now I make a living from the money I make. Many writers work at other jobs to pay their expenses.

Do you like to write? You have to enjoy language to be a good writer. I've always liked to read and write. Words are very important to me. I want people to learn things from my articles. I present information so it will be interesting. Nobody wants to read a boring magazine article.

I just finished writing an article about animal astronauts. Did you know that dogs and monkeys have traveled to space? I learned important information about the space program. I had to make sure my facts were correct. I worked hard to finish the story by the deadline. Editors need my articles by a certain date so they have time to edit them and lay them out before the magazine is printed. Writing is my life. I love what I do. I work very hard. I can't imagine doing anything else.

SALARY

= $25,001 to $50,000

JOB GROWTH

= 11% to 20%

EDUCATION

Four-year degree or more

SCHOOL SUBJECTS

reading	computers
spelling	social studies
writing	

X-Ray and Radiologic Technicians

- ## SALARY
 = $25,001 to $50,000

- ## JOB GROWTH
 = 21% or more

- ## EDUCATION
  Two-year degree

SCHOOL SUBJECTS

science	writing
math	computers
reading	

HEALTH

Just call me Bones. I'm a radiologic technician. We take X rays at hospitals. I know a lot about the human body. I can check to see if you have a broken bone. I take a picture of it with X rays.

X rays are pictures that show the bones inside of your body. We call them X rays because the cameras use X-radiation to shoot the picture. We don't use enough radiation to cause your body any harm. I have to be very careful working with radiation.

I work in the emergency room. I see people who are in pain. I take the X rays very quickly so a doctor can look at them. I get the patient to lie in the right position to take the picture. I only want to take an X ray of the injured area. Then I put the film in a machine to be developed. X rays are developed a lot like regular photographs. I give the X rays to a doctor so he or she can see what is wrong.

I wear a uniform a lot like a nurse's. I am important at the hospital.

Yardmasters

Hello! My name is Jerry. I'm a yardmaster. I don't work in a backyard. I work in a railroad yard. Have you seen a model train switch tracks? I switch real trains to different tracks all day long.

I direct all the railroad traffic here. I am in charge of the train activity. Sometimes I put rail cars together to make a long train. Sometimes I break them apart. Trains with cargo to unload go to special tracks. I tell engineers where to move their cars.

It's like a big chess game. It's like leading a band. I must know about every train movement. I must know where cars are in the yard. Everything must work together.

We use computers and switches with remote controls to move many locomotives and cars. I pay careful attention to every detail. I have a good memory to keep track of train movements. I hear and see very well. I follow safety rules. I love trains, don't you?

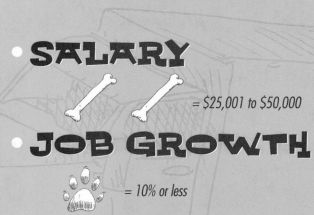

- **SALARY**

  = $25,001 to $50,000

- **JOB GROWTH**

  = 10% or less

- **EDUCATION**

  Training after high school

SCHOOL SUBJECTS

reading	geography
math	
computers	

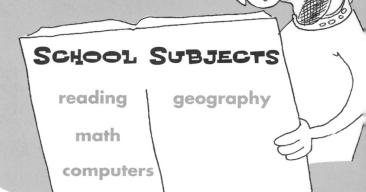

Zoologists

- # SALARY

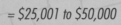

= $25,001 to $50,000

- # JOB GROWTH

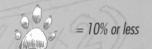

= 10% or less

- # EDUCATION

Four-year degree or more

SCHOOL SUBJECTS

science	computers
math	social studies
reading	

I bet you've seen giraffes at the zoo. Aren't they weird looking? They have those long, skinny necks and legs. How would you like to study giraffes for a living? That's what I do. I'm a zoologist.

Zoology is the study of animal life. I know about a lot of different animals. I do research on giraffes in Africa. Giraffes still live wild on the plains there. I am leading a group of scientists. We want to find out how giraffes adapt to humans building cities near their habitats. We want to see if humans have changed the way giraffes live in the wild. Zoologists don't want giraffes to become extinct. We study the giraffes' behavior at all hours. We watch them very carefully. We watch what they eat. We observe the way they move.

I use a microscope and computer to analyze data. I write the information in a report. Scientific reports take years to develop. I include many details. I use scientific words and big numbers so other scientists can use the data. Giraffes are fascinating. It's interesting to look at animals in a scientific way instead of as pets. I hope my report keeps giraffes on the plains of Africa for a long time.

LEARN ABOUT JOB FAMILIES

Meet the...
Arts and Entertainment Job Family

People in arts and entertainment paint, sing, act, take photographs, and write. They keep other people amused, inspired, or informed. Careers in arts and entertainment pay people to be creative.

Would You Like to Work in This Job Family?

Are you creative? Do you like to sing or dance? Paint or draw? Write stories and poems? You would love a career in arts and entertainment.

Here are the jobs in this family that are described in this book:

Actors and Actresses
Art Directors
Artists
Athletic Trainers
Camera Operators
Clothes Designers
Community Affairs Representatives
Copywriters
Craftspeople
Curators
Dancers
Directors
Editors

Floral Designers
Furniture Designers
Graphic Designers
Industrial Designers
Interior Designers
Interpreters and Translators
Journalists
Models
Musicians
Novelists
Photographers
Piano Tuners
Production Assistants

Professional Athletes
Public Relations Workers
Radio and Television Announcers
Sound Engineers
Stunt Performers
Vocalists
Web Designers
Writers

Get a Head Start!

1 Write your own book. If you like reading, you might like writing. Maybe you could write about your last family vacation or your pet. Think of the most interesting thing about you, and put it on paper. You're probably more interesting than you realized. You can even draw pictures to go with the words. Share the book with your friends, family, and teachers. Many famous authors started writing when they were your age. Remember, everyone has something important to say.

2 Sing along to the radio. When you listen to the radio, sing along with your favorite songs. Learn all of the words. Practice hitting the right notes. Join a school or community chorus. Do whatever it takes to become a great singer. Who knows, you might be making your own music videos in a few years.

3 Run your own art show. Draw or paint pictures of your favorite things. You can make a painting of ice cream, your sister, your dog, or even yourself. The key to good art is expressing yourself. Don't worry if your work isn't perfect. When you have 10 complete pieces of art, put them up around your room or house. Invite your friends and family to view your creations. You could be on the way to becoming an artistic genius.

Look Up These Words

Are you interested in arts and entertainment as a possible career? Look up these words in the dictionary.

a
advertising
airwaves
antiques
applause
arrangement
article
audience

b
blueprint
brochure

c
camera
celebrity
character
choreographer
cinematographer
commercials
communicate
copy

d
details
dolly

f
fabrics
festival
footage

g
glamorous

h
headline

i
illustration

l
layout

m
media
musical
mysteries

n
newsroom

p
plot
pose
pottery
publish

r
recording
recruiter
rehearse
rights

s
script
shoot
sketches
special effects
style

t
theater

w
wallpaper
watercolors

Find Out More

Would you like to work in arts and entertainment? There are many ways to find out more about jobs that interest you.

Do you know anyone who works in arts and entertainment? Ask your family, relatives, or your friends' families. Talk to teachers, counselors, coaches, neighbors, or other adults you know. Most people like to talk about their jobs. They can give you some good advice.

You can go to the Web or write for more information about many jobs in arts and entertainment.

ACTORS, ACTRESSES, DIRECTORS

Theatre Communications Group, Inc.
520 8th Avenue, 24th Floor
New York, NY 10018-4156
www.tcg.org

ART DIRECTORS, ARTISTS, CLOTHES DESIGNERS, CRAFTSPEOPLE

The National Association of Schools of Art and Design
11250 Roger Bacon Drive, Suite 21
Reston, VA 20190-5248
http://nasad.arts-accredit.org

The Society of Illustrators
128 East 63rd Street
New York, NY 10021-7303
www.societyillustrators.org

CAMERA OPERATORS

Professional Photographers of America, Inc.
229 Peachtree Street NE, Suite 2200
Atlanta, GA 30303
www.ppa.com

COMMUNITY AFFAIRS REPRESENTATIVES, PUBLIC RELATIONS WORKERS

The Public Relations Society of America
33 Maiden Lane, 11th Floor
New York, NY 10038-5150
www.prsa.org

Ragan Communications
316 N. Michigan Avenue, Suite 400
Chicago, IL 60601
www.ragan.com

COPYWRITERS, EDITORS, WRITERS

The Dow Jones Newspaper Fund
P.O. Box 300
Princeton, NJ 08543-0300
http://djnewspaperfund.dowjones.com

Magazine Publishers of America
810 Seventh Avenue, 24th Floor
New York, NY 10019
www.magazine.org

Society for Technical Communication, Inc.
901 North Stuart Street, Suite 904
Arlington, VA 22203
www.stc.org

DANCERS

American Alliance for Health, Physical Education, Recreation, and Dance
1900 Association Drive
Reston, VA 22091-1598
www.aahperd.org

American Dance Guild
P. O. Box 2006, Lenox Hill Station
New York, NY 10021
www.americandanceguild.org

FLORAL DESIGNERS

Society of American Florists
1601 Duke Street
Alexandria, VA 22314
www.safnow.org

FURNITURE DESIGNERS

American Society of Furniture Designers
144 Woodland Drive
New London, NC 28127
www.asfd.com

GRAPHIC DESIGNERS

The American Institute of Graphic Arts
164 Fifth Avenue
New York, NY 10010
www.aiga.org

INDUSTRIAL DESIGNERS

Industrial Designers Society of America
45195 Business Court, Suite 250
Dulles, VA 20166-6717
www.idsa.org

INTERIOR DESIGNERS

American Society of Interior Designers
608 Massachusetts Avenue, NE
Washington, DC 20002-6006
www.asid.org

INTERPRETERS AND TRANSLATORS

American Translators Association
225 Reinekers Lane, Suite 590
Alexandria, VA 22314
www.atanet.org

Monterey Institute of International Studies
460 Pierce Street
Monterey, CA 93940
www.miis.edu

JOURNALISTS

Association for Education in Journalism and Mass Communication
234 Outlet Pointe Boulevard
Columbia, SC 29210-5667
www.aejmc.org

National Newspaper Association
P. O. Box 7540
Columbia, MO 65205-7540
www.nna.org

MUSICIANS, VOCALISTS

American Guild of Musical Artists
1430 Broadway, 14th Floor
New York, NY 10018
www.musicalartists.org

PHOTOGRAPHERS

Professional Photographers of America, Inc.
229 Peachtree Street NE, Suite 2200
Atlanta, GA 30303
www.ppa.com

PIANO TUNERS

Piano Technicians Guild, Inc.
4444 Forest Avenue
Kansas City, KS 66106-3750
www.ptg.org

PRODUCTION ASSISTANTS

The International Association of Theatrical Stage Employes, Moving Picture Technicians, Artists, and Allied Crafts
1430 Broadway, 20th Floor
New York, NY 10018
www.iatse-intl.org

PROFESSIONAL ATHLETES

National Association for Sport and Physical Education
1900 Association Drive
Reston, VA 22091-1598
www.aahperd.org

RADIO AND TELEVISION ANNOUNCERS, SOUND ENGINEERS

National Association of Broadcasters
1771 N Street, NW
Washington, DC 20036
www.nab.org

Radio-Television News Directors Association and Foundation
1600 K Street, NW, Suite 700
Washington, DC 20006-2838
www.rtndf.org

358 Learn About Job Families

National Workforce Center for
    Emerging Technologies
Bellevue Community College
3000 Landerholm Circle SE, N258
Bellevue, WA 98007-6484
www.nwcet.org

Meet the...
Business Job Family

Careers in business involve selling products. They involve managing and persuading other people. Business people have to talk to many other people. Some business people are leaders who often work long hours to get the job done.

Would You Like to Work in This Job Family?

Do you like to talk with other people? Do you like to be the leader when you are playing games? Are you good at convincing other people? Do you like to work with numbers? Maybe you would like to work in business when you get older.

Here are the jobs in this family that are described in this book:

Accountants
Actuaries
Administrative Assistants
Advertising Account
    Executives
Advertising Directors
Appraisers
Bank Managers
Bank Tellers
Bookkeepers
Business Executives
Business Service Salespeople
Buyers
Compensation Analysts
Computer Security
    Consultants

Credit Analysts
Customer Service
    Representatives
Data Entry Operators
E-Commerce Managers
Escrow Officers
Estimators
Executive Assistants
Fashion Merchandisers
Financial Planners
Front Desk Clerks
Fund-Raisers
Grocery Clerks
Hazardous Waste Managers
Hospital Administrators
Hospitality Managers

Human Resource Workers
Image Consultants
Importers and Exporters
Information Technology
    (IT) Managers
Insurance Adjusters
Insurance Salespeople
Legal Secretaries
Loan Officers
Mail Carriers
Market Researchers
Marketing Directors
Office Managers
Postal Clerks
Product Managers
Production Planners

Production Superintendents
Property Managers
Purchasing Agents
Real Estate Salespeople
Receptionists
Recruiters
Restaurant Managers
Retail Salespeople
Retail Store Managers
Route Salespeople
Sales and Service Managers
Sales Representatives
Securities Clerks
Shipping and Receiving
    Clerks
Small Business Owners

Stock Brokers
Stock Clerks
Talent Agents
Tax Preparers
Telephone Operators
Title Examiners
Underwriters
Warehouse Workers
Water and Sewage Plant
    Operators

Get a Head Start!

1. Be a salesperson for your next school fundraiser. You can volunteer to sell chocolate bars, raffle tickets, wrapping paper, or anything your school is selling. Try to explain to people why they would like your product. Selling is a very important part of business. By volunteering for your school now, you can learn if you would like to work in sales later.

2. Become a class officer at your school. Run for secretary, treasurer, or president. Leaders often go into business. Having responsibility at your school now is a good way to see whether you would like being a business executive. Who knows, one day you may be the president of a major corporation. Many business professionals held offices in their schools when they were your age.

3. Start your own business. Talk with your family about activities you can do to make money. Maybe you could wash cars, sell vegetables from your garden, or mow lawns. Open a bank account with the money you make. Use math to keep track of your costs and profits. You might be a future small business owner!

Look Up These Words

Are you interested in business as a possible career? Look up these words in the dictionary.

a
account
audience

b
bar code
best-seller
budget

c
calculate
commission
competition
contract

d
deadline
debt
display

e
estimate
expenditure

f
factory
freight

g
guideline

i
interview
inventory
invoice

l
labor
lease
ledger

m
manufacturer
merchandise
mortgage

n
negotiate

o
ownership

p
percentage
profit
property
purchasing

r
receipt
research

s
schedule
staff
strategy
supervise
supplies

t
tenant
trends

v
volunteer

w
working conditions

z
zoning

362 **Learn About Job Families**

Find Out More

Would you like to work in business? There are many ways to find out more about jobs that interest you.

Do you know anyone who works in business? Ask your family, relatives, or your friends' families. Talk to teachers, counselors, coaches, neighbors, or other adults you know. Most people like to talk about their jobs. They can give you some good advice.

You can go to the Web or write for more information about many jobs in business.

ACCOUNTANTS

American Institute of Certified Public Accountants
1211 Avenue of the Americas
New York, NY 10036-8775
www.aicpa.org

ACTUARIES

American Academy of Actuaries
1100 17th Street, NW, 7th Floor
Washington, DC 20036
www.actuary.org

ADMINISTRATIVE ASSISTANTS, EXECUTIVE ASSISTANTS

International Association of Administrative Professionals
P. O. Box 20404
Kansas City, MO 64195-0404
www.iaap-hq.org

ADVERTISING ACCOUNT EXECUTIVES, ADVERTISING DIRECTORS

American Marketing Association
311 South Wacker Drive, Suite 5800
Chicago, IL 60606
www.marketingpower.com

APPRAISERS

Appraisal Institute
550 Van Buren Street, Suite 1000
Chicago, IL 60607
www.appraisalinstitute.org

BANK MANAGERS, BANK TELLERS, LOAN OFFICERS

American Bankers Association
1120 Connecticut Avenue, NW
Washington, DC 20036
www.aba.com

BUYERS, PURCHASING AGENTS

American Purchasing Society, Inc.
North Island Center
8 E. Galena Boulevard, Suite 203
Aurora, IL 60506
www.american-purchasing.com

Institute for Supply Management, Inc.
P.O. Box 22160
Tempe, AZ 85285-2160
www.ism.ws

COMPENSATION ANALYSTS

WorldatWork
14040 N. Northsight Boulevard
Scottsdale, AZ 85260
www.worldatwork.org

CREDIT ANALYSTS

National Association of Credit Management
8840 Columbia 100 Parkway
Columbia, MD 21045
www.nacm.org

DATA ENTRY OPERATORS

American Society for Information Science and Technology
1320 Fenwick Lane, Suite 510
Silver Spring, MD 20910
www.asis.org

ESTIMATORS

American Society of Professional Estimators
2525 Perimeter Place Drive, Suite 103
Nashville, TN 37217
www.aspenational.com

Association for the Advancement of Cost Engineering
209 Prairie Avenue, Suite 100
Morgantown, WV 26501
www.aacei.org

FASHION MERCHANDISERS

American Apparel and Footwear Association
1601 N. Kent Street, Suite 1200
Arlington, VA 22209
www.americanapparel.org

FINANCIAL PLANNERS

Financial Managers Society
100 W. Monroe, Suite 810
Chicago, IL 60603
www.fmsinc.org

FRONT DESK CLERKS, HOSPITALITY MANAGERS

American Hotel & Lodging Association
1201 New York Avenue, NW, #600
Washington, D.C. 20005-3931
www.ahla.com

GROCERY CLERKS

United Food and Commercial Workers Union
1775 K Street, NW
Washington, DC 20006-1502
www.ufcw.org

HAZARDOUS WASTE MANAGERS

Environmental Careers Organization
30 Winter Street
Boston, MA 02108
www.eco.org

HOSPITAL ADMINISTRATORS

American College of Health Care Administrators
300 N. Lee Street, Suite 301
Alexandria, VA 22314
www.achca.org

HUMAN RESOURCE WORKERS, RECRUITERS

Society for Human Resource Management
1800 Duke Street
Alexandria, VA 22314
www.shrm.org

IMPORTERS AND EXPORTERS

American Association of Exporters and Importers
1200 G Street, NW, Suite 800
Washington, DC 20005
www.aaei.org

INFORMATION TECHNOLOGY (IT) MANAGERS

Association of Information Technology Professionals
401 N. Michigan Avenue, Suite 2400
Chicago, IL 60611-4267
www.aitp.org

INSURANCE ADJUSTERS

Insurance Information Institute
110 William Street
New York, NY 10038
www.iii.org

National Association of Independent Insurance Adjusters
825 W. State Street, Suite 117 C & B
Geneva, IL 60134
www.naiia.com

INSURANCE SALESPEOPLE

National Association of Insurance and Financial Advisors
2901 Telstar Court
P.O. Box 12012
Falls Church, VA 22042-1205
www.naifa.org

LEGAL SECRETARIES

National Association for Legal Professionals
314 East Third Street, Suite 210
Tulsa, OK 74120
www.nals.org

MARKETING DIRECTORS, PRODUCT MANAGERS, ROUTE SALESPEOPLE, SALES AND SERVICE MANAGERS, SALES REPRESENTATIVES

Sales and Marketing Executives International
P.O. Box 1390
Sumas, WA 98295-1390
www.smei.org

PROPERTY MANAGERS

National Property Management Association
1102 Pinehurst Road
Dunedin, FL 34698
www.npma.org

REAL ESTATE SALESPEOPLE

National Association of Realtors
430 N. Michigan Avenue
Chicago, IL 60611-4087
www.realtor.org

RESTAURANT MANAGERS

National Restaurant Association
1200 17th Street, NW
Washington, DC 20036
www.restaurant.org

RETAIL SALESPEOPLE, RETAIL STORE MANAGERS, SHIPPING AND RECEIVING CLERKS, STOCK CLERKS

National Retail Federation
325 7th Street, NW, Suite 1100
Washington, DC 20004
www.nrf.com

SECURITIES CLERKS, STOCK BROKERS

Securities Industry Association
120 Broadway, 35th Floor
New York, NY 10271-0080
www.sia.com

SMALL BUSINESS OWNERS

Small Business Administration
409 Third Street, SW
Washington, DC 20416
www.sba.gov

TELEPHONE OPERATORS

United States Telecom Association
1401 H Street, NW, Suite 600
Washington, DC 20005
www.usta.org

UNDERWRITERS

Chartered Property and Casualty Underwriters Society
Kahier Hall
729 Providence Road
Malvern, PA 19355-0709
www.cpcusociety.org

WAREHOUSE WORKERS

AFL-CIO
815 16th Street, NW
Washington, DC 20006
www.afl-cio.org

WATER AND SEWAGE PLANT OPERATORS

American Water Works Association
6666 W. Quincy Avenue
Denver, CO 80235
www.awwa.org

Meet the...

Construction Job Family

People in construction work on and build houses, office buildings, hospitals, schools, bridges, and roads. Workers in construction install carpets, plumbing, and electricity. Careers in construction involve using tools and equipment.

Would You Like to Work in This Job Family?

Do you like to use your hands? Do you enjoy making things? Are you good at putting things together? Maybe you would enjoy a career working in construction.

Here are the jobs in this family that are described in this book:

Architects
Bricklayers
Building and Home Inspectors
Building Contractors
Carpenters
Construction Laborers

Drywall Installers
Electricians
Glaziers
Heavy Equipment Operators
Painters
Petroleum Field Workers

Plumbers
Roofers
Stage Hands
Steelworkers
Utility Line Workers

Get a Head Start!

1 **Build a model house.** Use old boxes to make the walls. Cut out windows and doors with scissors. Use masking tape to put several boxes together. Draw designs on the outside with markers and crayons. Use your imagination to make the best house around. People who work in construction plan and make buildings and other structures. One day you may work on a skyscraper.

2 **Help your family paint a room in your house.** Ask if you can help pick out the color. Get your own paint brush and pitch in. Work along with your family to add a fresh new coat of paint. Be careful not to spill any on the floor. People who work in construction do chores like this every day. If you had fun painting with your family, you might enjoy working in construction.

3 **Use boxes or building blocks to build a brick wall.** Create a pattern with the bricks. Paint them red or brown. Make sure your wall is sturdy and doesn't fall down easily. People in construction assemble materials in patterns all the time. If you like figuring out how to build a wall, you might like a job in construction.

Look Up These Words

Are you interested in construction as a possible career? Look up these words in the dictionary.

a

apprentice

b

backdrop
blueprint
bulldozer

c

chisel
circuit
compound
conduit
contractor

d

dexterity
drywall

e

electricity
equipment
exterior

f

fiberglass
framework

g

girder

h

hydraulic

i

inspection
installation
insulation

m

mallet
masonry
molding
mortar
muscles

o

oil field

p

plaster
power
primer
prop

r

rebar

s

sanding
scaffold
score
shingle
siding
structure

t

terrazzo
transformer
trowel

w

weld
wiring

© JIST Works

Find Out More

Would you like to work in construction? There are many ways to find out more about jobs that interest you.

Do you know anyone who works in construction? Ask your family, relatives, or your friends' families. Talk to teachers, counselors, coaches, neighbors, or other adults you know. Most people like to talk about their jobs. They can give you some good advice.

You can go to the Web or write for more information about many jobs in construction.

GENERAL CONSTRUCTION

Associated Builders and Contractors of America
4250 N. Fairfax Drive, 9th Floor
Arlington, VA 22203-1607
www.abc.org

Associated General Contractors of America
333 John Carlyle Street, Suite 200
Alexandria, VA 22314
www.agc.org

National Association of Home Builders
1201 15th Street, NW
Washington, DC 20005
www.nahb.org

ARCHITECTS

The American Institute of Architects
1735 New York Avenue, NW
Washington, DC 20006-5292
www2.aia.org

BRICKLAYERS

Brick Industry Association
11490 Commerce Park Drive
Reston, VA 20191-1525
www.brickinfo.org

International Union of Bricklayers and Allied Craftsmen
1776 Eye Street, NW
Washington, DC 20006
www.bacweb.org

BUILDING AND HOUSE INSPECTORS

American Society of Home Inspectors
932 Lee Street, Suite 101
Des Plaines, IL 60016
www.ashi.com

International Code Council
5203 Leesburg Pike, Suite 600
Falls Church, VA 22041
www.iccsafe.org

CARPENTERS

United Brotherhood of Carpenters and Joiners of America
www.carpenters.org

CONSTRUCTION LABORERS

Laborers' International Union of North America
905 16th Street, NW
Washington, DC 20006
www.liuna.org

DRYWALL INSTALLERS

International Union of Painters and Allied Trades
1750 New York Avenue, NW
Washington, DC 20006
www.ibpat.org

ELECTRICIANS

Independent Electrical Contractors
4401 Ford Avenue, Suite 1100
Alexandria, VA 22302
www.ieci.org

International Brotherhood of Electrical Workers
1125 15th Street, NW
Washington, DC 20005
www.ibew.org

National Electrical Contractors Association
3 Bethesda Metro Center, Suite 1100
Bethesda, MD 20814
www.necanet.org

GLAZIERS

International Union of Painters and Allied Trades
1750 New York Avenue, NW
Washington, DC 20006
www.ibpat.org

National Glass Association
8200 Greensboro Drive, Suite 302
McLean, VA 22102-3881
www.glass.org

HEAVY EQUIPMENT OPERATORS

International Union of Operating Engineers
1125 17th Street, NW
Washington, DC 20036
www.iuoe.org

PAINTERS

International Union of Painters and Allied Trades
1750 New York Avenue, NW
Washington, DC 20006
www.ibpat.org

PETROLEUM FIELD WORKERS

International Association of Drilling Contractors
P.O. Box 4287
Houston, TX 77210-4287
www.iadc.org

PLUMBERS

Plumbing-Heating-Cooling Contractors Association
180 S. Washington Street
P.O. Box 6808
Falls Church, VA 22040
www.phccweb.org

ROOFERS

National Roofing Contractors Association
10255 West Higgins Road, Suite 600
Rosemont, IL 60018
www.nrca.net

United Union of Roofers, Waterproofers and Allied Workers
1660 L Street, NW, Suite 800
Washington, DC 20036-5646
www.unionroofers.com

STAGEHANDS

International Alliance of Theatrical Stage Employees, Moving Picture Technicians, Artists and Allied Crafts of the United States, Its Territories, and Canada
1430 Broadway, 20th Floor
New York, NY 10018
www.iatse-intl.org

STEELWORKERS

The Association of Union Constructors
1501 Lee Highway, Suite 202
Arlington, VA 22209-1109
www.nea-online.org

The Ironworkers Union
1750 New York Avenue, NW, Suite 400
Washington, DC 20006
www.ironworkers.org

UTILITY LINE WORKERS

Communications Workers of America
501 3rd Street, NW
Washington, DC 20001-2797
www.cwa-union.org

United States Telecom Association
1401 H Street, NW, Suite 600
Washington, DC 20005
www.usta.org

Meet the...
Education and Social Services Job Family

People in education and social services like to help and teach others. They usually enjoy research and reading. Careers in education and social services involve talking with people.

Would You Like to Work in This Job Family?

Do you like to read and study? Does it make you feel good to help people? A career in education and social services might be perfect for your future.

Here are the jobs in this family that are described in this book:

Anthropologists
Business Education Teachers
Career Counselors
Clergy
Court Reporters
Customs Inspectors
Economists
Education Program Specialists
Elementary School Teachers
Health and Safety Inspectors
Immigration Inspectors
Lawyers
Liberal Arts Teachers

Librarians
Math and Science Teachers
Mental Health Counselors
Paralegal Assistants
Parole and Probation Officers
Police Commissioners
Police Officers
Political Aides
Political Scientists
Politicians
Preschool Teachers
Psychologists
Recreation Aides

Rehabilitation Counselors
School Counselors
School Principals
Social Directors
Social Scientists
Social Service Aides
Social Workers
Sociologists
Special Education Teachers
Teacher Aides
Trainers and Adult Education Teachers
University and College Teachers
Urban Planners

Get a Head Start!

1 Read. Pick up a book and read just for fun. People who go into education and social services love to learn. What are your special interests? Check out a book from the library to learn about something that you find interesting. Tell your friends or family about what you learn. You may be a great teacher of tomorrow.

2 Talk with one of your friends about a problem. Maybe two of your friends got in a fight. Your friend might be having problems with a brother or sister. Careers in counseling and psychology involve talking to people about their problems. Really listen to what your friend tells you. See if you can offer advice. If you enjoy helping your friends with problems, you might enjoy working in education and social services. The world needs good counselors, psychologists, and social workers.

3 Join a team or club. If you are good at sports, join the softball team or play football. If you like to read, join a book club. Get involved in activities with other kids your age. People who work in education and social services usually work well with other people. Teamwork is important. You'll use this skill for the rest of your life.

Look Up These Words

Are you interested in education and social services as a possible career? Look up these words in the dictionary.

a

abide
academic
adopt
agency
assignment

b

border
Braille

c

census
citizen
community
counselor
culture

d

deport
development
disability

e

economy
elderly
election
emotion
experiment

f

funding

g

government

h

homeless

i

immigrant
inspect

l

language
legislation
literature

p

personality
population
predict
probation
protection
public

r

research

s

safety
self-defense
senior citizen
skill
society
spiritual

t

training
trial

u

university

w

welfare
worship

Find Out More

Would you like to work in education and social services? There are many ways to find out more about jobs that interest you.

Do you know anyone who works in education and social services? Ask your family, relatives, or your friends' families. Talk to teachers, counselors, coaches, neighbors, or other adults you know. Most people like to talk about their jobs. They can give you some good advice.

You can go to the Web or write for more information about many jobs in education and social services.

ANTHROPOLOGISTS

American Anthropological Association
2200 Wilson Boulevard, Suite 600
Arlington, VA 22201
www.aaanet.org

CAREER COUNSELORS

American Counseling Association
5999 Stevenson Avenue
Alexandria, VA 22304
www.counseling.org

National Career Development Association
10820 East 45th Street, Suite 210
Tulsa, OK 74146
www.ncda.org

CLERGY

Young people should seek the guidance and counsel of their own clergy members.

LAWYERS

American Bar Association
321 North Clark Street
Chicago, IL 60610
http://w3.abanet.org

LIBRARIANS

American Library Association
50 E. Huron Street
Chicago, IL 60611
www.ala.org

PARALEGAL ASSISTANTS

American Bar Association
32l North Clark Street
Chicago, IL 60610
www.abanet.org/legalservices/legalassistants/home.html

National Federation of Paralegal Associations
2517 Eastlake Avenue East, Suite 200
Seattle, WA 98102
www.paralegals.org

PAROLE AND PROBATION OFFICERS

American Probation and Parole Association
2760 Research Park Drive
Lexington, KY 40578
www.appa-net.org

POLICE COMMISSIONERS, POLICE OFFICERS

International Union of Police Associations
1421 Prince Street, Suite 400
Alexandria, VA 22314
www.iupa.org

POLITICAL SCIENTISTS

American Political Science Association
1527 New Hampshire Avenue, NW
Washington, DC 20036-1206
www.apsanet.org

POLITICIANS

Council of State Governments
2760 Research Park Drive
P.O. Box 11910
Lexington, KY 40578-1910
www.csg.org

International City/County Management Association
777 North Capitol Street, NE, Suite 500
Washington, DC 20002
www.icma.org

PSYCHOLOGISTS

American Psychological Association
750 First Street, NE
Washington, DC 20002-4242
www.apa.org

RECREATION AIDES

American Alliance for Health, Physical Education, Recreation and Dance
1900 Association Drive
Reston, VA 22091
www.aahperd.org

American Camping Association
5000 State Road 67 North
Martinsville, IN 46151
www.acacamps.org

National Recreation and Park Association
22377 Belmont Ridge Road
Ashburn, VA 20148-4150
www.nrpa.org

REHABILITATION COUNSELORS

National Rehabilitation Counseling Association
8007 Sudley Road, Suite 102
Manassas, VA 22110-4719
http://nrca-net.org

SCHOOL COUNSELORS

American School Counselor Association
1101 King Street, Suite 625
Alexandria, VA 22314
www.schoolcounselor.org

SOCIAL SCIENTISTS

American Political Science Association
1527 New Hampshire Avenue, NW
Washington, DC 20036-1206
www.apsanet.org

Organization of American Historians
112 North Bryan Street
P. O. Box 5457
Bloomington, IN 47408-5457
www.oah.org

SOCIAL SERVICE AIDES

National Organization for Human Service Education
5601 Brodie Lane, Suite 620-215
Austin, TX 78745
www.nohse.com

SOCIAL WORKERS

National Association of Social Workers
750 First Street, NE, Suite 700
Washington, DC 20002-4241
www.naswdc.org

National Network for Social Work Managers
c/o Jane Adams College of Social Work
M/C 309
1040 W. Harrison St., 4th Floor
Chicago, IL 60607-7134
www.socialworkmanager.org

SOCIOLOGISTS

American Sociological Association
1307 New York Avenue, NW, Suite 700
Washington, DC 20005
www.asanet.org

American Association of University Professors
1012 14th Street, NW, Suite 500
Washington, DC 20005
www.aaup.org

American Federation of Teachers
555 New Jersey Avenue, NW
Washington, DC 20001
www.aft.org

National Education Association
1201 16th Street, NW
Washington, DC 20036-3290
www.nea.org

TRAINERS AND ADULT EDUCATION TEACHERS

American Association for Adult and Continuing Education
4380 Forbes Boulevard
Lanham, MD 20706
www.aaace.org

Association for Career and Technical Education
1410 King Street
Alexandria, VA 22314
www.acteonline.org

URBAN PLANNERS

American Planning Association
1776 Massachusetts Avenue, NW
Washington, DC 20036-1904
www.planning.org

Planetizen
www.planetizen.com

Meet the... *Health* Job Family

People who work in health careers help people and animals stay healthy and get well. They go to school to learn about science and the body. Careers in health involve working with many people. People in health careers pay attention to important details.

Would You Like to Work in This Job Family?

Have you ever helped care for someone who is sick? Do you enjoy taking care of your pet? You might enjoy working in a health career.

Here are the jobs in this family that are described in this book:

Anesthesiologists
Chiropractors
Dental Hygienists
Dentists
Dietitians
Dispensing Opticians
Emergency Medical Technicians
Gerontologists
Health Therapists
Hospice Workers
Licensed Practical Nurses
Medical Assistants

Medical Laboratory Assistants
Medical Records Administrators
Medical Records Clerks
Medical Secretaries
Medical Technologists
Midwives
Nurse Practitioners
Nurses Aides and Orderlies
Occupational Therapists
Optometrists
Pathologists
Patient Account Representatives

Pharmacist Assistants
Pharmacists
Physical Therapists
Physical Therapy Aides
Physician Assistants
Physicians
Podiatrists
Prosthetists
Public Health Inspectors
Public Health Nurses
Registered Nurses
Respiratory Therapists

Speech Pathologists and
    Audiologists
Surgical Technicians
Ultrasound Technologists
Utilization-Review Coordinators
Veterinarians
X-Ray and Radiologic Technicians

© JIST Works

Get a Head Start!

1 **Go to the library and check out a book about human anatomy.** The human body is amazing. Look through the book to learn about the bones and muscles. Write 10 questions you have about the human body. Try to answer them by reading the book or searching on the Internet. If you can't find the answers, ask your family or teachers to help you with the project. They'd love to help you start a career in health.

2 **Ask your family for a science kit for your next birthday.** Maybe you would like to do experiments using a microscope or a chemistry set. There are many great science kits for kids. You also can find science experiments in books in your library. People in health are good thinkers. They analyze experiments to answer questions. Pathologists and medical laboratory technicians run tests using microscopes and chemicals every day.

3 **Buy your very own fish.** See if your family will let you be in charge of taking care of your new pet. You have to remember to keep the tank clean and feed the fish. Read a book or search the Internet to make sure you know all the details. The fish will rely on you for everything. People in health fields care for people and animals every day. If you enjoy caring for your pet, you might like to become a veterinarian or a nurse.

Look Up These Words

Are you interested in health as a possible career? Look up these words in the dictionary.

a
ambulance
anatomy
anesthesia
autopsy

b
blood pressure

c
cavity
chemistry

d
diagnosis
disability

e
emergency
exercise

f
forceps

g
germ
growth

h
heartbeat
hospital

m
medication
microscope
monitor
muscle

n
nerve
nutrition

o
operation
oxygen

p
patient
posture
pregnancy
prescription
prosthesis

s
scalpel
spinal column
sterilize
stethoscope
surgery

t
temperature
therapist
treatment

v
vaccine

w
wound

x
x-ray

Learn About Job Families

Find Out More

Would you like to work in health? There are many ways to find out more about jobs that interest you.

Do you know anyone who works in health? Ask your family, relatives, or your friends' families. Talk to teachers, counselors, coaches, neighbors, or other adults you know. Most people like to talk about their jobs. They can give you some good advice.

You can go to the Web or write for more information about many jobs in health.

ANESTHESIOLOGISTS

American Society of Anesthesiologists
510 N. Northwest Highway
Park Ridge, IL 60068-2573
www.asahq.org

CHIROPRACTORS

American Chiropractic Association
1710 Clarendon Boulevard
Arlington, VA 22209
www.amerchiro.org

International Chiropractors Association
1110 N. Glebe Road, Suite 1000
Arlington, VA 22201
www.chiropractic.org

World Chiropractic Alliance
2950 N. Dobson Road, Suite I
Chandler, AZ 85224
www.worldchiropracticalliance.org

DENTAL HYGIENISTS, DENTISTS

American Dental Association
211 East Chicago Avenue
Chicago, IL 60611-2678
www.ada.org

American Dental Hygienists' Association
444 North Michigan Avenue, Suite 3400
Chicago, IL 60611
www.adha.org

DIETITIANS

American Dietetic Association
120 South Riverside Plaza, Suite 2000
Chicago, IL 60606-6995
www.eatright.org

DISPENSING OPTICIANS

Opticians Association of America
441 Carlisle Drive
Herndon, VA 20170
www.oaa.org

EMERGENCY MEDICAL TECHNICIANS

National Association of Emergency Medical Technicians
P. O. Box 1400
Clinton, MS 39060-1400
www.naemt.org

GERONTOLOGISTS

**Association for Gerontology in
Higher Education**
1030 15th Street, NW, Suite 240
Washington, DC 20005
www.aghe.org

HOSPICE WORKERS

National Association Home Care and Hospice
228 Seventh Street, SE
Washington, DC 20003
www.nahc.org

LICENSED PRACTICAL NURSES, NURSE PRACTITIONERS, PUBLIC HEALTH NURSES, REGISTERED NURSES

**National Association for Practical Nurse
Education and Service, Inc.**
P.O. Box 25647
Alexandria, VA 22313
www.napnes.org

National League for Nursing
61 Broadway
New York, NY 10006
www.nln.org

MEDICAL LABORATORY ASSISTANTS, MEDICAL TECHNOLOGISTS

American Medical Technologists
710 Higgins Road
Park Ridge, IL 60068
www.amt1.com

American Society for Microbiology
1752 N Street, NW
Washington, DC 20036
www.asm.org

American Society for Clinical Pathology
2100 West Harrison Street
Chicago, IL 60612
www.ascp.org

MEDICAL RECORDS ADMINISTRATORS, MEDICAL RECORDS CLERKS, PATIENT ACCOUNT REPRESENTATIVES

**American Health Information Management
Association**
233 N. Michigan Avenue, Suite 2150
Chicago, IL 60601-5800
www.ahima.org

MIDWIVES

Midwives Alliance of North America
375 Rockbridge Road, Suite 172-313
Lilburn, GA 30047
www.mana.org

OCCUPATIONAL THERAPISTS

American Occupational Therapy Association
4720 Montgomery Lane
P.O. Box 31220
Bethesda, MD 20824-1220
www.aota.org

OPTOMETRISTS

American Optometric Association
243 North Lindbergh Boulevard
St. Louis, MO 63141
www.aoanet.org

PATHOLOGISTS, PHYSICIANS

American Medical Association
515 North State Street
Chicago, IL 60610
www.ama-assn.org

PHARMACISTS

**American Association of Colleges of
Pharmacy**
1426 Prince Street
Alexandria, VA 22314
www.aacp.org

PHYSICAL THERAPISTS, PHYSICAL THERAPY AIDES

American Physical Therapy Association
1111 North Fairfax Street
Alexandria, VA 22314-1488
www.apta.org

PHYSICIAN ASSISTANTS

American Academy of Physician Assistants
950 North Washington Street
Alexandria, VA 22314-1552
www.aapa.org

PODIATRISTS

American Podiatric Medicine Association
9312 Old Georgetown Road
Bethesda, MD 20814
www.apma.org

PROSTHETISTS

**American Academy of Orthotists and
Prosthetists**
526 King Street, Suite 201
Alexandria, VA 22314
www.oandp.org

RESPIRATORY THERAPISTS

American Association for Respiratory Care
9425 N. MacArthur Boulevard, Suite 100
Irving, TX 75063-4706
www.aarc.org

SPEECH PATHOLOGISTS AND AUDIOLOGISTS

**American Speech-Language-Hearing
Association**
10801 Rockville Pike
Rockville, MD 20852
www.asha.org

SURGICAL TECHNICIANS

Association of Surgical Technologists
7108-C South Alton Way
Centennial, CO 80112
www.ast.org

ULTRASOUND TECHNOLOGISTS

Society of Diagnostic Medical Sonography
2745 Dallas Parkway, Suite 350
Plano, TX 75093-8730
www.sdms.org

VETERINARIANS

American Veterinary Medical Association
1931 North Meacham Road, Suite 100
Schaumburg, IL 60173
www.avma.org

X-RAY AND RADIOLOGIC TECHNICIANS

American Society of Radiologic Technologists
15000 Central Avenue, SE
Albuquerque, NM 87123-3917
www.asrt.org

Meet the...
Mechanics and Repairers Job Family

Mechanics and repairers fix cars, airplanes, computers, appliances, and many other items. People who work in mechanics and repairing jobs use tools and special equipment to keep machines working.

Would You Like to Work in This Job Family?

Are you handy? Do you enjoy fixing things? You might be a perfect mechanic or repairer when you get older.

Here are the jobs in this family that are described in this book:

Aircraft Mechanics
Appliance Repairers
Auto Body Repairers
Automobile Mechanics
Cable and Satellite TV Installers
Computer Technicians

Farm Equipment Mechanics
Heating and Cooling Systems Mechanics
Instrument Mechanics
Locksmiths
Medical Equipment Repairers
Millwrights

Parts Managers
Security System Technicians
Solar Energy System Installers
Telephone Installers and Repairers
Vending Machine Mechanics

Get a Head Start!

1 **Experiment with an old or broken machine.** Be sure to ask for permission first. Then ask a family member to help you. Maybe you have a broken clock or old vacuum cleaner. Put on safety glasses. Next try to take it apart using a screwdriver. If the machine has an electrical cord, **DO NOT** plug it in. Electricity can be very dangerous. Never work on something that is plugged in. Look inside at all the parts. **DO NOT** plug the machine in after you have played with it. If you like working with machines and their parts, you might enjoy working as a mechanic. Mechanics make broken things work again.

2 **List everything you can think of that uses a motor.** Write down cars and trains to start the list. Do you have toys with motors? Look around your house for anything with a motor. Many machines use motors. See how long you can make your list. Mechanics and repairers work on these machines. You might find a machine that you would like to work on when you are older.

3 **Ask your family to show you some tools.** Use a notebook to create a dictionary of tools. Draw a picture of each tool and write its name. See how many different tools you can draw. Try to memorize them. People who work as mechanics and repairers work with many tools. Your knowledge of tools could help you on the job when you get older.

Look Up These Words

Are you interested in mechanics and repairing as a possible career? Look up these words in the dictionary.

a
adjustment
appliance

b
battery
blowtorch
blueprint

c
carburetor
circuit
combustion
connection
corrosion

d
defective
demagnetize
diagnosis
dolly
drill

e
electronic
energy
engine
equipment

f
fender
furnace

h
hard disk

i
ignition
inspection
instrument

m
maintenance
magnetic
mallet
measure
motor

p
piston

r
reception

s
sensor
solar panel
solder
spring
sturdy

t
technical
temperature
thermostat
transmission
troubleshoot
tumbler

v
valve
volt

w
warranty
weld

x
x-ray

© JIST Works

Find Out More

Would you like to work in mechanics and repairing? There are many ways to find out more about jobs that interest you.

Do you know anyone who works in mechanics and repairing? Ask your family, relatives, or your friends' families. Talk to teachers, counselors, coaches, neighbors, or other adults you know. Most people like to talk about their jobs. They can give you some good advice.

You can go to the Web or write for more information about many jobs in mechanics and repairing.

AIRCRAFT MECHANICS

Professional Aviation Maintenance Association
717 Princess Street
Alexandria, VA 22314
www.pama.org

APPLIANCE REPAIRERS

Appliance Service News
P.O. Box 809
St. Charles, IL 60174
www.asnews.com

National Appliance Service Association
P.O. Box 2514
Kokomo, IN 46904
www.nasa1.org

National Electronics Service Dealers Association
3608 Pershing Avenue
Fort Worth, TX 76107-4527
www.nesda.com

AUTO BODY REPAIRERS, AUTOMOBILE MECHANICS

Association of International Automobile Manufacturers
2111 Wilson Boulevard, Suite 1150
Arlington, VA 22201
www.aiam.org

Automotive Service Association, Inc.
P.O. Box 929
Bedford, TX 76095-0929
www.asashop.org

CABLE AND SATELLITE TV INSTALLERS

Communications Workers of America
501 3rd Street, NW
Washington, DC 20001-2797
www.cwa-union.org

Society of Cable Telecommunications Engineers
140 Philips Road
Exton, PA 19341-1318
www.scte.org

COMPUTER TECHNICIANS

Association of Computer Support Specialists
333 Mamaroneck Avenue, #129
White Plains, NY 10605
www.acss.org

Electronics Technicians Association
5 Depot Street
Greencastle, IN 46135
www.eta-i.org

FARM EQUIPMENT MECHANICS

Deere & Company World Headquarters
One John Deere Place
Moline, IL 61265
www.deere.com

North American Equipment Dealers Association
1195 Smizer Mill Road
Fenton, MO 63026-3480
www.naeda.com

HEATING AND COOLING SYSTEMS MECHANICS

Air Conditioning and Refrigeration Institute
4100 North Fairfax Drive, Suite 200
Arlington, VA 22203
www.ari.org

Associated Builders and Contractors
4250 N. Fairfax Drive, 9th Floor
Arlington, VA 22203-1607
www.abc.org

Mechanical Contractors Association of America
1385 Piccard Drive
Rockville, MD 20850
www.mcaa.org

Plumbing-Heating-Cooling Contractors— National Association
180 S. Washington Street, P.O. Box 6808
Falls Church, VA 22040
www.phccweb.org

INSTRUMENT MECHANICS

Electronics Technicians Association
5 Depot Street
Greencastle, IN 46135
www.eta-i.org

International Society of Certified Electronics Technicians
3608 Pershing Avenue
Fort Worth, TX 76107-4527
www.iscet.org

LOCKSMITHS

Associated Locksmiths of America Inc.
3003 Live Oak Street
Dallas, TX 75204
www.aloa.org

MEDICAL EQUIPMENT REPAIRERS

Association for the Advancement of Medical Instrumentation
1110 North Glebe Road, Suite 220
Arlington, VA 22201-4795
www.aami.org

MILLWRIGHTS

Association for Manufacturing Technology
7901 Westpark Drive
McLean, VA 22102-4206
www.amtonline.org

National Tooling and Machining Association
9300 Livingston Road
Fort Washington, MD 20744-4998
www.ntma.org

PARTS MANAGERS

National Automobile Dealers Association
8400 Westpark Drive
McLean, Virginia 22102
www.nada.org

SECURITY SYSTEM TECHNICIANS

Security Industry Association
635 Slaters Lane, Suite 110
Alexandria, VA 22314
www.siaonline.org

SOLAR ENERGY SYSTEM INSTALLERS

Solar Energy Industries Association
805 15th Street, NW, Suite 510
Washington, DC 20005
www.seia.org

TELEPHONE INSTALLERS AND REPAIRERS

Communications Workers of America
501 3rd Street, NW
Washington, DC 20001-2797
www.cwa-union.org

United States Telecom Association
1401 H Street, NW, Suite 600
Washington, DC 20005
www.usta.org

VENDING MACHINE MECHANICS

National Automatic Merchandising Association
20 North Wacker Drive, Suite 3500
Chicago, IL 60606-3102
www.vending.org

Meet the...
Natural Resources Job Family

People in natural resources work with nature and the environment. They work with trees, plants, animals, the earth, rocks, and water.

Would You Like to Work in This Job Family?

Do you like plants and animals? Do you enjoy hiking and being with nature? A career in natural resources might be perfect for you.

Here are the jobs in this family that are described in this book:

Agricultural Inspectors
Agricultural Scientists
Animal Health Technicians
Animal Trainers
Commercial Fishers
Environmental Analysts

Farmers
Fish and Wildlife Specialists
Foresters
Geologists
Horticultural Workers
Landscape Architects

Loggers
Oceanographers
Park Rangers
Range Managers
Soil Scientists
Tree Surgeons

Get a Head Start!

1 Plant your own garden. If you have a yard with extra space, ask your family if you can plant a flower garden. You can buy seeds at most hardware or discount stores. Check a book out of the library to learn how to take care of plants. You have to water, fertilize, and weed your garden. People who work in natural resources love plants and the earth. This project could get you started in a great career.

2 Start a rock collection. Find the most interesting rocks in your neighborhood. When you go on a family vacation, find rocks in different places. Library books can help you identify rocks. Do any of your rocks have fossil imprints? Can you make out layers in the rocks? Geologists study rocks. They learn about the earth's history from the rocks they collect.

3 Take a hike in the woods with your family. Explore the area as much as you can. Notice the different trees and plants. Bring a notebook to write down your observations. Park rangers and foresters work in the woods every day. Would you like to work with nature all the time?

Look Up These Words

Are you interested in natural resources as a possible career? Look up these words in the dictionary.

a
adapt
agriculture

b
behavior
biodiversity
biology

c
climate
combine
conservation
crop

e
earthquake
ecology
ecosystem
environment

f
fertilize
fossil

g
grazing
greenhouse

h
harvest

i
irrigation

k
kennel

l
livestock
lumber

m
mineral
mulch

o
observation
organism

p
pesticide
physics
pollution
population
preserve
prune

r
rescue

s
sapling
sedimentary
seed
shore
soil
swamp

t
trail

v
volcano

w
wildlife

Find Out More

Would you like to work in natural resources? There are many ways to find out more about jobs that interest you.

Do you know anyone who works in natural resources? Ask your family, relatives, or your friends' families. Talk to teachers, counselors, coaches, neighbors, or other adults you know. Most people like to talk about their jobs. They can give you some good advice.

You can go to the Web or write for more information about many jobs in natural resources.

AGRICULTURAL SCIENTISTS

American Society of Agronomy
677 South Segoe Road
Madison, WI 53711
www.agronomy.org

National Agricultural Library
U.S. Department of Agriculture
10301 Baltimore Boulevard
Beltsville, MD 20705
www.ars.usda.gov

Purdue University School of Agriculture
Agricultural Administration Building
615 W. State Street
West Lafayette, IN 47907-1140
www.agriculture.purdue.edu

ANIMAL HEALTH TECHNICIANS

American Veterinary Medical Association
1931 North Meacham Road, Suite 100
Schaumburg, IL 60173
www.avma.org

Humane Society of the United States
2100 L Street, NW
Washington, DC 20037
www.hsus.org

COMMERCIAL FISHERS

National Marine Fisheries Service
1315 East-West Highway, 9th Floor F/CS
Silver Spring, MD 20910
www.nmfs.noaa.gov

ENVIRONMENTAL ANALYSTS

Environmental Careers Organization
30 Winter Street
Boston, MA 02108
www.eco.org

FARMERS

American Farm Bureau Federation
600 Maryland Avenue, SW, Suite 800
Washington, DC 20024
www.fb.org

National FFA Organization
P.O. Box 68960, 6060 FFA Drive
Indianapolis, IN 46268-0960
www.ffa.org

FISH AND WILDLIFE SPECIALISTS

International Association of Fish and Wildlife Agencies
444 North Capitol Street, NW, Suite 725
Washington, DC 20001
www.iafwa.org

National Fish and Wildlife Foundation
1120 Connecticut Avenue, NW, Suite 900
Washington, DC 20036
www.nfwf.org

FORESTERS

Society of American Foresters
5400 Grosvenor Lane
Bethesda, MD 20814-2198
www.safnet.org

USDA Forest Service
1400 Independence Avenue, S.W.
Washington, DC 20250-0003
www.fs.fed.us

GEOLOGISTS

American Association of Petroleum Geologists
P.O. Box 979
Tulsa, OK 74101-0979
www.aapg.org

American Geological Institute
4220 King Street
Alexandria, VA 22302-1502
www.agiweb.org

Geological Society of America
P.O. Box 9140
Boulder, CO 80301-9140
www.geosociety.org

HORTICULTURAL WORKERS

American Nursery & Landscape Association
1000 Vermont Avenue, NW, Suite 300
Washington, DC 20005-4914
www.anla.org

LANDSCAPE ARCHITECTS

American Society of Landscape Architects
636 Eye Street, NW
Washington, DC 20001-3736
www.asla.org

LOGGERS

Forest Industry Suppliers and Logging Association
18008 - 107 Avenue
Edmonton, Alberta, Canada T5S 2J5
www.fisla.com

Forest Resources Association
600 Jefferson Plaza, Suite 350
Rockville, MD 20852
www.apulpa.org

OCEANOGRAPHERS

Marine Technology Society
5565 Sterrett Place, #108
Columbia, MD 21044
www.mtsociety.org

PARK RANGERS

National Park Service
1849 C Street, NW
Washington, DC 20240
http://www.nps.gov/

RANGE MANAGERS

Society for Conservation Biology
4245 N. Fairfax Drive, Suite 400
Arlington, VA, 22203-1651
www.conbio.org

Society of Range Management
445 Union Boulevard, Suite 230
Lakewood, CO 80228-1259
www.rangelands.org

SOIL SCIENTISTS

U.S. Bureau of Land Management
1849 C Street, NW, Room 406-LS
Washington, DC 20240
www.blm.gov

Soil and Water Conservation Society
945 SW Ankeny Road
Ankeny, IA 50021
www.swcs.org

TREE SURGEONS

International Society of Arboriculture
P.O. Box 3129
Champaign, IL 61826
www.isa-arbor.com

Tree Care Industry Association
3 Perimeter Road, Unit 1
Manchester, NH 03103
www.natlarb.com

Meet the...
Personal Services Job Family

Workers in personal services help, serve, and protect others. They enjoy talking with and caring for people. Careers in personal services make the world a nicer and safer place.

Would You Like to Work in This Job Family?

Do you like to help people? Do you enjoy meeting people? A career in personal services may be perfect for you.

Here are the jobs in this family that are described in this book:

Barbers
Building Maintenance Workers
Caterers
Chefs and Dinner Cooks
Child-Care Workers
Corrections Officers
Cosmetologists
Domestic Service Workers
Fast-Food Service Managers

Firefighters
Flight Attendants
Furniture Movers
Groundskeepers and Gardeners
Housekeeping Staff
Investigators
Kitchen Helpers
Massage Therapists

Personal Trainers
Pest Control Workers
Psychiatric Technicians
Security Guards
Short-Order Cooks
Tour Guides
Tourist Information Specialists
Wait Staff

Get a Head Start!

1. Make a list of how you help people every day. Do you take out the trash at home? Have you ever cleaned the blackboard for your teacher? Do you help your little brother or sister get dressed? You do many helpful things all the time. See how long you can make your list. If it makes you feel good to help people, you might enjoy working in personal services.

2. Pretend that you are a famous chef. Everyone wants to eat in your restaurant because you are very creative. Make up new recipes to serve to your customers. You don't have to cook anything. Just write your recipes on paper. Combine your favorite ingredients. Maybe you would like to mix strawberries and chocolate. Give each recipe a name. When you have 10 recipes, make your own cookbook. Share it with your family and friends. Chefs create recipes and cook meals. You may become a famous chef one day.

3. Ask a police officer or security guard about his or her work. Make a list of tasks that an officer does every day. Write a diary as if you were a police officer or guard. How much of your imaginary day is spent helping people? How much time is spent enforcing laws? Is your job ever dangerous? If the work sounds interesting, you might be a good police officer or security guard someday.

Look Up These Words

Are you interested in personal services as a possible career? Look up these words in the dictionary.

a
assist
appointment

b
beautify

c
caregiver
client
compassion
convenient
criminal
culinary

d
domestic

e
efficient
emergency
emotional
enforce
evidence
exterminate

g
gratuity

h
hazard

i
ingredient
inspect

l
listen

m
maintenance
massage
mental
menu

o
outgoing

p
pamper
passenger
patient
prisoner

r
reception
recipe
regulation
rescue
reservation
responsive

s
safety
sensitive
shrubbery
spa
stress
support

t
tourist

u
undercover
uniform

v
vandalism
vermin

Find Out More

Would you like to work in personal services? There are many ways to find out more about jobs that interest you.

Do you know anyone who works in personal services? Ask your family, relatives, or your friends' families. Talk to teachers, counselors, coaches, neighbors, or other adults you know. Most people like to talk about their jobs. They can give you some good advice.

You can go to the Web or write for more information about many jobs in personal services.

BARBERS, COSMETOLOGISTS

American Association of Cosmetology Schools
15825 N. 71st Street, Suite 100
Scottsdale, AZ 85254-1521
www.beautyschools.org/index2.html

National Accrediting Commission of Cosmetology Arts and Sciences
4401 Ford Avenue, Suite 1300
Arlington, VA 22203
www.naccas.org

National Cosmetology Association
401 N. Michigan Avenue
Chicago, IL 60601
www.salonprofessionals.org

BUILDING MAINTENANCE WORKERS

Building Service Contractors Association International
10201 Lee Highway, Suite 225
Fairfax, VA 22030
www.bscai.org

CATERERS

International Caterers Association
1200 17th Street, NW
Washington, DC 20036-3097
www.icacater.org

CHEFS AND DINNER COOKS, FAST-FOOD SERVICE MANAGERS, KITCHEN HELPERS, SHORT-ORDER COOKS, WAIT STAFF

American Culinary Federation
180 Center Place Way
St. Augustine, FL 32095
www.acfchefs.org

National Restaurant Association Educational Foundation
175 W. Jackson Boulevard, Suite 1500
Chicago, IL 60604-2814
www.nraef.org

CHILD-CARE WORKERS

Association for Childhood Education International
17904 Georgia Avenue, Suite 215
Olney, MD 20832
www.acei.org

Head Start Bureau
Administration for Children and Families
370 L'Enfant Promenade, SW
Washington, DC 20447
www2.acf.dhhs.gov/programs/hsb/

**National Association for the Education of
Young Children**
1509 16th Street, NW
Washington, DC 20036
www.naeyc.org

CORRECTIONS OFFICERS

American Correctional Association
4380 Forbes Boulevard
Lanham, MD 20706-4322
www.aca.org

American Probation and Parole Association
2760 Research Park Drive
Lexington, KY 40511-8410
www.appa-net.org

DOMESTIC SERVICE WORKERS,
HOUSEKEEPING STAFF

**International Executive Housekeepers
Association**
1001 Eastwind Drive, Suite 301
Westerville, OH 43081-3361
www.ieha.org

FIREFIGHTERS

International Association of Fire Chiefs
4025 Fair Ridge Drive
Fairfax, VA 22033
www.iafc.org

International Association of Fire Fighters
1750 New York Avenue, NW
Washington, DC 20006
www.iaff.org

FLIGHT ATTENDANTS

Association of Flight Attendants
One O'Hare Center
6250 N. River Road, Suite 4020
Rosemont, IL 60018
www.unitedafa.org

FURNITURE MOVERS

MovingRelocation.com
9221-5th Avenue
PMB 120
Brooklyn, NY 11209
www.movingrelocation.com

GROUNDSKEEPERS AND GARDENERS

American Nursery and Landscape Association
1000 Vermont Avenue, NW, Suite 300
Washington, DC 20005-4914
www.anla.org

Associated Landscape Contractors of America
950 Herndon Parkway, Suite 450
Herndon, VA 20170
www.alca.org

INVESTIGATORS, SECURITY GUARDS

**American Federation of Police and
Concerned Citizens**
6350 Horizon Drive
Titusville, FL 32780
www.aphf.org/afp_cc.html

Federal Bureau of Investigation
935 Pennsylvania Avenue, NW, Room 7350
Washington, DC 20535
www.fbi.gov

MASSAGE THERAPISTS

American Massage Therapy Association
500 Davis Street
Evanston, IL 60201
www.amtamassage.org

PERSONAL TRAINERS

American Council on Exercise
4851 Paramount Drive
San Diego, CA 92123
www.acefitness.org

**National Strength and Conditioning
Association**
1885 Bob Johnson Drive
Colorado Springs, CO 80906
www.nsca-lift.org

PEST CONTROL WORKERS

National Pest Management Association
8100 Oak Street
Dunn Loring, VA 22027
www.pestworld.org

PSYCHIATRIC TECHNICIANS

American Psychiatric Association
1000 Wilson Boulevard, Suite 1825
Arlington, VA 22209-3901
www.psych.org

TOUR GUIDES, TOURIST INFORMATION SPECIALISTS

Travel Industry Association of America
1100 New York Avenue, NW, Suite 450
Washington, DC 20005-3934
www.tia.org

Meet the...
Production Job Family

People in production careers handle, make, or assemble products. They work with materials like metal, jewels, glass, and fabric. People in production usually work in factories or shops.

Would You Like to Work in This Job Family?

Do you enjoy making things? Are you good with details? You might like to work in production when you get older.

Here are the jobs in this family that are described in this book:

Bakery Workers
Cabinetmakers
Chemical Processing Workers
Dental Laboratory Technicians
Electronic Assemblers
Forklift Operators
Furniture Makers
Jewelers
Machine Tool Operators
Machinists

Manufacturing Workers
Meat Cutters
Metal Refining Workers
Molders
Optical Technicians
Plastic Molders
Power Plant Operators
Prepress Workers
Quality Control Inspectors
Sewing Machine Operators

Sheet Metal Workers
Ship Fitters
Shoe Repairers
Tailors and Dressmakers
Textile Machine Operators
Tool and Die Makers
Upholsterers
Welders
Woodworkers

Get a Head Start!

1 **Be a baker.** Ask your family to help you bake a cake. You can buy a mix and frosting at the grocery store. Read the directions carefully. Be sure you have all the ingredients. Be careful when you measure ingredients. Everything has to be exactly right. Ask an adult to help you with the oven. Have fun frosting the cake. Print a message to yourself on top with icing. Bakers make many cakes every day. One day you might work in a bakery.

2 **Become a famous jewelry designer.** Use paper clips to make fun necklaces. Clip them together to make a string. Fasten the two ends to make a loop. You can attach other things like beads or small pieces of painted wood. Try adding pieces of foil to the chain for extra flash. Model your creations for your family. One day you may work with gold and diamonds. Jewelers create beautiful necklaces, bracelets, rings, and earrings.

3 **Become a molder and model maker.** Use modeling clay or dough to mold models. Get a picture of a car or plane out of a magazine. Make a model of it using your clay. Make sure you pay attention to the details. Molders and model makers work with similar materials every day. It's one job where you can play while you work.

Look Up These Words

Are you interested in production as a possible career? Look up these words in the dictionary.

a
accurate
adjustment
alteration
artificial
assemble
assembly line

b
blowtorch

c
cast
chemical
clasp

d
dimension
dowel

f
fabric
fabricate
factory
faulty
fiber
furnace

h
hinge
hydroelectric

i
imperfection
instrument

l
lathe
lithography
lubricate

m
magnify
measurement
microchip
model

p
pattern
pigment
plaster
plastic
prefabricate
processing

r
refinery
rivet

s
safety
sanitary
sealer
seam
silver
solder
stitch
strenuous

t
thread
torch

v
veneer

ind Out More

Would you like to work in production? There are many ways to find out more about jobs that interest you.

Do you know anyone who works in production? Ask your family, relatives, or your friends' families. Talk to teachers, counselors, coaches, neighbors, or other adults you know. Most people like to talk about their jobs. They can give you some good advice.

You can go to the Web or write for more information about many jobs in production.

BAKERY WORKERS

International Dairy-Deli-Bakery Association
313 Price Place, Suite 202
P.O. box 5528
Madison, WI 53705-0528
www.iddba.org

CABINETMAKERS, FURNITURE MAKERS, WOODWORKERS

American Home Furnishings Alliance
P.O. Box HP-7
High Point, NC 27261
www.ahfa.us/index.htm

Association of Woodworking and Furnishing Suppliers
5733 Rickenbacker Road
Commerce, CA 90040
www.awfs.org

Certified Custom Woodworkers Association
101 Constitution Avenue, NW
Washington, D.C. 20001
www.woodindustry.org

CHEMICAL PROCESSING WORKERS

International Chemical Workers Union
1655 West Market Street
Akron, OH 44313
www.icwuc.org

DENTAL LABORATORY TECHNICIANS

National Association of Dental Laboratories
1530 Metropolitan Boulevard
Tallahassee, FL 32308
www.nadl.org

FORKLIFT OPERATORS

Industrial Truck Association
1750 K Street, NW, Suite 460
Washington, DC 20006
www.indtrk.org

JEWELERS

Gemological Institute of America
The Robert Mouawad Campus
5345 Armada Drive
Carlsbad, CA 92008
www.gia.edu

Jewelers of America
52 Vanderbilt Avenue, 19th Floor
New York, NY 10017
www.jewelers.org

Manufacturing Jewelers and Suppliers of America
45 Royal Little Drive
Providence, RI 02904
www.mjsainc.com

MACHINE TOOL OPERATORS, MACHINISTS, PLASTIC MOLDERS, TOOL AND DIE MAKERS

Association for Manufacturing Excellence
380 Palatine Road West
Wheeling, IL 60090-5863
www.ame.org

National Tooling and Machining Association
9300 Livingston Road
Fort Washington, MD 20744-4998
www.ntma.org

Precision Metalforming Association
6363 Oak Tree Boulevard
Independence, OH 44131-2500
www.metalforming.com

Tooling and Manufacturing Association
1177 South Dee Road
Park Ridge, IL 60068
www.tmanet.com

MEAT CUTTERS

United Food and Commercial Workers International Union
1775 K Street, NW
Washington, DC 20006
www.ufcw.org

MOLDERS

Glass, Molders, Pottery, Plastics and Allied Workers International Union
P.O. Box 607
608 East Baltimore Pike
Media, PA 19603-0607
www.gmpiu.org

OPTICAL TECHNICIANS

Commission on Opticianry Accreditation
P.O. Box 3073
Merrifield, VA 22116-3073
www.coaccreditation.com

POWER PLANT OPERATORS

International Brotherhood of Electrical Workers
1125 15th Street, NW
Washington, DC 20005
www.ibew.org

Utility Workers Union of America
815 16th Street, NW
Washington, DC 20006
www.uwua.org

PREPRESS WORKERS

Graphic Communications Council
1899 Preston White Drive
Reston, Virginia 20191-4367
www.npes.org/../edcouncil.html

Printing Industries of America/Graphic Arts Technical Foundation Headquarters
200 Deer Run Road
Sewickley, PA 15143
www.gain.net

QUALITY CONTROL INSPECTORS

American Society for Quality
600 North Plankinton Avenue
Milwaukee, WI 53203
www.asq.org

SEWING MACHINE OPERATORS, TAILORS AND DRESSMAKERS, TEXTILE MACHINE OPERATORS, UPHOLSTERERS

Custom Tailors and Designers Association of America
P.O. Box 53052
Washington, DC 20009
www.ctda.com

Textile News
Mullen Publications, Inc.
9629 Old Nations Ford Road
Charlotte, NC 28273-5719
www.textilenews.com

SHEET METAL WORKERS

Associated Builders and Contractors
4250 North Fairfax Drive, 9th Floor
Arlington, VA 22203-1607
www.abc.org

Sheet Metal and Air Conditioning Contractors' National Association
4201 Lafayette Center Drive
Chantilly, VA 20151-1209
www.smacna.org

Sheet Metal Workers International Association
1750 New York Avenue, NW
Washington, DC 2006
www.smwia.org

SHIP FITTERS

International Brotherhood of Boilermakers, Iron Ship Builders, Blacksmiths, Forgers and Helpers
753 State Avenue, Suite 570
Kansas City, KS 66101
www.boilermakers.org

SHOE REPAIRERS

Shoe Service Institute of America
18 School Street
North Brookfield, MA 01535
www.ssia.info

WELDERS

American Welding Society
550 NW LeJeune Road
Miami, FL 33126
www.aws.org

Meet the...
Science and Engineering Job Family

Careers in science and engineering involve math and science. Scientists and engineers use their knowledge to design everything from bridges to robots. They do research and analysis. They have to be very good at math and science.

Would You Like to Work in This Job Family?

Do you like science and math? Do you enjoy working with computers? Science and engineering might be a great path for you to choose.

Here are the jobs in this family that are described in this book:

Aerospace Engineers
Astronomers
Biomedical Engineers
Biotechnical Researchers
Chemical Engineers
Chemists
Civil Engineers
Electrical Engineers
Ergonomics Engineers

Fiber-optic Engineers
Industrial Engineers
Information Abstractors and Indexers
Materials Engineers
Mathematicians
Mechanical Engineers
Meteorologists
Microbiologists
Mining Engineers

Nuclear Engineers
Nuclear Technicians
Operations Research Analysts
Physicists
Seismologists
Statisticians
Telecommunications Analysts
Zoologists

© JIST Works

Get a Head Start!

1 **Design a spaceship so you can fly to Jupiter.** You have to consider many things. Remember that you will be in the ship for a long time. Include a kitchen, a TV, and everything you will need. But a spaceship doesn't have much space. Find out more about spaceships at the library or on the Internet. Engineers design important projects like rockets, buildings, and machines. You may work as an aerospace engineer when you get older.

2 **Take a trip to the zoo.** Zoos are full of exotic animals. Bring a notebook so you can jot down your observations. Animals are fascinating. Watch the way they move. A gorilla moves differently from a giraffe. What do the animals eat? Every animal has a favorite food. Are any of the animals endangered? If you have questions, ask someone who works at the zoo. You can find animal information at the library and online. Biologists and zoologists study animals. Maybe you will work in the wilds of Africa when you get older.

3 **Build a model of a bridge.** Check a book out of the library to learn about famous bridges. You can use anything around the house make the bridge. Old tennis balls, Styrofoam, and aluminum foil work well. You might want to paint the bridge. Learn about different types of bridges, like suspension bridges. Find out what makes a bridge stay up. Engineers plan and build bridges. You might build a famous bridge someday.

ook Up These Words

Are you interested in science and engineering as a possible career? Look up these words in the dictionary.

a

algorithm
analyze

c

calculate
cell
circuit
composition
compound
compute

d

data
database

e

earthquake
electricity
element
energy
equation
estimate
experiment
extrapolate

f

fault line
force
forecast
formula

g

galaxy
geology
gravity

l

laboratory
laser

m

matter
microscope
motion

n

nuclear

o

organism

p

petroleum
pharmaceutical
poisonous
population
pressure

r

radiation

s

satellite
simulate
solar system
statistic
structure
survey

t

telescope
transmit

w

workflow

Find Out More

Would you like to work in science and engineering? There are many ways to find out more about jobs that interest you.

Do you know anyone who works in science and engineering? Ask your family, relatives, or your friends' families. Talk to teachers, counselors, coaches, neighbors, or other adults you know. Most people like to talk about their jobs. They can give you some good advice.

You can go to the Web or write for more information about many jobs in science and engineering.

AEROSPACE ENGINEERS

American Institute of Aeronautics and Astronautics
1801 Alexander Bell Drive, Suite 500
Reston, VA 20191-4344
www.aiaa.org

ASTRONOMERS

American Astronomical Society
2000 Florida Avenue, NW, Suite 400
Washington, DC 20009-1231
www.aas.org

BIOMEDICAL ENGINEERS

Biomedical Engineering Society
8401 Corporate Drive, Suite 225
Landover, MD 20785-2224
www.bmes.org

BIOTECHNICAL RESEARCHERS

Biotechnology Industry Organization
1225 Eye Street, NW, Suite 400
Washington, DC 20005
www.bio.org

CHEMICAL ENGINEERS, CHEMISTS

American Chemical Society
1155 16th Street, NW
Washington, DC 20036
www.chemistry.org

American Institute of Chemical Engineers
3 Park Avenue
New York, NY 10016-5991
www.aiche.org

CIVIL ENGINEERS

American Society of Civil Engineers
1801 Alexander Bell Drive
Reston, VA 20191-4400
www.asce.org

ELECTRICAL ENGINEERS

Institute of Electrical and Electronics Engineers
3 Park Avenue, 17th Floor
New York, NY 10016-5997
www.ieee.org

FIBER-OPTIC ENGINEERS

The Fiber Optic Association
1119 S. Mission Road, #355
Fallbrook, CA 92028
www.thefoa.org

INDUSTRIAL ENGINEERS

Institute of Industrial Engineers
3577 Parkway Lane, Suite 200
Norcross, GA 30092
www.iienet.org

INFORMATION ABSTRACTORS AND INDEXERS

American Society of Indexers
10200 West 44th Avenue, Suite 304
Wheat Ridge, CO 80033
www.asindexing.org

MATERIALS ENGINEERS

ASM International
9639 Kinsman Road
Materials Park, OH 44073-0002
www.asm-intl.org

The Minerals, Metals and Materials Society
184 Thorn Hill Road
Warrendale, PA 15086
www.tms.org

MATHEMATICIANS

American Mathematical Society
201 Charles Street
Providence, RI 02904-2294
www.ams.org

Mathematical Association of America
1529 18th Street, NW
Washington, DC 20036-1385
www.maa.org

MECHANICAL ENGINEERS

American Society of Heating, Refrigerating, and Air-Conditioning Engineers
1791 Tullie Circle, NE
Atlanta, GA 30329
www.ashrae.org

American Society of Mechanical Engineers
Three Park Avenue
New York, NY 10016-5990
www.asme.org

METEOROLOGISTS

American Meteorological Society
45 Beacon Street
Boston, MA 02108-3693
www.ametsoc.org

National Weather Service
1325 East West Highway
Silver Spring, MD 20910
www.nws.noaa.gov

MICROBIOLOGISTS

American Society for Microbiology
1752 N Street, NW
Washington, DC 20036-2904
www.asm.org

MINING ENGINEERS

Society for Mining, Metallurgy, and Exploration
8307 Shaffer Parkway
P.O. Box 277002
Littleton, CO 80127
www.smenet.org

NUCLEAR ENGINEERS

American Nuclear Society
555 North Kensington Avenue
La Grange Park, IL 60526
www.ans.org

OPERATIONS RESEARCH ANALYSTS

Institute for Operations Research and the Management Sciences
901 Elkridge Landing Road, Suite 400
Linthicum, MD 21090-2909
www.informs.org

PHYSICISTS

American Institute of Physics
One Physics Ellipse
College Park, MD 20740-3843
www.aip.org

Institute of Mathematical Statistics
P.O. Box 22718
Beachwood, OH 44122
www.imstat.org

SEISMOLOGISTS

American Geological Institute
4220 King Street
Alexandria, VA 22302-1502
www.agiweb.org

Geological Society of America
P.O. Box 9140
Boulder, CO 80301-9140
www.geosociety.org

STATISTICIANS

American Statistical Association
1429 Duke Street
Alexandria, VA 22314-3415
www.amstat.org

TELECOMMUNICATIONS ANALYSTS

**National Cable and Telecommunications
  Association**
1724 Massachusetts Avenue, NW
Washington, DC 20036
www.ncta.com

ZOOLOGISTS

The American Institute of Biological Sciences
1444 I Street, NW, Suite 200
Washington, DC 20005
www.aibs.org

Meet the... *Technology* Job Family

People in technology work with computers and electrical equipment. They are very good at paying attention to details. They use technology to make the world a better place.

Would You Like to Work in This Job Family?

Do you like to use computers? Would you like to invent a new and exciting machine? You might become a leader in technology in the future.

Here are the jobs in this family that are described in this book:

Astronauts
Broadcast Technicians
CAD Technicians
Computer Engineers
Computer Graphics Specialists
Drafters
Electromechanical Technicians

Laser Technicians
Metallographic Technicians
Military Enlisted Personnel
Military Officers
Network Administrators
Programmers
Robotics Technicians

Surveyors
Technical Illustrators
Technical Support Specialists
Technical Writers
Webmasters
Wireless Technology Product Managers

414 **Learn About Job Families**

© JIST Works

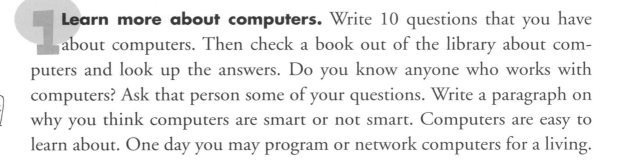

1 Learn more about computers. Write 10 questions that you have about computers. Then check a book out of the library about computers and look up the answers. Do you know anyone who works with computers? Ask that person some of your questions. Write a paragraph on why you think computers are smart or not smart. Computers are easy to learn about. One day you may program or network computers for a living.

2 Design a robot. Imagine what you want this robot to do. Maybe this robot can get you out of bed in the morning or play with your little brother. Draw a picture of the robot. What does the robot look like from the front? The back? The side? Write a paragraph about your special robot. Describe everything about it. Go online and research what kinds of robot kits are available. Hundreds of people might want a robot like yours. People who work in technology create exciting machines.

3 Learn about the United States space program and NASA. There are many exciting books, movies, and Web sites about astronauts. Pretend that you will be an astronaut on the next space flight. Write a story about your mission. Will you do experiments? How long will you be in orbit? Include all of the important details about your flight. It is important for astronauts to log their activities. You might want to work with NASA as a career.

Look Up These Words

Are you interested in technology as a possible career? Look up these words in the dictionary.

a
alloy
altimeter
animate
artificial intelligence
atmosphere

b
backup
blueprint

c
calculate
calibrate
circuit
code
complex

d
database
debug

e
equipment

g
global
graph

i
illustration
innovate
interface
interpret
intranet

l
laptop
laser

m
modem

o
object
orbit

p
portal
precision
program
prototype

r
radiation
repetitive
robotic

s
satellite
scanner
schematic
signal
simulate
specification
support
system

t
theodolite

u
user

v
virtual reality
visualize

w
wireless
workstation

Find Out More

Would you like to work in technology? There are many ways to find out more about jobs that interest you.

Do you know anyone who works in technology? Ask your family, relatives, or your friends' families. Talk to teachers, counselors, coaches, neighbors, or other adults you know. Most people like to talk about their jobs. They can give you some good advice.

You can go to the Web or write for more information about many jobs in technology.

ASTRONAUTS

National Aeronautics and Space Administration Headquarters
300 E St. SW
Washington, DC 20546
www.nasa.gov

National Space Society
1620 I (Eye) Street NW, Suite 615
Washington, DC 20006
www.nss.org

BROADCAST TECHNICIANS

National Association of Broadcasters
1771 N Street, NW
Washington, DC 20036
www.nab.org

Society of Broadcast Engineers
9247 North Meridian Street, Suite 305
Indianapolis, IN 46260
www.sbe.org

CAD TECHNICIANS, DRAFTERS

American Design Drafting Association
105 E. Main Street
Newbern, TN 38059
www.adda.org

CADwire.net
c/o Cyon Research Corporation
8220 Stone Trail Drive
Bethesda, MD 20817-4556
www.cadwire.net

COMPUTER ENGINEERS, NETWORK ADMINISTRATORS, PROGRAMMERS

Association for Computing Machinery
1515 Broadway
New York, NY 10036
www.acm.org

National Workforce Center for Emerging Technologies
Bellevue Community College
3000 Landerholm Circle SE, N258
Bellevue, WA 98007-6484
www.nwcet.org

System Administrators Guild
2560 9th Street, Suite 215
Berkeley, CA 94710
www.sage.org

COMPUTER GRAPHICS SPECIALISTS

Graphic Communications Council
1899 Preston White Drive
Reston, VA 20191-4367
www.npes.org/../edcouncil.html

ELECTROMECHANICAL TECHNICIANS, LASER TECHNICIANS, METALLOGRAPHIC TECHNICIANS

Junior Engineering Technical Society
1420 King Street, Suite 405
Alexandria, VA 22314
www.jets.org

National Institute for Certification in Engineering Technologies
1420 King Street
Alexandria, VA 22314-2794
www.nicet.org

MILITARY ENLISTED PERSONNEL, MILITARY OFFICERS

www.todaysmilitary.com

ROBOTICS TECHNICIANS

Robotics Education Project
robotics.nasa.gov

Robotic Industries Association
900 Victors Way, Suite 140
P.O. Box 3724
Ann Arbor, MI 48106
www.roboticsonline.com

SURVEYORS

American Congress on Surveying and Mapping
6 Montgomery Village Avenue, Suite #403
Gaithersburg, MD 20879
www.acsm.net

TECHNICAL ILLUSTRATORS

National Association of Schools of Art and Design
11250 Roger Bacon Drive, Suite 21
Reston, VA 20190-5248
www.nasad.arts-accredit.org

The Society of Illustrators
128 East 63rd Street
New York, NY 10021-7303
www.societyillustrators.org

TECHNICAL SUPPORT SPECIALISTS

Association of Computer Support Specialists
333 Mamaroneck Avenue, #129
White Plains, NY 10605
www.acss.org

National Workforce Center for Emerging Technologies
Bellevue Community College
3000 Landerholm Circle SE, N258
Bellevue, WA 98007-6484
www.nwcet.org

Network and Systems Professionals Association
7044 S. 13th Street
Oak Creek, WI 53154
www.naspa.com

TECHNICAL WRITERS

Society for Technical Communication
901 North Stuart Street, Suite 904
Arlington, VA 22203
www.stc.org

WEBMASTERS

International Webmasters Association
119 E. Union Street, Suite F
Pasadena, CA 91103
www.iwanet.org

National Workforce Center for Emerging Technologies
Bellevue Community College
3000 Landerholm Circle SE, N258
Bellevue, WA 98007-6484
www.nwcet.org

WIRELESS TECHNOLOGY PRODUCT MANAGERS

Wi-Fi Alliance
3925 W. Braker Lane
Austin, TX 78759
www.wi-fi.org

Wireless Developer Network
4588 East Highway 20, Suite A
Niceville, FL 32578
www.wirelessdevnet.com

Meet the...
Transportation Job Family

Transportation careers involve moving items and people from one place to another. Some people who work in transportation get to travel every day.

Would You Like to Work in This Job Family?

Do you enjoy taking trips? Do you look forward to getting your driver's license? Have you dreamed about traveling around the world? You might consider a job in transportation.

Here are the jobs in this family that are described in this book:

Air Traffic Controllers
Airport Security Workers
Baggage Handlers
Bus Drivers
Delivery Truck Drivers

Dispatchers
Pilots
Railroad Engineers
Ship's Crew Members
Ship's Officers

Taxi Drivers
Ticket and Reservation Agents
Travel Agents
Truck Drivers
Yardmasters

420 *Learn About Job Families*

Get a Head Start!

1 Notice the many types of transportation jobs. Join your family members the next time they go to the airport or train station. Count the number of different jobs you see. You will see ticket agents, baggage handlers, and people who drive the train or pilot the plane. Bring a notebook to write your observations. Look at the schedules of arrivals and departures. Make a list of every place you would like to go. If you work in transportation, you may visit those places.

2 Look at a map or a globe of the world. Pick any two countries. Find them on the map. Now figure out the best way to get from one country to the other in a plane. What other countries do you have to cross? Will you fly over oceans? Use travel Web sites to find actual flights and figure out how long the trip would take. Pilots fly from country to country all the time. One day you may fly the paths you just charted.

3 Imagine that you are a truck driver. Pretend you have to get a shipment of ice cream from Chicago, Illinois, to New Orleans, Louisiana. Use a road atlas to figure out the roads you need to take. If your family does not have a road atlas, find one at the library or online. Then find the right roads to other cities. Travel from San Francisco, California, to Denver, Colorado. Travel from New York City to Boston. Knowing how to read a map is a good skill. People in transportation work with maps every day.

Look Up These Words

Are you interested in transportation as a possible career? Look up these words in the dictionary.

a
accident

b
baggage

c
cargo
construction
customs

d
destination
detour
diesel
direction
dispatch

e
emergency

f
fare
flight plan
fuel

g
gauge

h
hangar
highway

i
inspection
intersection
interstate
itinerary

l
license
locomotive
luggage

m
maintenance
manifest
merge

p
passport
port

r
radar
reservation
roadblock
runway

s
scenery
schedule
security
shipment

t
throttle
ticket
toll
traffic
transfer
transit
transport

v
vacation
visibility
voyage

422 **Learn About Job Families** © JIST Works

Find Out More

Would you like to work in transportation? There are many ways to find out more about jobs that interest you.

Do you know anyone who works in transportation? Ask your family, relatives, or your friends' families. Talk to teachers, counselors, coaches, neighbors, or other adults you know. Most people like to talk about their jobs. They can give you some good advice.

You can go to the Web or write for more information about many jobs in transportation.

AIR TRAFFIC CONTROLLERS

Federal Aviation Administration
800 Independence Avenue, SW
Washington, DC 20591
www.faa.gov

National Air Traffic Controllers Association
1325 Massachusetts Avenue, NW
Washington, DC 20005
www.natca.org

AIRPORT SECURITY WORKERS

Air Transport Association of America
1301 Pennsylvania Avenue, NW, Suite 1100
Washington, DC 20004-1707
www.airlines.org

Transportation Security Administration
601 South 12th Street
Arlington, VA 22202-4220
www.tsa.gov

BUS DRIVERS

American Public Transportation Association
1666 K Street, NW
Washington, DC 20006
www.apta.com

National School Transportation Association
625 Slaters Lane, Suite 205
Alexandria, VA 22314
www.schooltrans.com

DELIVERY TRUCK DRIVERS, TRUCK DRIVERS

American Trucking Association
2200 Mill Road
Alexandria, VA 22314-4677
www.trucking.org

DISPATCHERS

Associated Public-Safety Communications Officials
351 N. Williamson Boulevard
Daytona Beach, FL 32114-1112
www.apcointl.org

National Academies of Emergency Dispatch
139 E. South Temple, Suite #530
Salt Lake City, UT 84111
www.emergencydispatch.org

PILOTS

Air Line Pilots Association
1625 Massachusetts Avenue, NW
Washington, DC 20036
www.alpa.org

International Council of Aircraft Owner and Pilot Associations
421 Aviation Way
Frederick, MD 21701
www.iaopa.org

RAILROAD ENGINEERS

Association of American Railroads
50 F Street, NW
Washington, DC 20001-1564
www.aar.org

Federal Railroad Administration
1120 Vermont Avenue NW
Washington, DC 20590
www.fra.dot.gov

SHIP'S CREW MEMBERS, SHIP'S OFFICERS

Maritime Administration
U.S. Department of Transportation
400 7th Street, SW
Washington, DC 20590
www.marad.dot.gov

Paul Hall Center for Maritime Training and Education
P.O. Box 75
Piney Point, MD 20674-0075
www.seafarers.org/phc

TAXI DRIVERS

Write to local taxi services or state employment service offices.

National Limousine Association
49 South Maple Avenue
Marlton, NJ 08053
www.limo.org

TICKET AND RESERVATION AGENTS

Air Transport Association of America
1301 Pennsylvania Avenue, NW, Suite 1100
Washington, DC 20004-1707
www.airlines.org

TRAVEL AGENTS

American Society of Travel Agents
1101 King Street, Suite 200
Alexandria, VA 22314
www.astanet.com

The Travel Institute
148 Linden Street, Suite 305
Wellesley, MA 02482
www.icta.com

YARDMASTERS

Association of American Railroads
50 F Street, NW
Washington, DC 20001-1564
www.aar.org

Transportation Commmunications Union
3 Research Place
Rockville, MD 20850
www.tcunion.org

424   **Learn About Job Families**